Also by David Remnick

HOLDING THE NOTE

Holding the Note

PROFILES IN POPULAR MUSIC

DAVID REMNICK

Alfred A. Knopf   *New York*   2023

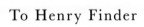
To Henry Finder

Contents

Preface

Sometimes, when I go to hear music, I feel like a weekend natural-
ist of the Anthropocene feverishly trying to catch a last glimpse of
some glorious species: James Brown ringing out New Year's Eve
at the Apollo; Paul Simon in a rainstorm in Forest Hills; Aretha
Franklin fronting a pickup orchestra at a casino in Ontario. The
urge to see aging performers while we still can is an inheritance. My
parents suffered from neurological ailments that eventually made it
impossible for them to work or get around easily—my mother with
MS in her early thirties, my father with Parkinson's in his fifties—
and yet they somehow managed to bring my brother and me, who
were children in the era of the Beatles, to see Louis Armstrong, Ella
Fitzgerald, Dizzy Gillespie, Dave Brubeck, Nina Simone. Before my
father had to shut down his small practice, he was surely the only
dentist in the New York metropolitan area who replaced Muzak
with Big Mama Thornton and Screamin' Jay Hawkins to accompany the sound of the drill and the spit sink.

On a typical grownup venture—this one about a quarter century in the past—I emerged from the subway in the Village on a June
afternoon and headed to a now-defunct club called Sweet Basil to
see Doc Cheatham, a top-flight trumpet player from the very early

days of jazz, who played a brunch gig there on Sundays. Cheatham was just shy of ninety. To miss him would be unforgivable. His first appearance on a record was as a sideman for Ma Rainey.

It was hot out on Seventh Avenue but the club was comfortingly dark and cool. I took a seat at a shared table near the back of the bar. Cheatham, trailed by his bandmates, made his way to the bandstand. He walked with the aid of a collapsible cane and wore oversized aviator glasses. What few strands of hair he had left he dyed chestnut and combed forward over the crown of his skull. The crowd, drinking mimosas and Bloody Marys, came dressed in jeans, shorts, T-shirts. This was not Cheatham's style. He was pin sharp, gaily professional, wearing an apricot shirt, a red-print tie, a green linen jacket, and cream-colored slacks held up by skinny red galluses.

Cheatham was born in 1905, in Nashville. He went by Adolphus until he started playing music for patients at a medical clinic and won his nickname for life. Doc's father played mandolin and was a barber on riverboats. His mother was a teacher. He took up music at fourteen, playing drums and coronet in school and church bands, and then, first as a sax player, then as a trumpet player, started hooking up with small-time professional gigs: carnivals, parade wagons, coal-mine dances. He played in the pit of the Bijou Theatre behind Bessie Smith and Ethel Waters. Following the Great Migration north to Chicago, he got work at the Dreamland Café, where the Prohibition-era clientele drank bathtub gin out of teacups. One day, he encountered King Oliver on the street and expressed his admiration. Oliver, who had been Armstrong's mentor, gave Doc a gift, a beat-up tarnished copper mute that Cheatham stuffed in his horn for the next seventy-odd years. Doc even played behind the man who claimed to have invented jazz itself, Jelly Roll Morton. On the bandstand, at Sweet Basil, he paid homage:

"This next one's by Jelly Roll Morton," he said. "Not everyone used to like him. He'd stand on the corner all day bragging about being the greatest composer in the world. Of course, he could back it up. He wore a diamond in his front tooth. Wore a twenty-dollar gold piece in the tips of his shoes. He didn't play in places like this. Didn't play in the Waldorf-Astoria. Mostly, he played in bodegas . . ."

"Bordellos, Doc, bordellos," the pianist Chuck Folds said, with a practiced roll of the eyes.

"Yeah, bordellos," Cheatham said. "'Cause, he was also a pimp."

Cheatham played for an hour or so, mainly New Orleans standards from his youth. In his off-hours, he was making music with much younger musicians. He was not stuck in the past. He'd just met Nicholas Payton, a quicksilver trumpet player in his twenties, and soon they'd win a Grammy for their collaboration.

Cheatham was mindful of time: he tapped his foot to the gunshot of the snare, he played just behind the pillowy pulse of the bass. He soloed in measured steps. He knew better than to overextend himself. His solos were brief, witty, resonant; he took his leave before he lost his breath or his way. He did not need to strain in order to glow. When he used King Oliver's mute, it was to summon that distant elder, but always with attention to the song—nothing maudlin or academic about it.

After the set, I had a chance to talk with Cheatham at a table in the back. "The truth is, I was a late bloomer," he said. "I didn't even know there was a place called New Orleans until 1926. Nashville was a two-college town, nothing to listen to, dead as hell in those days. But when I got to Chicago, that town was filled with New Orleans musicians. Louis Armstrong was inspiring everyone, me included."

Before Cheatham headed back to the bandstand I asked him if he'd be playing Sunday brunches at Sweet Basil in ten years, when he'd be a hundred. "I don't know," he said. "This place may not be standing in ten years. But we'll see."

———•———

The pieces in this volume were written over time for *The New Yorker* and are the result of my earliest enthusiasms. In every case, I encountered these artists in late career. The voices had weathered. In *nearly* every case, the best songs and the best performances were well in the past. They were all grappling, in music and in their own lives, with their diminishing gifts and mortality. Yet there was never any diminishment in the desire to make music—to hold the note.

Just as I was collecting these pieces, one songwriter and performer who had long dodged my requests to meet with her, Joni Mitchell, emerged at the Newport Folk Festival to play her first full set of music in two decades. Mitchell had been dealing for years with various ailments; in 2015, she suffered a brain aneurysm that nearly killed her. When she was a child, polio left her unable to walk for a while. But, as she told a reporter, "the aneurysm took away a lot more, really. Took away my speech and my ability to walk. And, you know, I got my speech back quickly, but the walking I'm still struggling with."

Mitchell warmed up to playing in public again slowly. She began hosting private jams—"Joni jams"—at her house in Los Angeles. Brandi Carlisle, Paul McCartney, Chaka Khan, Bonnie Raitt, Herbie Hancock, and others came by to play, to talk, to sing.

At Newport, a festival she last played in 1969, Mitchell took the stage in front of ten thousand people and was surrounded by a raft of musicians, including Carlisle, Celisse Henderson, Wynonna Judd, and Blake Mills. She sat in a magnificently garish armchair and sang a full set, from "Carey" to "The Circle Game." She pleased herself with songs of her own past—Frankie Lymon & the Teenagers' "Why Do Fools Fall in Love," Gershwin's "Summertime," the Clovers' "Love Potion No. 9." Her voice was far deeper than it was when she recorded *Blue,* her masterpiece, but Brandi Carlisle was there to provide the soprano filigree. Celisse Henderson, playing guitar with the attack of Sister Rosetta Tharpe, delighted Joni with a uniquely jagged version of "Help Me." Mitchell loved it all: the crowd, the companionship onstage, the sheer aliveness of the moment. And in the end, from the open air of Newport to the rest of us getting the full report on YouTube, it was the spectacle of Joni, determined and joyful, singing "Both Sides Now" that left every listener not just moved and grateful, but altered.

> But now old friends are acting strange
> They shake their heads, they say I've changed
> Well, something's lost, but something's gained
> In living every day.

A young woman's song, written in 1966 after she'd read *Henderson the Rain King* on a flight above a bank of clouds, had reshaped itself. Something was lost, something was gained.

———·———

For musicians late in their careers, it's the spirit of *sostenuto*, of sustain, that prevails: writing, playing, and performing keeps them in the game, helping to replenish what age has attenuated. For listeners like my father, music is also a source of resilience. Music had long ago ceased being a matter of cool or fashion, of keeping up. He listened to what he loved, no matter the period. When he told me some detail of his past—hearing Sidney Bechet at a club in Paris when he was in the Army—or when he recommended something to me or, less often, took a recommendation of mine, the pleasure was so evident it seemed almost illicit.

When I was in college, he called to tell me that a singer named Alberta Hunter was performing at a club in the Village called the Cookery. I should be sure to go see her, he said, and, as a way of insisting, he sent me a check for twenty dollars to pay the cover charge. Hunter, who was a contemporary of Bessie Smith's, was the Memphis-born daughter of a Pullman porter. As a girl, she ran off to Chicago to sing the blues, and she became friends with Armstrong, Ma Rainey, Sophie Tucker, and King Oliver. She cowrote "Downhearted Blues" with Lovie Austin: *Trouble, trouble, I've had it all my days.* After Hunter's mother died, in 1954, she spent the next couple of decades working as a registered nurse at a hospital on Roosevelt Island. Now that she had retired from nursing, Hunter decided that she would sing again. My father had led me once more to the blues, to one of the originals, in her last years. Hunter, that night at the Cookery, was bawdy, fearless, magnificently alive. The voice was ragged, but the wear hardly detracted from the feeling. She would go out singing. Years later, at my father's funeral, we set up a boom box and played his favorite music. People left the synagogue to the strains of "Downhearted Blues."

HOLDING THE NOTE

HOW THE LIGHT GETS IN

When Leonard Cohen was twenty-five, he was living in London, sitting in cold rooms writing sad poems. He got by on a three-thousand-dollar grant from the Canada Council for the Arts. This was 1960, long before he played the festival at the Isle of Wight in front of six hundred thousand people. In those days, he was a Jamesian Jew, the provincial abroad, a refugee from the Montreal literary scene. Cohen, whose family was both prominent and cultivated, had an ironical view of himself. He was a bohemian with a cushion whose first purchases in London were an Olivetti typewriter and a blue raincoat at Burberry. Even before he had much of an audience, he had a distinct idea of the audience he wanted. In a letter to his publisher, he said that he was out to reach "inner-directed adolescents, lovers in all degrees of anguish, disappointed Platonists, pornography-peepers, hair-handed monks and Popists."

Cohen was growing weary of London's rising damp and its gray skies. An English dentist had just yanked one of his wisdom teeth. After weeks of cold and rain, he wandered into a bank and asked the teller about his deep suntan. The teller said that he had just returned from a trip to Greece. Cohen bought an airline ticket.

Not long afterward, he alighted in Athens, visited the Acropolis, made his way to the port of Piraeus, boarded a ferry, and disembarked at the island of Hydra. With the chill barely out of his bones, Cohen took in the horseshoe-shaped harbor and the people drinking cold glasses of retsina and eating grilled fish in the cafés by the water; he looked up at the pines and the cypress trees and the whitewashed houses that crept up the hillsides. There was something mythical and primitive about Hydra. Cars were forbidden. Mules humped water up the long stairways to the houses. There was only intermittent electricity. Cohen rented a place for fourteen dollars a month. Eventually, he bought a whitewashed house of his own, for fifteen hundred dollars, thanks to an inheritance from his grandmother.

Hydra promised the life Cohen had craved: spare rooms, the empty page, eros after dark. He collected a few paraffin lamps and some used furniture: a Russian wrought-iron bed, a writing table, chairs like "the chairs that van Gogh painted." During the day, he worked on a sexy, phantasmagoric novel called *The Favorite Game* and the poems in a collection titled *Flowers for Hitler.* He alternated between extreme discipline and the varieties of abandon. There were days of fasting to concentrate the mind. There were drugs to expand it: pot, speed, acid. "I took trip after trip, sitting on my terrace in Greece, waiting to see God," he said years later. "Generally, I ended up with a bad hangover."

Here and there, Cohen caught glimpses of a beautiful Norwegian woman. Her name was Marianne Ihlen, and she had grown up in the countryside near Oslo. Her grandmother used to tell her, "You are going to meet a man who speaks with a tongue of gold." She thought she already had: Axel Jensen, a novelist from home, who wrote in the tradition of Jack Kerouac and William Burroughs. She had married Jensen, and they had a son, little Axel. Jensen was not a constant husband, however, and, by the time their child was four months old, Jensen was, as Marianne put it, "over the hills again" with another woman.

One spring day, Ihlen was with her infant son in a grocery store and café. "I was standing in the shop with my basket waiting to pick up bottled water and milk," she recalled decades later, on a Norwegian radio program. "He is standing in the doorway with the sun behind him." Cohen asked her to join him and his friends outside. He was wearing khaki pants, sneakers, a shirt with rolled sleeves, and a cap. The way Marianne remembered it, he seemed to radiate "enormous compassion for me and my child." She was taken with him. "I felt it throughout my body," she said. "A lightness had come over me."

Cohen had known some success with women. He would know a great deal more. For a troubadour of sadness—"the godfather of gloom," he was later called—Cohen found frequent respite in the arms of others. As a young man, he had a kind of Michael Corleone Before the Fall look, sloe-eyed, dark, a little hunched, but high courtesy and verbal fluency were his charm. When he was thirteen, he read a book on hypnotism. He tried out his new discipline on the family housekeeper. She took off her clothes. Not everyone over the years was quite as bewitched. Nico spurned him, and Joni Mitchell, who had once been his lover, remained a friend but dismissed him as a "boudoir poet." But these were the exceptions.

Leonard began spending more and more time with Marianne. They went to the beach, made love, kept house. Once, when they were apart—Marianne and Axel in Norway, Cohen in Montreal scraping up some money—he sent her a telegram: "Have house all I need is my woman and her son. Love, Leonard."

There were times of separation, times of argument and jealousy. When Marianne drank, she could go into a dark rage. And there were infidelities on both sides. ("Good gracious. All the girls were panting for him," Marianne recalled. "I would dare go as far as to say that I was on the verge of killing myself due to it.")

In the mid-sixties, as Cohen started to record his songs and win worldly success, Marianne became known to his fans as that antique figure—the muse. A memorable photograph of her, dressed only in a towel, and sitting at the desk in the house on Hydra, appeared on the back of Cohen's second album, *Songs from a Room*. But, after they'd been together for eight years, the relationship came apart, little by little—"like falling ashes," as Cohen put it.

Cohen was spending more time away from Hydra pursuing his career. Marianne and Axel stayed on awhile on Hydra, then left for Norway. Eventually, Marianne married again. But life had its burdens, particularly for Axel, who has had persistent health problems. What Cohen's fans knew of Marianne was her beauty and what it had inspired: "Bird on the Wire," "Hey, That's No Way to Say Goodbye," and, most of all, "So Long, Marianne." She and Cohen stayed in touch. When he toured in Scandinavia, she visited him backstage. They exchanged letters and emails. When they spoke to journalists and to friends of their love affair, it was always in the fondest terms.

In late July this year, Cohen received an email from Jan Christian Mollestad, a close friend of Marianne's, saying that she was suffering from cancer. In their last communication, Marianne had told Cohen that she had sold her beach house to help ensure that Axel would be taken care of, but she never mentioned that she was sick. Now, it appeared, she had only a few days left. Cohen wrote back immediately:

> Well Marianne, it's come to this time when we are really so old and our bodies are falling apart and I think I will follow you very soon. Know that I am so close behind you that if you stretch out your hand, I think you can reach mine. And you know that I've always loved you for your beauty and your wisdom, but I don't need to say anything more about that because you know all about that. But now, I just want to wish you a very good journey. Goodbye old friend. Endless love, see you down the road.

Two days later, Cohen got an email from a friend in Norway:

Dear Leonard

Marianne slept slowly out of this life yesterday evening. Totally at ease, surrounded by close friends.

Your letter came when she still could talk and laugh in full consciousness. When we read it aloud, she smiled as only Marianne can. She lifted her hand, when you said you were right behind, close enough to reach her.

It gave her deep peace of mind that you knew her condition. And your blessing for the journey gave her extra strength . . . In her last hour I held her hand and hummed "Bird on the Wire," while she was breathing so lightly. And when we left the room, after her soul had flown out of the window for new adventures, we kissed her head and whispered your everlasting words.

So long, Marianne . . .

———•———

Leonard Cohen lives on the second floor of a modest house in Mid-Wilshire, a diverse, unglamorous precinct of Los Angeles. He is eighty-two. Between 2008 and 2013, he was on tour more or less continuously. It is highly unlikely that his health will permit such rigors ever again. Cohen has an album coming out in October—obsessed with mortality, God-infused, yet funny, called *You Want It Darker*—but friends and musical associates say they'd be surprised to see him onstage again except in a limited way: a single performance, perhaps, or a short residency at one venue. When I emailed ahead to ask Cohen out for dinner, he said that he was more or less "confined to barracks."

Not long ago, one of Cohen's most frequent visitors, and an old friend of mine—Robert Faggen, a professor of literature—brought me by the house. Faggen met Cohen twenty years ago in a grocery store, at the foot of Mt. Baldy, the highest of the San Gabriel Mountains, an hour and a half east of Los Angeles. They were both living near the top of the mountain: Bob in a cabin where he wrote about Frost and Melville and drove down the road to teach his classes at Claremont McKenna College; Cohen in a small Zen Buddhist monastery, where he was an ordained monk. As Faggen was shopping for cold cuts, he heard a familiar basso voice across the store; he looked down the aisle and saw a small, trim man, his head shaved, talking intently with a clerk about varieties of potato salad. Faggen's musical expertise runs more to Mahler's lieder than to popular song. But he is an admirer of Cohen's work and introduced himself. They have been close friends ever since.

Cohen greeted us. He sat in a large blue medical chair, the better to ease the pain from compression fractures in his back. He is now very thin, but he is still handsome, with a full head of gray-white hair and razory dark eyes. He wore a well-tailored midnight-blue suit—even in the sixties he wore suits—and a stickpin through his collar. He extended a hand like a courtly retired capo.

"Hello, friends," he said. "Please, please, sit right there." The depth of his voice makes Tom Waits sound like Eddie Kendricks.

And then, like my mother, he offered what could only have been the complete catalog of his larder: water, juice, wine, a piece of chicken, a slice of cake, "maybe something else." In the hours we spent together, he offered many refreshments, and, always, kindly. "Would you like some slices of cheese and olives?" is not an offer you are likely to get from Axl Rose. "Some vodka? A glass of milk? Schnapps?" And, as with my mother, it is best, sometimes, to say yes. One day, we had cheeseburgers-with-everything ordered from a Fatburger down the street and, on another, thick slices of gefilte fish with horseradish.

Marianne's death was only a few weeks in the past, and Cohen was still amazed at the way his letter—an email to a dying friend—

had gone viral, at least in the Cohen-ardent universe. He hadn't set out to be public about his feelings, but when one of Marianne's closest friends, in Oslo, asked to release the note, he didn't object. "And since there's a song attached to it, and there's a story . . ." he said. "It's just a sweet story. So, in that sense, I'm not displeased."

Like anyone of his age, Cohen counts the losses as a matter of routine. He seemed not so much devastated by Marianne's death as overtaken by the memory of their time together. "There would be a gardenia on my desk perfuming the whole room," he said. "There would be a little sandwich at noon. Sweetness, sweetness everywhere."

Cohen's songs are death-haunted, but then they have been since his earliest verses. A half century ago, a record executive said, "Turn around, kid. Aren't you a little old for this?" But, despite his diminished health, Cohen remains as clear-minded and hardworking as ever, soldierly in his habits. He gets up well before dawn and writes. In the small, spare living room where we sat, there were a couple of acoustic guitars leaning against the wall, a keyboard synthesizer, two laptops, a sophisticated microphone for voice recording. Working with an old collaborator, Pat Leonard, and his son, Adam, who has the producer's credit, Cohen did much of his work for *You Want It Darker* in the living room, emailing recorded files to his partners for additional refinements. Age and the end of age provide a useful, if not entirely desired, air of quiet.

"In a certain sense, this particular predicament is filled with many fewer distractions than other times in my life and actually enables me to work with a little more concentration and continuity than when I had duties of making a living, being a husband, being a father," he said. "Those distractions are radically diminished at this point. The only thing that mitigates against full production is just the condition of my body.

"For some odd reason," he went on, "I have all my marbles, so far. I have many resources, some cultivated on a personal level, but circumstantial, too: my daughter and her children live downstairs, and my son lives two blocks down the street. So I am extremely blessed. I have an assistant who is devoted and skillful. I have a friend like Bob and another friend or two who make my life very rich. So in a certain sense I've never had it better. At a certain point, if you still have your marbles and are not faced with serious financial challenges, you have a chance to put your house in order. It's a cliché, but it's underestimated as an analgesic on all levels. Putting your house in order, if you can do it, is one of the most comforting activities, and the benefits of it are incalculable."

————•————

Cohen came of age after the war. His Montreal, however, was nothing like Philip Roth's Newark or Alfred Kazin's Brownsville. He was brought up in Westmount, a predominantly Anglophone neighborhood, where the city's well-to-do Jews lived. The men in his family, particularly on his father's side, were the "dons" of Jewish Montreal. His grandfather, Cohen told me, "was probably the most significant Jew in Canada," the founder of a range of Jewish institutions; in the wake of anti-Semitic pogroms in the Russian imperium, he saw to it that countless refugees made it to Canada. Nathan Cohen, Leonard's father, ran Freedman Company, the family clothing business. His mother, Masha, came from a family of more recent immigrants. She was loving, depressive, "Chekhovian" in her emotional range, according to Leonard: "She laughed and wept deeply." Masha's father, Solomon Klonitzki-Kline, was a distinguished Talmudic scholar from Lithuania who completed a "Lexicon of Hebrew Homonyms." Leonard went to fine schools, including McGill and, for a while, Columbia. He never resented the family's comforts.

"I have a deep tribal sense," he said. "I grew up in a synagogue that my ancestors built. I sat in the third row. My family was decent.

They were good people, they were handshake people. I never had a sense of rebellion."

When Leonard was nine, his father died; this moment, a primal wound, was when he first used language as a kind of sacrament. "I have some memories of him," Cohen said, and recounted the story of his father's funeral, which was held at their house. "We came down the stairs, and the coffin was in the living room." Contrary to Jewish custom, the funeral workers had left the coffin open. It was winter, and Cohen thought of the gravediggers: it would be difficult to break the frozen ground. He watched his father lowered into the earth. "Then I came back to the house and I went to his closet and I found a premade bow tie. I don't know why I did this, I can't even own it now, but I cut one of the wings of the bow tie off and I wrote something on a piece of paper—I think it was some kind of farewell to my father—and I buried it in a little hole in the backyard. And I put that curious note in there. It was just some attraction to a ritual response to an impossible event."

Cohen's uncles made sure that Masha—and her two children, Leonard and his sister, Esther—did not suffer any financial decline after her husband's death. Leonard studied; he worked in an uncle's foundry, W. R. Cuthbert & Company, pouring metal for sinks and piping, and at the clothing factory, where he picked up a useful skill for his career as a touring musician: he learned to fold suits so they didn't wrinkle. But, as he wrote in a journal, he always imagined himself as a writer, "raincoated, battered hat pulled low above intense eyes, a history of injustice in his heart, a face too noble for revenge, walking the night along some wet boulevard, followed by the sympathy of countless audiences . . . loved by two or three beautiful women who could never have him."

And yet a rock-and-roll life was far from his mind. He set out to be an author. As Sylvie Simmons makes plain in her excellent biography, *I'm Your Man*, Cohen's apprenticeship was in letters. As a teenager, his idols were Yeats and Lorca (he named his daughter after Lorca). At McGill, he read Tolstoy, Proust, Eliot, Joyce, and Pound, and he fell in with a circle of poets, particularly Irving Layton. Cohen, who published his first poem, "Satan in Westmount," when he was nineteen, once said of Layton, "I taught him how to dress, he taught me how to live forever."

Cohen was also taken with music. As a kid, he had learned the songs in the old lefty folk compendium *The People's Song Book*, listened to Hank Williams and other country singers on the radio, and, at sixteen, dressed in his father's old suede jacket, he played in a country music combo called the Buckskin Boys. He took some informal guitar lessons in his twenties from a Spaniard he met next to a local tennis court. After a few weeks, he picked up a flamenco chord progression. When the man failed to appear for their fourth lesson, Cohen called his landlady and learned that the man had killed himself. In a speech many years later, in Asturias, Cohen said, "I knew nothing about the man, why he came to Montreal . . . why he appeared at that tennis court, why he took his life . . . It was those six chords, it was that guitar pattern, that has been the basis of all my songs, and all my music."

Cohen loved the masters of the blues—Robert Johnson, Sonny Boy Williamson, Bessie Smith—and the French storyteller-singers like Édith Piaf and Jacques Brel. He put coins in the jukebox to listen to "The Great Pretender," "Tennessee Waltz," and anything by Ray Charles. And yet when the Beatles came along he was indifferent. "I'm interested in things that contribute to my survival," he said. "I had girlfriends who really irritated me by their devotion to the Beatles. I didn't begrudge them their interest, and there were songs like 'Hey Jude' that I could appreciate. But they didn't seem to be essential to the kind of nourishment that I craved."

The same set of ears that first tuned in to Bob Dylan, in 1961, discovered Leonard Cohen, in 1966. This was John Hammond, a patrician related to the Vanderbilts, and by far the most perceptive scout and producer in the business at that time. He was instrumental in the first recordings of Count Basie, Big Joe Turner, Benny Goodman, Aretha Franklin, and Billie Holiday. Tipped off by friends who were following the folk scene downtown, Hammond called Cohen and asked if he would play for him.

Cohen was thirty-two, a published poet and novelist, but, though a year older than Elvis Presley, a musical novice. He had turned to songwriting largely because he wasn't making a living as a writer. He was staying on the fourth floor of the Chelsea Hotel, on West Twenty-third Street, and filled notebooks during the day. At night, he sang his songs in clubs and met people on the scene: Patti Smith, Lou Reed (who admired Cohen's novel *Beautiful Losers*), Jimi Hendrix (who jammed with him on, of all things, "Suzanne"), and, if just for a night, Janis Joplin ("giving me head on the unmade bed / while the limousines wait in the street").

After taking Cohen to lunch one day, Hammond suggested that they go to Cohen's room, and, sitting on his bed, Cohen played "Suzanne," "Hey, That's No Way to Say Goodbye," "The Stranger Song," and a few others.

When Cohen finished, Hammond grinned and said, "You've got it."

A few months after his audition, Cohen put on a suit and went to the Columbia recording studios in midtown to begin work on his first album. Hammond was encouraging after every take. And after one he said, "Watch out, Dylan!"

Cohen's links to Dylan were obvious—Jewish, literary, a penchant for Biblical imagery, Hammond's tutelage—but the work was divergent. Dylan, even on his earliest records, was moving toward more surrealist, free-associative language and the furious abandon of rock and roll. Cohen's lyrics were no less imaginative or charged, no less ironic or self-investigating, but he was clearer, more economical and formal, more liturgical.

Over the decades, Dylan and Cohen saw each other from time to time. In the early eighties, Cohen went to see Dylan perform in Paris, and the next morning in a café they talked about their latest work. Dylan was especially interested in "Hallelujah." Even before three hundred other performers made "Hallelujah" famous with their cover versions, long before the song was included on the soundtrack for *Shrek* and as a staple on *American Idol*, Dylan recognized the beauty of its marriage of the sacred and the profane. He asked Cohen how long it took him to write.

"Two years," Cohen lied.

Actually, "Hallelujah" had taken him five years. He drafted many dozens of verses and then it was years more before he settled on a final version. In several writing sessions, he found himself in his underwear, banging his head against a hotel room floor.

Cohen told Dylan, "I really like 'I and I,'" a song that appeared on Dylan's album *Infidels*. "How long did it take you to write that?"

"About fifteen minutes," Dylan said.

When I asked Cohen about that exchange, he said, "That's just the way the cards are dealt." As for Dylan's comment that Cohen's songs at the time were "like prayers," Cohen seemed dismissive of any attempt to plumb the mysteries of creation.

"I have no idea what I am doing," he said. "It's hard to describe. As I approach the end of my life, I have even less and less interest in examining what have got to be very superficial evaluations or opinions about the significance of one's life or one's work. I was never given to it when I was healthy, and I am less given to it now."

Although Cohen was steeped more in the country tradition, he was swept up when he heard Dylan's *Bringing It All Back Home* and *Highway 61 Revisited*. One afternoon, years later, when the two had become friendly, Dylan called him in Los Angeles and said he wanted to show him a piece of property he'd bought. Dylan did the driving.

"One of his songs came on the radio," Cohen recalled. "I think it was 'Just Like a Woman' or something like that. It came to the bridge of the song, and he said, 'A lot of eighteen-wheelers crossed that bridge.' Meaning it was a powerful bridge."

Dylan went on driving. After a while, he told Cohen that a famous songwriter of the day had told him, "Okay, Bob, you're Number 1, but I'm Number 2."

Cohen smiled. "Then Dylan says to me, 'As far as I'm concerned, Leonard, *you're* Number 1. I'm Number Zero.' Meaning, as I understood it at the time—and I was not ready to dispute it—that his work was beyond measure and my work was pretty good."

Dylan doesn't often play the role of music critic, but he proved eager to discuss Leonard Cohen. I put a series of questions to him about Number 1, and he answered in a detailed, critical way—nothing cryptic or elusive.

"When people talk about Leonard, they fail to mention his melodies, which to me, along with his lyrics, are his greatest genius," Dylan said. "Even the counterpoint lines—they give a celestial character and melodic lift to every one of his songs. As far as I know, no one else comes close to this in modern music. Even the simplest song, like 'The Law,' which is structured on two fundamental chords, has counterpoint lines that are essential, and anybody who even thinks about doing this song and loves the lyrics would have to build around the counterpoint lines.

"His gift or genius is in his connection to the music of the spheres," Dylan went on. "In the song 'Sisters of Mercy,' for instance, the verses are four elemental lines which change and move at predictable intervals . . . but the tune is anything but predictable. The song just comes in and states a fact. And after that anything can happen and it does, and Leonard allows it to happen. His tone is far from condescending or mocking. He is a tough-minded lover who doesn't recognize the brush-off. Leonard's always above it all. 'Sisters of Mercy' is verse after verse of four distinctive lines, in perfect meter, with no chorus, quivering with drama. The first line begins in a minor key. The second line goes from minor to major and steps up, and changes melody and variation. The third line steps up even higher than that to a different degree, and then the fourth line comes back to the beginning. This is a deceptively unusual musical theme, with or without lyrics. But it's so subtle a listener doesn't realize he's been taken on a musical journey and dropped off somewhere, with or without lyrics."

In the late eighties, Dylan performed "Hallelujah" on the road as a roughshod blues with a sly, ascending chorus. His version sounds less like the prettified Jeff Buckley version than like a work by John Lee Hooker. "That song 'Hallelujah' has resonance for me," Dylan said. "There again, it's a beautifully constructed melody that steps up, evolves, and slips back, all in quick time. But this song has a connective chorus, which when it comes in has a power all of its own. The 'secret chord' and the point-blank I-know-you-better-than-you-know-yourself aspect of the song has plenty of resonance for me."

I asked Dylan whether he preferred Cohen's later work, so colored with intimations of the end. "I like all of Leonard's songs, early or late," he said. " 'Going Home,' 'Show Me the Place,' 'The Darkness.' These are all great songs, deep and truthful as ever and multidimensional, surprisingly melodic, and they make you think and feel. I like some of his later songs even better than his early ones. Yet there's a simplicity to his early ones that I like, too."

Dylan defended Cohen against the familiar critical reproach that his is music to slit your wrists by. He compared him to the Russian Jewish immigrant who wrote "Easter Parade." "I see no disenchantment in Leonard's lyrics at all," Dylan said. "There's always a direct sentiment, as if he's holding a conversation and telling you something, him doing all the talking, but the listener keeps listening. He's very much a descendant of Irving Berlin, maybe the only songwriter in modern history that Leonard can be directly related to. Berlin's songs did the same thing. Berlin was also connected to some kind of celestial sphere. And, like Leonard, he probably had no classical music training, either. Both of them just hear melodies that most of us can only strive for. Berlin's lyrics also fell into place and consisted of half lines, full lines at surprising intervals, using simple elongated words. Both Leonard and Berlin are incredibly crafty. Leonard particularly uses chord progressions that seem classical in shape. He is a much more savvy musician than you'd think."

———•———

Cohen has always found performing unnerving. His first major attempt came in 1967, when Judy Collins asked him to play at Town Hall, in New York, at an anti–Vietnam War benefit. The idea was that he would make his stage debut by singing "Suzanne," an early song of his that Collins had turned into a hit after he sang it to her on the telephone.

"I can't do it, Judy," he told her. "I would die from embarrassment."

As Collins writes in her memoir, she finally cajoled him into it, but that night, from the wings, she could see that Cohen, "his legs shaking inside his trousers," was in trouble. He got halfway through the first verse and then stopped and mumbled an apology. "I can't go on," he said, and walked off into the wings.

Out of sight, Cohen rested his head on Collins's shoulder as she tried to get him to respond to the encouraging shouts from the crowd. "I can't do it," he said. "I can't go back."

"But you will," she said, and, finally, he acceded. He went out, with the crowd cheering, and finished singing "Suzanne."

Since then, Cohen has played thousands of concerts all over the world, but it did not become second nature until he was in his seventies. He was never one of those musicians who talk about feeling most alive and at home onstage. Although he has had many successful performance strategies—wry self-abnegation, drugs, drink—the act of giving concerts often made him feel like "some parrot chained to his stand." He is also a perfectionist; a classic like "Famous Blue Raincoat" still feels "unfinished" to him.

"It stems from the fact that you are not as good as you want to be—that's really what nervousness is," Cohen told me. "That first time I went out with Judy Collins, it wasn't to be the last time I felt this."

In 1972, Cohen, now accompanied by a full complement of musicians and singers, arrived in Jerusalem at the end of a long tour. Just to be in that city was, for Cohen, a charged situation. (The following year, during the war with Egypt, Cohen showed up in Israel, hoping to replace someone who had been drafted. "I am committed to the survival of the Jewish people," he told an interviewer at the time. He ended up performing, often many times a day, for the troops on the front.) Out onstage, Cohen started singing "Bird on the Wire." He stopped after the audience greeted the opening chords and phrase with applause.

"I really enjoy your recognizing these songs," he said. "But I'm scared enough as it is out here, and I think something is wrong every time you begin to applaud. So if you do recognize this song, would you just wave your hands?"

He fumbled again, and what at first had seemed like performative charm now appeared to signal genuine anxiety. "I hope you bear with me," he said. "These songs become meditations for me and sometimes, you know, I just don't get high on it and I feel that I'm cheating you. I'll try it again. If it doesn't work, I'll stop in the middle. There's no reason why we should mutilate a song just to save face."

Cohen began singing "One of Us Cannot Be Wrong."

"I lit a thin green candle . . ."

He stopped again, laughing, unnerved. More fumbling, more deflective jokes.

"I have my rights up here, too, you know," he said, still smiling. "I can sit around and talk if I want to."

By then, it was apparent that there was a problem. "Look, if it doesn't get any better, we'll just end the concert and I'll refund your money," Cohen said. "I really feel that we're cheating you tonight. Some nights, one is raised off the ground, and some nights you just can't get off the ground. And there's no point in lying about it. And tonight we just haven't been getting off the ground, and it says in the Kabbalah . . ." The Jerusalem audience laughed at the mention of the Jewish mystical text. "It says in the Kabbalah that if you can't get off the ground you should stay on the ground! No, it says in the Kabbalah that, unless Adam and Eve face each other, God does not sit on his throne, and somehow the male and female parts of me refuse to encounter one another tonight—and God does not sit on his throne. And this is a terrible thing to have happen in Jerusalem. So, listen, we're going to leave the stage now and try to profoundly meditate in the dressing room to get ourselves back into shape."

I recalled this incident to Cohen—it's captured on a documentary film that floats around the internet—and he remembered it well.

"It was at the end of the tour," he told me. "I thought I was doing very poorly. I went back to the dressing room, and I found some acid in my guitar case." He took the acid. Meanwhile, out in the hall, the audience started singing to Cohen as if to inspire him and call him back. The song was a traditional one, "Hevenu Shalom Aleichem," "We Have Brought Peace Upon You."

"How sweet can an audience possibly be?" Cohen recalled. "So I go out on the stage with the band . . . and I started singing 'So Long, Marianne.' And I see Marianne straight in front of me and I started crying. I turned around and the band was crying, too. And then it turned into something in retrospect quite comic: the entire audience turned into one Jew! And this Jew was saying, 'What else can you show me, kid? I've seen a lot of things, and this don't move the dial!' And this was the entire skeptical side of our tradition, not just writ large but manifested as an actual gigantic being! Judging me hardly begins to describe the operation. It was a sense of invalidation and irrelevance that I felt was authentic, because those feelings have always circulated around my psyche: Where do you get to stand up and speak? For what and whom? And how deep is your experience? How significant is anything you have to say? . . . I think it really invited me to deepen my practice. Dig in deeper, whatever it was, take it more seriously."

Back inside the dressing room, Cohen wept fiercely. "I can't make it, man," he said. "I don't like it. Period. So I'm splitting."

He went out one last time to speak to the audience.

"Listen, people, my band and I are all crying backstage. We're too broken up to go on. But I just want to tell you, thank you and good night."

The next year, he told the press, half-seriously, that the "rock life" was overwhelming him. "I don't find myself leading a life that has many good moments in it," he told a reporter for *Melody Maker*. "So I've decided to screw it. And go."

————•————

For many years, Cohen was more revered than bought. Although his albums generally sold well enough, they did not move on the scale of big rock acts. In the early eighties, when he presented his record company with *Various Positions*—a magnificent album that included "Hallelujah," "Dance Me to the End of Love," and "If It Be Your Will"—Walter Yetnikoff, the head of CBS Records, argued with him about the mix.

"Look, Leonard," he said, "we know you're great, but we don't know if you're any good." Eventually, Cohen learned that CBS had decided not to release the album in the U.S. Years later, accepting an award, he thanked his record company by saying, "I have always been touched by the modesty of their interest in my work."

Suzanne Vega, a singer-songwriter who is in her late fifties, sometimes tells a funny story onstage about Cohen's secret-handshake appeal. When she was eighteen, she was teaching dance and folk singing at a summer camp in the Adirondacks. One night, she met a handsome young man, a counselor from another camp up the road. He was from Liverpool. And his opening line was "Do you like Leonard Cohen?"

This was nearly four decades ago, and, in Vega's memory, admirers of Leonard Cohen in those days were a kind of "secret society." What's more, there was a particular way to answer the young man's semi-innocent question: "Yes, I *love* Leonard Cohen—but only in certain moods." Otherwise, your new friend might think you were a depressive.

But because the young man was English, and not given to the "fake cheer" of Americans, he replied, "I love Leonard Cohen all the time." The result, she says, was an affair that lasted for the rest of the summer.

In the years to come, Cohen's songs were fundamental to Vega's own sense of lyrical precision and possibility. "It was the way he wrote about complicated things," Vega told me. "It was very intimate and personal. Dylan took you to the far ends of the expanding universe, eight minutes of 'one hand waving free,' and I loved that, but it didn't sound like anything I did or was likely to do—it wasn't very earthly. Leonard's songs were a combination of very real details and a sense of mystery, like prayers or spells."

And there was the other thing, too. Once, after Cohen and Vega became friendly, he called and asked her to visit him at his hotel. They met out by the pool. He asked if she wanted to hear his latest song.

"And as I listened to him recite this song—it was a long one—I watched as one woman after another, all in bikinis, arranged themselves on beach chairs behind Leonard," Vega recalled. "After he finished reciting, I said to Leonard, 'Have you noticed these women in bikinis arranging themselves here?' And completely deadpan, without glancing around, Leonard said, 'It works every time.'"

A world of such allurements had costs as well as rewards. In the seventies, Cohen had two children, Lorca and Adam, with his common-law wife, Suzanne Elrod. That relationship fizzled when the decade did. Touring had its charms, but it, too, wore down his spirits. After a tour in 1993, Cohen felt utterly depleted. "I was drinking at least three bottles of Château Latour before performances," he said, allowing that he always poured a glass for others. "The wine bill was enormous. Even then, I think, Château Latour was over three hundred bucks a bottle. But it went so beautifully with the music! I don't know why. When I tried to drink it when there wasn't a performance coming, it meant nothing! I might as well have been drinking Wild Duck or whatever they call it. I mean, it had no significance."

At the same time, a long relationship with the actress Rebecca De Mornay was beginning to come undone. "She got wise to me," Cohen has said. "Finally she saw I was a guy who just couldn't come across. In the sense of being a husband and having more children and the rest." De Mornay, who remains friends with Cohen, told the biographer Sylvie Simmons that he was "having all these relationships with women and not really committing . . . and having this long relationship to his career and yet feeling like it's the last thing he wants to be doing."

———•———

Since his days davening next to his uncles in his grandfather's synagogue, Cohen has been a spiritual seeker. "Anything, Roman Catholicism, Buddhism, LSD, I'm for anything that works," he once said. In the late sixties, when he was living in New York, he studied briefly at a Scientology center and emerged with a certificate that declared him "Grade IV Release." In recent years, he spent many Shabbat mornings and Monday evenings at Ohr HaTorah, a synagogue on Venice Boulevard, talking about Kabbalistic texts with the rabbi there, Mordecai Finley. Sometimes, on Rosh Hashanah and Yom Kippur, Finley, who says that he considers Cohen "a great liturgical writer," read from the pulpit passages from *Book of Mercy*, a 1984 collection of Cohen's that is steeped in the Psalms. "I participated in all these investigations that engaged the imagination of my generation at that time," Cohen has said. "I even danced and sang with the Hare Krishnas—no robe, I didn't join them, but I was trying everything."

To this day, Cohen reads deeply in a multivolume edition of the Zohar, the principal text of Jewish mysticism; the Hebrew Bible; and Buddhist texts. In our conversations, he mentioned the Gnostic Gospels, Lurianic Kabbalah, books of Hindu philosophy, Carl Jung's *Answer to Job*, and Gershom Scholem's biography of Sabbatai Sevi, a self-proclaimed messiah of the seventeenth century. Cohen is also very much at home in the spiritual reaches of the internet, and he listens to the lectures of Yakov Leib HaKohain, a Kabbalist who has converted, serially, to Islam, Catholicism, and Hinduism, and lives in the San Bernardino Mountains with two pit bulls and four cats.

For forty years, Cohen was associated with a Japanese Zen master named Kyozan Joshu Sasaki Roshi. ("Roshi" is an honorific for a venerated teacher, and Cohen always refers to him that way.) Roshi, who died a couple of years ago at the age of a hundred and seven, arrived in Los Angeles in 1962 but never quite learned the language of his adoptive home. Through his translators, though, he adapted traditional Japanese koans for his American students: "How do you realize Buddha nature while driving a car?" Roshi was short, stout, a drinker of sake and expensive Scotch. "I came to have a good time," he once said of his sojourn in the States. "I want Americans to learn how to truly laugh."

Until the early nineties, Cohen used to study with Roshi at the Zen Center, on Mt. Baldy, for periods of learning and meditation that stretched over two or three months a year. He considered Roshi a close friend, a spiritual master, and a deep influence on his work. And so, not long after getting home from the Château Latour tour, in 1993, Cohen went up to Mt. Baldy. This time, he stayed for nearly six years.

"Nobody goes into a Zen monastery as a tourist," Cohen told me. "There are people who do, but they leave in ten minutes because the life is very rigorous. You are getting up at two-thirty in the morning; the camp wakes up at three, but you have to light fires in the *zendo*. The cabins are only heated a few hours a day. There's snow coming in under the badly carpentered doors. You're shoveling snow half the day. And the other half of the day you're sitting in the *zendo*. So in a certain sense you toughen up. Whether it has a spiritual aspect is debatable. It helps you endure, and it makes whining the least appropriate response to suffering. Just on that level it's very valuable."

Cohen lived in a tiny cabin that he outfitted with a coffeemaker, a menorah, a keyboard, and a laptop. Like the other adepts, he cleaned toilets. He had the honor of cooking for Roshi and eventually lived in a cabin that was linked to his teacher's by a covered walkway. For many hours a day, he sat in half lotus, meditating. If he, or anyone else, nodded off during meditation or lost the proper position, one of the monks would come by and rap him smartly on the shoulder with a wooden stick.

"People have the idea that a monastery is a place of serenity and contemplation," Cohen said. "It isn't that at all. It's a hospital, and a lot of the people who end up there can barely walk or speak. So a lot of the activity there is to get people to learn how to walk and speak and breathe and prepare their own meals or shovel their own paths in the winter."

Allen Ginsberg once asked Cohen how he could reconcile his Judaism with Zen. Cohen said that he wasn't looking for a new religion, that he was well satisfied with the religion he had. Zen made no mention of God; it demanded no scriptural devotion. For him, Zen was a discipline rather than a religion, a practice of investigation. "I put on those robes because that was Roshi's school and that was the uniform," he said. Had Roshi been a professor of physics at the University of Heidelberg, Cohen says, he would have learned German and moved to Heidelberg.

Roshi, toward the end of his life, was accused of sexual misconduct. He was never charged with any crime, but some former students, writing in internet chat rooms and in letters to Roshi himself, said that he had sexually groped or coerced many Buddhist students and nuns. An independent Buddhist panel determined that the behavior had been going on since the seventies, and that those "who chose to speak out were silenced, exiled, ridiculed, or otherwise punished," according to *The New York Times*.

One morning, Bob Faggen drove me up the mountain to the Zen Center. A former Boy Scout camp, the center comprises a series of rough-hewn cabins surrounded by pines and cedars. It was striking how few people were around. One monk told me that Roshi had left no successor and that the center had not yet recovered from the scandal. Cohen, for his part, took pains to explain Roshi's multiple transgressions without excusing them. "Roshi," he said, "was a very naughty guy."

In 1996, Cohen became a monk, but that did not safeguard him from depression, a lifelong nemesis; two years later, it overwhelmed him. "I've dealt with depression ever since my adolescence," he said. "Moving into some periods, which were debilitating, when I found it hard to get off the couch, to periods when I was fully operative but the background noise of anguish still prevailed." Cohen tried antidepressants. He tried throwing them out. Nothing worked. Finally, he told Roshi he was "going down the mountain." In a collection of poems called *Book of Longing,* he wrote:

> I left my robes hanging on a peg
> in the old cabin
> where I had sat so long
> and slept so little.
> I finally understood
> I had no gift
> for Spiritual Matters.

In fact, Cohen was hardly done with his searching. Just a week after returning home, he boarded a flight to Mumbai to study with another spiritual guide. He took a room in a modest hotel and went to daily *satsangs,* spiritual discussions, at the apartment of Ramesh Balsekar, a former president of the Bank of India and a teacher of Advaita Vedanta, a Hindu discipline. Cohen read Balsekar's book *Consciousness Speaks,* which teaches a single universal consciousness, no "you" or "me," and denies a sense of individual free will, any sense that any one person is a "doer."

Cohen spent nearly a year in Mumbai, calling on Balsekar in the mornings, and spending the rest of the day swimming, writing, and wandering the city. For reasons that he now says are "impossible to penetrate," his depression lifted. He was ready to come home. The story, and the way Cohen tells it now, full of uncertainty and modesty, reminded me of the chorus of "Anthem," a song that took him ten years to write and that he recorded just before he first headed up the mountain:

> Ring the bells that still can ring
> Forget your perfect offering
> There is a crack in everything
> That's how the light gets in.

Even if he was now freed of depression, the next crisis was not far off. Aside from a few indulgences, Cohen was not obsessed with luxury. "My project has been completely different than my contemporaries'," he says. His circle in Montreal valued modesty. "The minimum environment that would enable you to do your work with the least distraction and the most aesthetic deliverance came from a modest surrounding. A palace, a yacht would be an enormous distraction from the project. My fantasies went the other way. The way I lived on Mt. Baldy was perfect for me. I liked the communal life, I liked living in a little shack."

And yet he had made a considerable fortune from album sales, concerts, and the publishing rights to his songs. "Hallelujah" was recorded so often and so widely that Cohen jokingly called a moratorium on it. He certainly had enough money to feel secure about his two children and their mother, and a few other dependents.

Before he left on his spiritual adventures, Cohen had ceded nearly absolute control of his financial affairs to Kelley Lynch, his business manager for seventeen years and, at one time, briefly, his lover. In 2004, however, he discovered that his accounts had been emptied. Millions of dollars were gone. Cohen fired Lynch and sued her. The court ruled in Cohen's favor, awarding him more than five million dollars.

In Los Angeles County Superior Court, Cohen testified that Lynch had been so outraged by the suit that she started calling him twenty, thirty times a day and inundating him with emails, some directly threatening, eventually ignoring a restraining order. "It makes me feel very conscious about my surroundings," Cohen said, according to *The Guardian*'s account of the trial. "Every time I see a car slow down, I get worried." Lynch was sentenced to eighteen months in prison and five years' probation.

After thanking the judge and his attorney in his usual high style, Cohen turned to his antagonist. "It is my prayer," Cohen told the court, "that Ms. Lynch will take refuge in the wisdom of her religion, that a spirit of understanding will convert her heart from hatred to remorse, from anger to kindness, from the deadly intoxication of revenge to the lowly practices of self-reform."

Cohen has never managed to collect the awarded damages, and, because the situation is still a matter of litigation, he does not like to talk about it. But one result was plain: he would need to return to the stage. Even a Zen monk has to earn some coin.

————•————

There is something irresistible about Cohen's charm. For proof, take a look at a YouTube clip called "Why It's Good to Be Leonard Cohen": a filmmaker follows Cohen backstage as a beautiful German-accented actress tries to coax him, in front of a full dressing room, to "go somewhere" with her as he wryly rebuffs her. He is no less charming with men.

So it was more than a little surprising when Faggen and I returned to the house one afternoon thinking that we were on time and were informed, in the sternest terms imaginable, that we were not. In fact, Cohen, wearing a dark suit and a fedora, settled into his medical chair and gave us the most forbidding talking-to I have experienced since grade school. I'm one of those tiresome people who are rarely, if ever, late; who show up, old-mannishly, for flights much too early. But there had apparently been a misunderstanding about the time of our visit, and a text to him and his assistant seemed to have gone unseen. Every effort to apologize or explain, mine and Faggen's, was dismissed as "not the point." Cohen reminded us of his poor health. This was an abuse of his time. A violation. Even "a form of elder abuse." More apologies, more rebuffs. This wasn't about anger or apology, he went on. He felt no rage, no, but we had to understand that we were not "doers," none of us have free will . . . And so on. I recognized the language of his teacher in Mumbai. But that didn't make it sting any less. The lecture—steely, ominous, high-flown—went on quite a long time. I felt humiliated, but also defensive. In the dynamic of people getting something off their chest, the speaker feels cleansed, the listener accused and miserable.

Finally, Cohen eased into other matters. And the subject that he was happiest to talk about was the tour that began as a means of restoring what had been stolen from him. In 2007, he started conceiving a tour with a full band: three backup singers, two guitarists, drummer, keyboard player, bassist, and saxophonist (later replaced by a violinist). He rehearsed the band for three months.

"I hadn't played any of these songs for fifteen years," he said. "My voice had changed. My range had changed. I didn't know what to do. There was no way I could transpose the positions that I knew." Instead, Cohen tuned the strings on his guitar down two whole steps, so, for instance, the low E was now a low C. Cohen had always had a deep, intimate voice, but now, with age, and after countless cigarettes, it is a fantastical growl, confiding, lordly. In concert, he always got a knowing laugh with this line from "Tower of Song": "I was born like this, I had no choice / I was born with the gift of a golden voice."

Neil Larsen, who played keyboards in Cohen's band, said that the preparation was meticulous. "We rehearsed very close to the way you would record," he told me. "We did one song over and over and made adjustments. He was locking the lyrics into his memory, too. Usually it takes a while before a tour jells. Not this one. We went out ready."

The tour started in Canada, and then went everywhere during the next five years—three hundred and eighty shows, from New York to Nice, Moscow to Sydney. Cohen began every performance saying that he and the band would give "everything we've got," and they did. "I think he was competing with Springsteen," Sharon Robinson, a singer and frequent cowriter, joked about the length of the shows. "They were close to four hours some nights."

Cohen was in his mid-seventies by this time, and his manager did everything possible for the performer to marshal his energies. It was a first-class operation: a private plane, where Cohen could write and sleep; good hotels, where he could read and compose on a keyboard; a car to take him to the hotel the minute he stepped off the stage.

"Everybody was rehearsed not only in the notes but also in something unspoken," he said. "You could feel it in the dressing room as you moved closer to the concert, you could feel the sense of commitment, tangible in the room." This time, there was no warmup with Château Latour. "I didn't drink at all. Occasionally, I'd have half a Guinness with Neil Larsen, but I had no interest in alcohol."

The show that I saw, at Radio City, was among the most moving performances I've ever experienced. Here was Cohen, an old master of his art, serving up the thick cream of his catalog with a soulful corps of exacting musicians. Time and again, he would enact the song as well as sing it, taking one knee in gratitude to the object of affection, taking both knees to emphasize his devotion, to the audience, to the musicians, to the song.

The tour not only restored Cohen's finances (and then some); it also brought a sense of satisfaction rarely associated with him. "One time I asked him on the bus, 'Are you enjoying this?' And he would never really own up to enjoying it," Sharon Robinson recalled. "But after we finished I was at his house one day, and he admitted to me that there was something extremely fulfilling about that tour, something that brought his career full circle that he hadn't expected."

In 2009, Cohen gave his first performance in Israel since 1985, at a stadium in Ramat Gan, donating the proceeds to Israeli-Palestinian peace organizations. He had wanted to perform in Ramallah, in the West Bank, too, but Palestinian groups decided that this was politically untenable. And yet he persisted, dedicating the concert to the cause of "reconciliation, tolerance, and peace," and the song "Anthem" to the bereaved. At the end of the show,

Cohen raised his hands, rabbinically, and recited in Hebrew the *birkat kohanim*, the priestly blessing, over the crowd.

"It's not self-consciously religious," Cohen told me. "I know that it's been described that way, and I am happy with that. It's part of the intentional fallacy. But when I see James Brown it has a religious feel. Anything deep does."

When I asked him if he intended his performances to reflect a kind of devotion, he hesitated before he answered. "Does artistic dedication begin to touch on religious devotion?" he said. "I start with artistic dedication. I know that if the spirit is on you it will touch on to the other human receptors. But I dare not begin from the other side. It's like pronouncing the holy name—you don't do it. But if you are lucky, and you are graced, and the audience is in a particular salutary condition, then these deeper responses will be produced."

The final night of the tour happened to be in Auckland, in late December 2013, and the last songs were exit songs: the prayerful "If It Be Your Will," and then "Closing Time," "I Tried to Leave You," and, finally, a cover of the Drifters song "Save the Last Dance for Me."

The musicians all knew this was not only the last night of a long voyage but, for Cohen, perhaps the last voyage. "Everybody knows that everything has to end sometime," Sharon Robinson told me. "So, as we left, there was the thought: This is it."

———•———

There is probably no more touring ahead. What is on Cohen's mind now is family, friends, and the work at hand. "I've had a family to support, so there's no sense of virtue attached to it," he said. "I've never sold widely enough to be able to relax about money. I had two kids and their mother to support and my own life. So there was never an option of cutting out. Now it's a habit. And there's the element of time, which is powerful, with its incentive to finish up. Now I haven't gotten near finishing up. I've finished up a few things. I don't know how many other things I'll be able to get to, because at this particular stage I experience deep fatigue. . . . There are times when I just have to lie down. I can't play anymore, and my back goes fast also. Spiritual things, *baruch Hashem*"—thank God—"have fallen into place, for which I am deeply grateful."

Cohen has unpublished poems to arrange, unfinished lyrics to finish and record or publish. He's considering doing a book in which poems, like pages of the Talmud, are surrounded by passages of interpretation.

"The big change is the proximity to death," he said. "I am a tidy kind of guy. I like to tie up the strings if I can. If I can't, that's okay. But my natural thrust is to finish things that I've begun."

Cohen said he had a "sweet little song" that he'd been working through, one of many, and, suddenly, he closed his eyes and began reciting the lyrics:

Listen to the hummingbird
Whose wings you cannot see
Listen to the hummingbird
Don't listen to me.
Listen to the butterfly
Whose days but number three
Listen to the butterfly
Don't listen to me.
Listen to the mind of God
Which doesn't need to be
Listen to the mind of God
Don't listen to me.

He opened his eyes, paused awhile. Then he said, "I don't think I'll be able to finish those songs. Maybe, who knows? And maybe

I'll get a second wind, I don't know. But I don't dare attach myself
to a spiritual strategy. I don't dare do that. I've got some work to do.
Take care of business. I am ready to die. I hope it's not too uncom-
fortable. That's about it for me."

Cohen's hand has been bothering him, so he plays the guitar
less than he did—"I've lost my 'chop'"—but he was eager to show
me his synthesizer. He sets a chord progression going with his left
hand, flips some switches to one mode or another, and plays a melody with his right. At one point, he flipped on the "Greek" mode,
and suddenly he was singing a Greek fisherman's song, as if we had
suddenly transported ourselves back in time, to Dousko's Taverna,
"in the deep night of fixed and falling stars" on the island of Hydra.

In his chair, Cohen waved away any sense of what might follow
death. That was beyond understanding and language: "I don't ask
for information that I probably wouldn't be able to process even if
it were granted to me." Persistence, living to the last, loose ends,
work—that was the thing. A song called "Going Home" made clear
his sense of limits: "He will speak these words of wisdom / Like a
sage, a man of vision / Though he knows he's really nothing / But
the brief elaboration of a tube."

The new record opens with the title track, "You Want It
Darker," and in the chorus, the singer declares:

Hineni Hineni
I'm ready my Lord.

Hineni is Hebrew for "Here I am," Abraham's answer to the
summons of God to sacrifice his son Isaac; the song is an announcement of readiness, a man at the end preparing for his service and
devotion. Cohen asked Gideon Zelermyer, the cantor at Shaar
Hashomayim, the synagogue of his youth in Montreal, to sing the
backing vocals. And yet the man sitting in his medical chair was
anything but haunted or defeated.

"I know there's a spiritual aspect to everybody's life, whether they want to cop to it or not," Cohen said. "It's there, you can feel it in people—there's some recognition that there is a reality that they cannot penetrate but which influences their mood and activity. So that's operating. That activity at certain points of your day or night insists on a certain kind of response. Sometimes it's just like: 'You are losing too much weight, Leonard. You're dying, but you don't have to cooperate enthusiastically with the process.' Force yourself to have a sandwich.

"What I mean to say is that you hear the *Bat Kol*." The divine voice. "You hear this other deep reality singing to you all the time, and much of the time you can't decipher it. Even when I was healthy, I was sensitive to the process. At this stage of the game, I hear it saying, 'Leonard, just get on with the things you have to do.' It's very compassionate at this stage. More than at any time of my life, I no longer have that voice that says, 'You're fucking up.' That's a tremendous blessing, really."

October 2016

Leonard Cohen, who was suffering from leukemia, died on November 7, 2016. He was buried in the family plot in Montreal.

SOUL SURVIVOR

Late on a winter night, Aretha Franklin sat in the dressing room of Caesars Windsor Hotel and Casino, in Ontario. She did not wear the expression of someone who has just brought boundless joy to a few thousand souls.

"What was with the sound?" she said, in a tone somewhere between perplexity and irritation. Feedback had pierced a verse of "My Funny Valentine," and before she sat down at the piano to play "Inseparable," a tribute to the late Natalie Cole, she narrowed her gaze and called on a "Mr. Lowery" to fix the levels once and for all. Miss Franklin, as nearly everyone in her circle tends to call her, was distinctly, if politely, displeased. "For a time up there, I just couldn't hear myself right," she said.

On the counter in front of her, next to her makeup mirror and hairbrush, were small stacks of hundred-dollar bills. She collects on the spot or she does not sing. The cash goes into her handbag and the handbag either stays with her security team or goes out onstage and resides, within eyeshot, on the piano. "It's the era she grew up in—she saw so many people, like Ray Charles and B.B. King, get ripped off," a close friend, the television host and author Tavis Smiley, told me. "There is the sense in her very often that people are out to harm you. And she won't have it. You are not going to disrespect her."

Franklin has won eighteen Grammy awards, sold tens of millions of records, and is generally acknowledged to be the greatest singer in the history of postwar popular music. James Brown, Sam Cooke, Etta James, Otis Redding, Ray Charles: even they cannot match her power, her range from gospel to jazz, R&B, and pop. At the 1998 Grammys, Luciano Pavarotti called in sick with a sore throat and Aretha, with twenty minutes' notice, sang "Nessun dorma" in his place. What distinguishes her is not merely the breadth of her catalog or the cataract force of her vocal instrument; it's her musical intelligence, her way of singing behind the beat, of spraying a wash of notes over a single word or syllable, of constructing, moment by moment, the emotional power of a three-minute song. "Respect" is as precise an artifact as a Ming vase.

"There are certain women singers who possess, beyond all the boundaries of our admiration for their art, an uncanny power to evoke our love," Ralph Ellison wrote in a 1958 essay on Mahalia Jackson. "Indeed, we feel that if the idea of aristocracy is more than mere class conceit, then these surely are our natural queens." In 1967, at the Regal Theatre, in Chicago, the DJ Pervis Spann presided over a coronation in which he placed a crown on Franklin's head and pronounced her the Queen of Soul.

The Queen does not rehearse the band—not for a casino gig in Windsor, Ontario. She leaves it to her longtime musical director, a seventy-nine-year-old former child actor and doo-wop singer named H. B. Barnum, to assemble her usual rhythm section and backup singers and pair them with some local union horn and string players, and run them through a three-hour scan of anything Franklin might choose to sing: the hits from the late sixties and early seventies—"Chain of Fools," "Spirit in the Dark," "Think"—along with more recent recordings. Sometimes, Franklin will switch things up and pull out a jazz tune—"Cherokee" or "Skylark"—

but that is rare. Her greatest concern is husbanding her voice and her energies. When she wears a fur coat onstage, it's partly to keep warm and prevent her voice from closing up. But it's also because that's what the old I've-earned-it-now-I'm-gonna-wear-it gospel stars often did: they wore the mink. Midway through her set, she makes what she calls a "false exit," and slips backstage and lets the band noodle while she rests. "It's a fifteen-round fight, and so she paces herself," Barnum says. "Aretha is not thirty years old." She is seventy-four.

Franklin doesn't get around much anymore. For the past thirty-four years, she has refused to fly, which means that she hasn't been able to perform in favorite haunts from the late sixties, like the Olympia, in Paris, or the Concertgebouw, in Amsterdam. When she does travel, it's by bus. Not a Greyhound, exactly, but, still, it's exhausting. A trip not long ago from her house, outside Detroit, to Los Angeles proved too much to contemplate again. "That one just wore me out," she said. "It's a nice bus, but it took *days!*" She has attended anxious-flyer classes and said that she's determined to get on a plane again soon. "I'm thinking about making the flight from Detroit to Chicago," she said. "Baby steps."

Even if the concert in Windsor was a shadow of her stage work a generation ago, there were intermittent moments of sublimity. Naturally, she has lost range and stamina, but she is miles better than Sinatra at a similar age. And she has survived longer than nearly any contemporary. In Windsor, she lagged for a while and then ripped up the B.B. King twelve-bar blues "Sweet Sixteen." Performing "Chain of Fools," a replica of the Reverend Elijah Fair's gospel tune "Pains of Life," she managed to make it just as greasy as when she recorded it, in 1968.

Before the show, I was talking with people in the aisles. More than a few said they hadn't seen Franklin or paid much attention to her recordings for years. It was an older crowd, but they hadn't come to see an oldies show. What reawakened them, they said, was precisely what had reawakened me: a video, gone viral, of Franklin singing "(You Make Me Feel Like) A Natural Woman" at last December's Kennedy Center Honors. Watch it if you haven't: in under five minutes, your life will improve in the moment by a minimum of forty-seven percent. Aretha comes out onstage looking like the fanciest church lady in Christendom: fierce red lipstick, floor-length mink, a brocaded pink-and-gold dress that Bessie Smith would have worn if she'd sold tens of millions of records. Aretha sits down at the piano. She adjusts the mike. Then she proceeds to punch out a series of gospel chords in 12/8 time, and, if you have an ounce of sap left in you, you are overcome. A huge orchestra wells up beneath her, and four crack backup singers sliver their perfectly timed accents ("Ah-hoo!") in front of her lines. Aretha is singing with a power that rivals her own self of three or four decades ago.

Up in the first tier, sitting next to the Obamas, Carole King is about to fall over the rail. She is an honoree, and wrote "A Natural Woman" with her first husband, Gerry Goffin. From the moment Franklin starts the first verse—"Looking out on the morning rain, / I used to feel . . . so uninspired"—King is rolling her eyes back in her head and waving on the music as if in a kind of ecstatic possession. She soon spots Obama wiping a tear from his cheek. ("The cool cat wept!" King told me later. "I loved that.")

King hadn't seen Franklin in a long time, and when she had Franklin was not performing at this level of intensity. "Seeing her sit down to play the piano put me rungs higher on the levels of joy," King says. And when Franklin gets up from the piano bench to finish off the song—"That's a piece of theatre, and she's a diva in the best sense, so, of *course*, she had to do that at the perfect moment"—the joy deepens.

King recalls how the song came about. It was 1967, and she and Goffin were in Manhattan, walking along Broadway, and Jerry Wexler, of Atlantic Records, pulled up beside them in a limousine, rolled down the window, and said, "I'm looking for a really big hit for Aretha. How about writing a song called 'A Natural Woman'?" He rolled up the window and the car drove off. King and Goffin went home to Jersey. That night, after tucking their kids into bed, they sat down and wrote the music and the lyrics. By the next morning, they had a hit.

"I hear these things in my head, where they *might* go, how they *might* sound," King says. "But I don't have the chops to do it myself. So it was like witnessing a dream realized."

Beyond the music itself, the moment everyone talked about after Franklin's performance at the Kennedy Center was the way, just before the final chorus, as she was reaching the all-out crescendo, she stripped off her mink and let it fall to the floor. *Whoosh!* Dropping the fur—it's an old gospel move, a gesture of emotional abandon, of letting loose. At Mahalia Jackson's wake, Clara Ward, one of Aretha's greatest influences, threw her mink stole at the open casket after she sang "Beams of Heaven." The fur is part of the drama, the royal persona. When Franklin went to see Diahann Carroll in a production of *Sunset Boulevard*, in Toronto, she had two seats: one for her, one for the mink.

Backstage in Windsor, I asked Franklin about that night in D.C. Her mood brightened. "One of the three or four greatest nights of my life," she said.

The cool cat wept, King had marveled. When I emailed a question to President Obama via his press office about Aretha Franklin and that night, Obama wasn't reticent in his reply. "Nobody embodies more fully the connection between the African American spiritual, the blues, R. & B., rock and roll—the way that hardship and sorrow were transformed into something full of beauty and vitality and hope," he wrote back. "American history wells up when Aretha sings. That's why, when she sits down at a piano and sings 'A Natural Woman,' she can move me to tears—the same way that Ray Charles's version of 'America the Beautiful' will always be in my view the most patriotic piece of music ever performed—because it captures the fullness of the American experience, the view from the bottom as well as the top, the good and the bad, and the possibility of synthesis, reconciliation, transcendence."

———•———

So much of this history—the transformation of hardship and sorrow, the spiritual uplift after boundless pain, gospel after blues—is a particular inheritance of the Black church. In *The Souls of Black Folk*, W. E. B. Du Bois writes that, "despite caricature and defilement," the music of the Black church "remains the most original and beautiful expression of human life and longing yet born on American soil." From the days of slavery, the Black church was a refuge, a safe house of community, worship, and speech, and as the decades passed the music of Sunday morning became increasingly associated with the music of the night before. Thomas A. Dorsey, a father of modern gospel, was a whorehouse piano player and the musical director of the Pilgrim Baptist Church, in Chicago. His songs were sung at rent parties, and at the funeral of Dr. King. His gospel and his barrelhouse blues—"Take My Hand, Precious Lord" and "It's Tight Like That," "Peace in the Valley" and "Big Fat Mama"—possess, in his words, "the same feeling, a grasping of the heart."

Aretha's father, Clarence LaVaughn Franklin, was the most famous Black preacher of his day, and by far the most profound influence on the course of her life. He was born in 1915 and grew up in Sunflower County, in the Mississippi Delta. This was the same landscape that bred Robert Johnson, Son House, Howlin' Wolf, Muddy Waters, and Fannie Lou Hamer. B.B. King, another Delta neighbor, described in his memoirs that common ground: the Klan and the cross burnings; the fury suppressed in every child who encountered a lynching—the "strange fruit" hanging from a tree near the courthouse: "I feel disgust and disgrace and rage and every emotion that makes me cry without tears and scream without sound."

When C. L. Franklin was around fifteen, he experienced a vision: he saw a single plank on the wall of his house engulfed in flames. "A voice spoke to me from behind the plank," he told the ethnomusicologist Jeff Todd Titon, "and said something like 'Go and preach the gospel to all the nations.'" By the time he was eighteen, he was a circuit rider, an itinerant preacher hitchhiking from church to church.

Eventually, he landed a pulpit in Memphis, where he attracted notice as "the king of the young whoopers," a style of preaching that begins with a relatively measured exposition of a passage from Scripture and then crescendos into an ecstatic, musical flight, with the kind of call-and-response that became embedded in the music of James Brown.

Franklin left Memphis in 1944 and, after a two-year residence at a church in Buffalo, settled in Detroit, at the New Bethel Baptist Church. There he established a reputation, acquiring one nickname after another—the Black Prince, the Jitterbug Preacher, the Preacher with the Golden Voice. In those days, New Bethel was on Hastings Street, the spine of Paradise Valley, which was the center of the Black community. Detroit had swelled with Black migrants from the South, and Hastings Street was dense with churches and Black-run beauty salons, barbershops, funeral homes; around the corner from New Bethel was the Flame Show Bar and Lee's Sensation. Franklin was, in the phrase of one of his congregants, "stinky sharp." He drove a Cadillac and took to wearing slick suits and alligator shoes.

Franklin, his wife, Barbara Siggers, and their four children—Erma, Cecil, Carolyn, and Aretha—lived in a parsonage house on East Boston Boulevard, among Black professionals and businesspeople. There were six bedrooms and a living room with silk curtains and a grand piano. Yet, while Franklin lived large, he preached a kind of Black liberation theology—Baptist, but inflected at times with the accents of the Pentecostal, or "sanctified," church. As his scrupulous biographer Nick Salvatore writes, he was "unique among his fellow ministers in that he welcomed all of the residents of Hastings Street—prostitutes, drug dealers and pimps as well as the businessmen, professionals, and the devout working classes."

Franklin gained national fame by recording his sermons. The albums sold in the hundreds of thousands. On Sunday nights, he could be heard on WLAC, a Nashville-based station that covered half the country. John Lewis, a leader of the SNCC and a congressman since 1987, recalls listening to Franklin on the radio when he was growing up, in Pike County, Alabama. "He was a master at building his sermon, pacing it, layering it, lifting it level by level to a climax and then finally bringing it *home*," Lewis wrote in his memoir *Walking with the Wind*. "No one could bring it home like the Reverend Franklin."

As a girl, Aretha was thoroughly absorbed in the church life of New Bethel and in the cultural life of her living room, which, at times, seemed to represent the epicenter and genealogy of African American music. Sitting on the stairs, she watched Art Tatum and Nat Cole play the piano. Oscar Peterson, Duke Ellington, Della Reese, Ella Fitzgerald, Billy Eckstine, and Lionel Hampton came to visit. Dinah Washington coached the girls on their singing. The Reverend James Cleveland, a pillar of the gospel world, showed Aretha how to play gospel chords. The kids nearby included Diana Ross, Smokey Robinson, and the roster of what became Motown.

As C. L. Franklin's fame grew, Salvatore writes, so did his penchant for drinking, womanizing, and worse. In 1940, he had fathered a child with a twelve-year-old girl, and he remained unrepentant. He could also be abusive to the women in his life. In 1948, when Aretha was six, her mother left Detroit to live in Buffalo. The children saw her occasionally, but there was always a looming and powerful sadness in the house. As Mahalia Jackson, a close friend of the Franklins, put it, "The whole family wanted for love." C. L. Franklin's mother helped care for the children, as did a string of friends, secretaries, and lovers, including Clara Ward, of the Ward Singers, one of the great gospel vocalists of her time. Barbara Siggers died in 1952.

In the mid-fifties, Franklin started the C. L. Franklin Gospel Caravan and toured the country for weeks at a time, preaching his greatest hits: "The Eagle Stirreth Her Nest," "Dry Bones in the Valley," "The Man at the Pool." Little Sammy Bryant, a dwarf who was a preternaturally talented singer, often opened the show and appeared alongside gospel stars like the Dixie Hummingbirds, Sister Rosetta Tharpe, and the Soul Stirrers, featuring Sam Cooke. Aretha was in his entourage, playing piano and singing. The voice—ringing, powerful, soulful—and the musical guile were there from the start. She could riff, bending notes as if high on the neck of a guitar; she had fantastic range and command of every effect, from melisma to circling the beat. These techniques came into play in her career in R&B, soul, and pop, but "all that was *echt* gospel," according to the scholar Anthony Heilbut.

When Aretha was fifteen, she recorded several gospel songs, among them "Never Grow Old" and "While the Blood Runs Warm." She also saw a great deal of life, including the libertine atmosphere surrounding the gospel music scene. By the time she recorded those first songs, she was pregnant with her second child. She left school and went on the road for, more or less, the rest of her life.

Aretha did not inherit a purely religious and musical legacy. The Franklin house was also political. She was, by the standards of Paradise Valley, a young woman of status and privilege, but she suffered the same humiliations as any Black woman traveling through the South or venturing into the white precincts of Detroit. By the time of the murder of Emmett Till, in 1955, C. L. Franklin had opened New Bethel up to the movement, and, from his pulpit, he denounced segregation and white supremacy. When Dr. King came to Detroit, he stayed with the Franklins.

Aretha, too, joined the movement. At the same time, she yearned for larger stages. She saw how Sam Cooke had crossed over into R&B as if it were the most natural of passages. In 1960, when she was eighteen, she moved to New York and signed with Columbia Records. This marked the start of an extended apprenticeship under John Hammond, who had been behind the careers of Billie Holiday and Count Basie. Hammond had it in his mind that Aretha should be the next great jazz singer, even though the form was no longer ascendant. It wasn't until 1966, when Franklin went to work with Jerry Wexler and Ahmet Ertegun, at Atlantic Records, that she really made her hits in R&B. But at Columbia, even singing standards like "Skylark" and "How Deep Is the Ocean," she broke into the secular world. Franklin had her father's support and the example of Cooke, but she felt compelled to publish a column, in 1961, in the *Amsterdam News*, saying, "I don't think that in any matter I did the Lord a disservice when I made up my mind two years ago to switch over." She went on, "After all, the blues is a music born out of the slavery day sufferings of my people."

On June 23, 1963, C. L. Franklin helped Dr. King organize the Walk to Freedom, a march of more than a hundred thousand people through downtown Detroit. At Cobo Hall, King, acknowledging "my good friend" C. L. Franklin, delivered a speech filled with passages that he recycled, two months later, at the March on Washington. "This afternoon I have a dream," he told the crowd. "I have a dream," that "little white children and little Negro children" will be "judged by the content of their character and not the color of their skin."

King later confided to C. L. Franklin, "Frank, I will never live to see forty." At Dr. King's funeral, in April 1968, Aretha was asked to sing Thomas Dorsey's "Precious Lord." She was now a central voice both in the Black community, eclipsing her father, and in the musical world. She had crossed over.

The songs on her first records for Atlantic—"Do Right Woman, Do Right Man," "Respect," "Dr. Feelgood," "(You Make Me Feel Like) A Natural Woman," "Think," "Chain of Fools"—were the resolution of her apprenticeship. As she landed on just the right blend of the church and the blues, she was now celebrated as the greatest voice in popular music. "Respect" and "Think" became anthems of feminism and Black power and stand alongside "Mississippi Goddamn," "Busted," and "A Change Is Gonna Come." "Daddy had been preaching Black pride for decades," she told the writer David Ritz, "and we as a people had rediscovered how beautiful Black truly was and were echoing, 'Say it loud, I'm Black and I'm proud.'"

At the same time, Franklin found that the strains of life as a star, as a mother, as a daughter to her tempestuous father were at times unbearable. Ted White, her first husband—they married in 1961 and divorced eight years later—was a jumped-up street hustler who abused her. In 1969, when her father let a radical organization called the Republic of New Africa use the sanctuary at New Bethel, the night ended in a bloody gun battle between the group and the Detroit police. The next year, she came out onstage, in St. Louis, and started singing "Respect" but then walked off, unable to continue. The promoter announced that Franklin had suffered "a nervous breakdown from extreme personal problems." She soon recovered enough to perform, but she rarely seemed unburdened, except in the studio and onstage.

"I think of Aretha as Our Lady of Mysterious Sorrows," Wexler wrote in his memoirs. "Her eyes are incredible, luminous eyes covering inexplicable pain. Her depressions could be as deep as the dark sea. I don't pretend to know the sources of her anguish, but anguish surrounds Aretha as surely as the glory of her musical aura."

———•———

Franklin's vulnerability has brought with it an intense desire for control that often leads to still more anguish. When it came time to do an autobiography, she enlisted David Ritz, who had produced fascinating books with Ray Charles, Etta James, Bettye LaVette, and Smokey Robinson. He found her a singularly resistant subject. She insisted on stripping the book of nearly anything gritty or dark. Published in 1999, it reads like an extended press release. "Denial is her strategy for emotional survival," Ritz told me. It was only at the microphone, in her music, he concluded, that Franklin felt in command. There are reports that she has, in recent years, been struggling with cancer, but her friends say she'd never admit to such a thing, "not even on her deathbed."

Fifteen years after the autobiography was published, and flopped, Ritz published an unauthorized biography, filled with material that he had accumulated over time from intimate personal and professional sources. The woman who emerges is a musical genius and a pivotal figure in the cultural history of the Black freedom movement; she is also someone who has suffered countless losses, been mistreated in many ways, and at times has reactions that try the patience of her associates, creditors, family, and friends. Franklin denounced the book: "Lies and more lies!" But none of the sources, including those closest to her, have backed away.

Even Beyoncé has had the experience of displeasing Franklin. The occasion was the 2008 Grammy Awards. Beyoncé, working from lines on a teleprompter that were likely not of her own devising, introduced Tina Turner to the audience as "the Queen." With due respect to Tina Turner, this is Aretha's title, as surely as it is

Elizabeth II's, and Franklin, who is easily wounded, issued a scathing proclamation. It was a "cheap shot," she said.

A larger consequence of Franklin's craving for control is that her audience has been denied one of her greatest treasures. Not long ago, Ahmir Khalib Thompson, the drummer and bandleader better known as Questlove, posted this on his Instagram feed: "Of all the 'inside industry' stuff I've been privy to learn about NOTHING has tortured my soul more than knowing one of the GREATEST recorded moments in gospel history was just gonna sit on the shelf and collect dust."

Questlove was referring to the holy grail of Aretha Studies—a filmed version, never seen in public, of "Amazing Grace," two gospel concerts that Franklin gave in January 1972 at the New Temple Missionary Baptist Church, in south-central Los Angeles. Pop music has long tantalized its completist fans with rumors of "rare footage": there was "Eat the Document," featuring a scene in which a stoned John Lennon teases an even more stoned Bob Dylan ("Do you suffer from sore eyes, groovy forehead, or curly hair?"); and there was "Cocksucker Blues," Robert Frank's collaboration with the Rolling Stones, featuring Mick Jagger snorting coke. Both films are now pretty easy to find—and neither is essential.

The film of "Amazing Grace" is another matter. Atlantic issued a recording from the concerts as a double LP, in 1972, and it has sold two million copies, double platinum, making it the best-selling gospel record of all time. It is perhaps her most shattering and indispensable recording. As Franklin has said repeatedly, "I never left the church." The Black church was, and is, in everything she sings, from a faltering "My Country, 'Tis of Thee" at Obama's first inaugural to a knockout rendition of Adele's "Rolling in the Deep" on the David Letterman show.

By 1971, Franklin was at her peak, with a string of hits and Grammys, but she was also preparing for a return to gospel. In March, she played the Fillmore West, in San Francisco, the ultimate hippie venue. The film of that date is on YouTube, and you can hear her singing her hits, fronting King Curtis's astonishing band, the Kingpins. She wins over a crowd more accustomed to the Mixolydian jams of the Grateful Dead. And her surprise duet with Ray Charles on "Spirit in the Dark" is far from the highlight.

A few songs into the set, Franklin plays on a Fender Rhodes the opening chords of Paul Simon's "Bridge Over Troubled Water," weaving hypnotic gospel phrases between her backup singers ("Still waters run deep . . .") and the B-3 organ lines of Billy Preston, a huge figure in gospel but recognized by the white audience as the "fifth Beatle," for his playing on the *Let It Be* album. Just as Otis Redding quit singing "Respect" after hearing Aretha's version ("From now on, it belongs to her"), Simon and Art Garfunkel forever had to compete with the memory of this performance. Simon, who wrote the song a year before, was inspired by a gospel song, Claude Jeter and the Swan Silvertones' version of "Mary, Don't You Weep." Jeter included an improvised line—"I'll be your bridge over deep water if you trust in my name"—and Simon was so clearly taken with it that he eventually gave Jeter a check. Daphne Brooks, who teaches African American studies at Yale, aptly describes the Fillmore West performance as a "bridge" to the "Amazing Grace" concerts that were just a few months away.

Franklin enlisted her Detroit mentor, the Reverend James Cleveland, to sing and play piano, and the pastor Alexander Hamilton to conduct the Southern California Community Choir. The gospel concert in Los Angeles opens with "Mary, Don't You Weep," a spiritual based on Biblical narratives of liberation and resurrection, and recorded, in 1915, by the Fisk Jubilee Singers. It is possibly the most wrenching music on the album. Countless performers have recorded the song—the Soul Stirrers, Inez Andrews, Burl Ives, James Brown, Bruce Springsteen—but Franklin, who was never in better voice, seems possessed by it. She delivers a pulsing, haunted version, taking flights of lyrical improvisation, note after note soaring over single syllables. In her reading, the blues always resides in gospel, and somehow this is her version of grace.

Chuck Rainey, her bass player in the early seventies, told me that Aretha's voice was so emotionally powerful that at times she would throw the band out of its groove. "Aretha came to me once and held my hand and she said to me, 'Chuck, don't listen to me too intensely. I know what I do to people. I need for the bass to be where it is so I can sing.'" Bernard (Pretty) Purdie, the drummer on the "Amazing Grace" sessions, told me that Franklin, having sung for so long with the Reverend Cleveland at New Bethel and in her living room, was absolutely sure of herself. "She didn't have to worry about what to think about or sing," he said. "She knew what she was doing from jump street."

There's no arguing with that. Aretha sang songs in Los Angeles that she first sang and recorded as a girl, including "Never Grow Old" and "Precious Lord." There is a ten-minute-long "Amazing Grace," part song, part sermon, that could come only from someone steeped in the tradition of her father's Delta whooping.

The record is an enduring achievement, but the event, like Woodstock, was something that also deserved to be seen. Sydney Pollack, who had directed Jane Fonda in *They Shoot Horses, Don't They?* and had been nominated for an Academy Award, wanted to make that happen. Pollack and his crew filmed both nights. The 16 mm color footage was shot in the most straightforward way, but there was a problem: Pollack was not an experienced documentarian, and he and his crew failed to use clapper boards to synchronize the sound with the images. After a months-long effort to fix the problem, Warner Bros. shelved the project. Pollack went on to direct *The Way We Were*, *Three Days of the Condor*, and *Out of Africa*. He lost interest in *Amazing Grace*. The film stayed in a vault for forty years.

In 2007, Alan Elliott, a record producer, approached Pollack about the film. Pollack had cancer, and Warner Bros. sold Elliott the rights to the film. Pollack agreed to work on it with him, but he died the next year.

Elliott succeeded in getting the film synchronized, but he has not yet won over the subject and star of the film. For years, he and Franklin have tussled over permissions, rights, and contracts. The Telluride Film Festival was scheduled to show *Amazing Grace* last September, but Franklin's lawyers filed suit. Judge John Kane, of the U.S. District Court in Colorado, held a slapped-together seventy-one-minute hearing the afternoon before the screening. Franklin testified by telephone.

"For them to show that film" and for Elliott "to just completely and totally and blatantly ignore me where my name and reputation, my concern, it would be terrible," she said. "This is my fifty-fifth year in the business, and he is all but fearless."

Elliott was proposing only to show the film to a couple of hundred people at Telluride, where the goal was to find a distributor. He told me that he has offered to pay her far more—a million dollars and half the proceeds—than she was originally promised. As they negotiated, Elliott and his representatives also encountered a quality of chaos that often surrounds Franklin's business affairs. Lawyers and agents came and went. Franklin, who is the wariest of personalities, deflected and delayed, even as some of her closest friends encouraged her to settle the deal and enjoy the inevitable attention that would come with *Amazing Grace*.

"Aretha gets offended when she thinks you think you're getting over on her," Tavis Smiley told me. "It's hard to know why that line gets blurred from time to time, between making people respect you and self-sabotage. But don't ever underestimate the power of the personal. 'Respect' is not just a song to Aretha. It's the mantra for her life.

"Aretha authorizes her own reality, and sometimes it's hard to juxtapose that reality to *the* reality," he went on. "We're all guilty of that at times, but Aretha does that to a greater extent, and it can be dangerous. Sometimes, in life, we can unwittingly self-sabotage when we want ultimate control."

In Denver, Judge Kane was protective of Franklin, issuing the injunction against the screening in Telluride for that evening. In his ruling, he quoted *Othello*: "He that filches from me my good name robs me of that which not enriches him and makes me poor indeed." Elliott and Franklin have meanwhile inched toward a settlement. When the hope arose that *Amazing Grace* was a possibility for the Tribeca Film Festival, coming next month, Robert De Niro called Franklin and implored her to make it happen. That is unlikely to occur.

Watching Aretha Franklin sing from the pulpit and at the piano somehow intensifies everything heard on the record. It's almost too much to absorb in one or two viewings. I've watched it a half-dozen times, and it never fails to leave me in tears. The most touching moment in the film comes when James Cleveland gestures to C. L. Franklin, who is sitting up front, next to Clara Ward. The Reverend cannot resist a prideful star turn at the pulpit.

"It took me all the way back to the living room at home when she was six and seven years of age, it took me back to about eleven, when she started traveling with me on the road, singing gospel," he says. "I saw you crying and I saw you responding, but I was just about to bust wide open. You talk about being moved, not only because Aretha is my daughter . . . Aretha is just a *stone* singer."

Then Aretha sits at the piano and leans hard into "Never Grow Old." As she sweats under the lights, her father approaches her at the piano and tenderly mops her forehead with a handkerchief.

"You can hear Aretha's influence across the landscape of American music, no matter the genre," Obama had said in his note. "What other artist had that kind of impact? Dylan. Maybe Stevie, Ray Charles. The Beatles and the Stones—but, of course, they're imports. The jazz giants like Armstrong. But it's a short list. And if I'm stranded on a desert island, and have ten records to take, I know she's in the collection. For she'll remind me of my humanity. What's essential in all of us. And she just sounds so damn good. Here's a tip: when you're deejaying a party, open with 'Rock Steady.' "

———•———

With the breadth of Aretha's influence comes the regularity of musical homage. The titans of hip-hop adore her. Mos Def sampled "One Step Ahead," on *Ms. Fat Booty*. Kanye West sampled "Spirit in the Dark," on *School Spirit*. Alicia Keys sampled "A Natural Woman," and Dr. Dre and Outkast, in accordance with the sage advice of their commander in chief, sampled "Rock Steady." The Fugees, Public Enemy, Slum Village—Aretha is everywhere. There is no "Formation" without "Respect." One queen follows another.

Beyoncé may have overstepped on one occasion, but she knew the score. A singer like her, who can provide flawless versions of both "Precious Lord" and "Bootylicious," understands the variousness of her roots and the specificity of her debts. "The soulfulness comes from the gospel," she once said. "It comes from Aretha, who listened to all of that, who sang in the church."

The morning after the Windsor concert, I went to Sunday services at the Franklins' old church, New Bethel Baptist. Arriving half an hour early, I met C. L. Franklin's successor, Pastor Robert Smith Jr., a stout gray-haired man in a dark three-piece suit. Pastor Smith led me to "the history room," which was filled with photographs and souvenirs of the Franklins. The sanctuary can hold a couple of thousand worshippers, but the stream of people arriving was modest. The days of vitality, of Paradise Valley and Black Bottom, are long gone. The workers for Ford and General Motors went south. There are few middle-class parishioners left at New Bethel. "My appeal is largely to the broken," Pastor Smith said. "People coming from prison, drugs. My style of preaching doesn't appeal to the professionals. A lot of them are going off to the megachurches."

It's been a long time since New Bethel echoed with "The Eagle Stirreth Her Nest." Early one morning in 1979, six burglars broke into C. L. Franklin's house. Franklin kept a gun in his room and fired two errant shots. One of the burglars fired back, hitting him once in the knee and once in the groin, rupturing his femoral artery. He spent five years in a coma and died. His funeral was among the largest in the history of Detroit.

Like others, Pastor Smith has had his rocky moments with Aretha Franklin over the years, and is careful not to offend her. Aretha is supportive of New Bethel—sending money and food packages, organizing the occasional gospel concert—and their relations, he says, "are better now than they've been, but it's a day-to-day thing." The importance of Aretha Franklin, he made clear, is the "sense of higher things" that her music inspires. The rest is dross. Her genius, her central place in American music and spirit, is undeniable.

"I don't care what they say about Aretha," Billy Preston, who died in 2006, once said. "She can be hiding out in her house in Detroit for years. She can go decades without taking a plane or flying off to Europe. She can cancel half her gigs and infuriate every producer and promoter in the country. She can sing all kinds of jive-ass songs that are beneath her. She can go into her diva act and turn off the world. But on any given night, when that lady sits down at the piano and gets her body and soul all over some righteous song, she'll scare the shit out of you. And you'll know—you'll swear—that she's still the best fuckin' singer this fucked-up country has ever produced."

March 2016

Aretha Franklin died on August 16, 2018. *Amazing Grace* was released worldwide the following year.

HOLDING THE NOTE

It's a winter night in Chicago. Buddy Guy is sitting at the bar of Legends, the spacious blues emporium on South Wabash Avenue. He hangs out at the bar because he owns the place and his presence there is good for business. The tourists who want a "blues experience" as part of their trip to the city come to hear the music and to buy a T-shirt or a mug at the souvenir shop near the door. If they're nervy, they sidle up to Guy and ask to take a picture. Night after night, he poses with customers—from Helsinki, Madrid, Tokyo—who inform him, not meaning to offend, that he is "an icon."

"Thank you," he says. "Now, let's smile!"

Buddy Guy is eighty-two and a master of the blues. What weighs on him is the idea that he may be the last. Several years ago, in 2015, after the funeral of B.B. King, he was overcome not only with grief for a friend but also with a suffocating sense of responsibility. Late into his eighties, King went on touring incessantly with his band. It was only at the end that his wandering mind led him to play the same song multiple times in a single set. With King gone, Guy says, he suddenly "felt all alone in this world." The way Guy sees it, he is like one of those aging souls who find themselves the last fluent speaker of an obscure regional language. In conversation, he has a habit of recalling the names of all the blues players who have died in recent years: Otis Rush, Koko Taylor, Etta James, James Cotton, Bobby Bland, and many others. "All of 'em gone."

Guy admits that no matter how many Grammys he's collected (eight) or invitations he's had to the White House (four), no matter how many hours he has spent onstage and in recording studios (countless), he has always been burdened with insecurity. Before he steps onstage, he has a couple of shots of cognac. The depth of the blues tradition makes him feel unworthy. "I've never made a record I liked," he says. As far as his greater burden is concerned, he radiates no certainty that the blues will outlast him as anything other than a source of curatorial interest. Will the blues go the way of Dixieland or epic poetry, achievements firmly sealed in the past? "How can you ever know?" he says.

As he talks, he keeps his eyes fixed on the stage, where a young guitar player is strenuously performing an overstuffed solo on "Sweet Home Chicago." In this club, you are as likely to hear that song as you are to hear "When the Saints Go Marching In" at Preservation Hall. The youngster is a reverent preservationist, playing the familiar licks and enacting the familiar exertions: the scrunched face, the eyes squeezed shut, the neck craned back, all the better to advertise emotional transport and the demands of technical virtuosity. It's fair to say that Buddy Guy, having done much to invent these licks and these moves, is not impressed. The homage being paid seems only to embarrass him. He is generous to young musicians who earn his notice—he even brings them up onstage, giving them a chance to shine in his reflected prestige—but he does not grade on a curve. The tradition will not allow it. Guy turns away from the stage and takes another sip of his drink, Heineken diluted by a glass full of ice.

"The young man might consider another song," he says.

Guy has always been a handsome presence: slick, fitted suits in the nineteen-sixties; Jheri curls in the eighties. These days, he is bald, twinkly, and preternaturally cool. He wears a powder-blue fedora and a long black leather jacket, a gift from Carlos Santana. He flashes two blocky rings, one with his initials and the other with the word "BLUES," each spelled out in diamonds.

His influence over time has been as outsized as his current sense of responsibility. In the sixties, when Jimi Hendrix went to hear him play at a blues workshop, Hendrix brought along a reel-to-reel recorder and shyly asked Guy if he could tape him; anyone with ears could hear Buddy Guy's influence in Hendrix's playing—in the overdrive distortion, the frenetic riffs high up on the neck of the guitar.

Guy can mimic any of his forerunners and sometimes he will emulate B.B. King, interrupting a prolonged silence with a single heartbreaking note sustained with a vibrato as singular as a human voice. But more often he throws in as much as the listener can take: Guy is a putter-inner, not a taker-outer. His solos are a rich stew of everything-at-once-ness—all the groceries, all the spices thrown into the pot, notes and riffs smashing together and producing the combined effect of pain, endurance, ecstasy. All blues guitar players bend notes, altering the pitch by stretching the string across the fretboard; Guy will bend a note so far that he produces a feeling of uneasy disorientation, and then, when he has decided the moment is right, he'll let the string settle into pitch and relieve the tension.

Even on a night when he is coasting through a routine set list, it is hard to leave his show without a sense of joy. He cuts an extravagant figure onstage, wearing polka-dot shirts to match his polka-dot Fender Stratocaster. He is a superb singer, too, with a falsetto scream nearly as expressive as James Brown's. Joking around between songs, he can be as bawdy as his favorite comedians, Moms Mabley and Richard Pryor. This is not Miles Davis; he does not turn his back to the audience. He is eager to entertain. The unschooled think of blues as sad music, but it is the opposite. "The blues is an impulse to keep the painful details and episodes of a brutal experience alive in one's aching consciousness, to finger its jagged grain, and to transcend it, not by the consolation of philosophy, but by squeezing from it a near-tragic, near-comic lyricism." That's how Ralph Ellison defined it. Guy puts it more simply: "Funny thing about the blues—you play 'em 'cause you got 'em. But, when you play 'em, you lose 'em."

———•———

Three chords. The "one," the "four," and the "five." Twelve bars, more or less. Guy's devotion and sense of obligation to the blues form began long before the death of B.B. King. The story goes like this.

The son of sharecroppers, George (Buddy) Guy was born in 1936, in the town of Lettsworth, Louisiana, not far from the Mississippi River. On September 25, 1957, he boarded a train and arrived in Chicago, another addition to the Great Migration, the northward exodus of Black southerners that began four decades earlier. But Guy hadn't come to Chicago to work in the slaughterhouses or the steel mills; he came to play guitar in the blues clubs on the South Side and the West Side. He was twenty-one. He had served his musical apprenticeship in juke joints and roadhouses in and around Baton Rouge and knew the real action was in Chicago, in smoke-choked bars so cramped that the stage was often not much bigger than a tabletop. If all went well, Guy hoped to get a contract at Chess Records, the hot independent label run by Leonard and Phil Chess, Jewish immigrants from Poland who were assembling an astonishing stable of artists, including Little Walter, Willie Dixon, Howlin' Wolf, Etta James, John Lee Hooker, Sonny Boy Williamson, Bo Diddley, and Chuck Berry. Most important, for Guy, Chess was the record label of the king of the Chicago bluesmen, McKinley Morganfield, better known as Muddy Waters.

In his first months in town, Guy found a place to crash, but he was hungry much of the time and he missed his family. He played as often as he could at blues hangouts like Theresa's and the Squeeze Club, but it wasn't easy to make an impression when there were so many topflight musicians around. And some nights could be scary. Guy was playing at the Squeeze when a man in the audience buried an ice pick in a fellow patron's neck. "When the cops saw the dead man, they couldn't have cared less," Guy recalled years later. "Didn't even investigate. To them it meant only one more dead nigger. In those days cops came around for their bribes and nothing else."

One evening, emboldened by a drink or three, Guy went to the 708 Club, a blues bar on Forty-seventh Street. The owner's name was Ben Gold. Clubs along Forty-seventh Street weren't so difficult to crack. They stayed open deep into the morning; workers coming off the night shift were ready to drink and hear some music. A guy like Ben Gold needed all the musical talent he could get to fill the hours, whether it was from stalwarts like Muddy Waters and Otis Rush or from a nervous newcomer from Louisiana. That night, Guy was feeling desperate, and he decided to perform "The Things That I Used to Do," a hit by one of his idols, an eccentric, self-destructive musician named Guitar Slim. When Guy was fifteen or sixteen, he bought a fifty-cent ticket to see Slim at the Masonic Temple, in Baton Rouge. He wedged himself close to the stage, hoping to watch the man's hands, to study his moves. He waited through the opening acts until, finally, the announcer declared, "Ladies and gentlemen, Guitar Slim!" When the band started into "The Things That I Used to Do," you could hear Slim's guitar—but where was he? "I thought they were all full of shit and all they were doing was playing the record," Guy told me. It was only after a while that anyone could see Slim, his hair dyed flaming red to match his suit, being carried forward through the crowd like a toddler by a hulking roadie. Using a three-hundred-foot-long cord to connect his guitar to his amplifier, he played a frenzied solo as his one-man caravan inched him toward the stage. And, once he joined the band, Slim pulled every stunt imaginable, playing with the guitar between his legs, behind his back. He raised it to his face and plucked the strings with his teeth. Many years later, Jimi Hendrix would pull some of the same stunts to dazzle white kids from London to Monterey, but these tricks had been around since the beginning of the Delta blues. As Guy watched Guitar Slim, he made a decision: "I want to play like B.B. King, but I want to act like Guitar Slim."

That night at the 708 Club, Guy did his best to fulfill that teenage ambition. He remembers playing "The Things That I Used to Do" as if "possessed": "Maybe I knew my life depended on tearing up this little club until folks wouldn't forget me."

When the set was over, Ben Gold came up to him and said, "The Mud wants you."

Guy did not quite understand. Gold explained that Muddy Waters had been in the club, watching. Now he was waiting for Guy on the street.

Guy went outside, and spotted a cherry-red station wagon parked nearby. He saw his idol sitting in the back seat, his pompadour done up high and shiny. Muddy Waters rolled down the window and told him to get in.

Waters said, "You like salami?"

"I like anything," Guy said. He hadn't eaten for a few days.

Waters knew the feeling. He produced a loaf of bread, a knife, and a thick package of sliced meat wrapped in butcher paper. "You won't complain none about this salami," he said. "Comes from a Jewish delicatessen where they cut it special for me. Have a taste."

As Guy recalls in his 2012 memoir, *When I Left Home*, he and Waters talked for a long time, about picking cotton in the Delta, about music, about the clubs on the South Side. Guy admitted that things had been tough. Lonely, broke, and frustrated, he was thinking of heading back to Lettsworth.

Muddy waved that off. Look at me, he said. He'd grown up on the Stovall Plantation, near Clarksdale, Mississippi. He played blues for nickels and dimes, and figured that he'd have to make his livelihood in the fields. But he kept at his music and developed a local reputation. In the summer of 1941, two outsiders, Alan Lomax, representing the Library of Congress, and John Work, a music scholar from Fisk University, came to Coahoma County with a portable disk recorder. Lomax asked folks where he could find a singer he'd been hearing about, Robert Johnson. He was told that Johnson was dead, but that a young fellow named Muddy Waters was just as good. Lomax and Work set up the recording equipment at the commissary of the Stovall Plantation and persuaded Waters to come around. Muddy knew all kinds of songs, including Gene Autry's "Missouri Waltz" and pop hits like "Chattanooga Choo-Choo," but Lomax and Work didn't want the whole jukebox. They wanted the local stuff, and recorded Waters singing "Country Blues." When Waters heard the recording, he had a realization. "I can do it," he said. "I can do it." He headed north, in 1943, to make a life in the blues.

In his early days in Chicago, Waters played for change alongside the pushcarts in "Jewtown," a bustling commercial district on Maxwell Street. Some nights, he played in bars. There were a few good acts around—Big Bill Broonzy, Memphis Minnie, Memphis Slim, Eddie Boyd—but it was a dispiriting scene. "There was nothing happening," he said at the time. You couldn't play the country blues and expect to make a living at it. Waters made his living driving a truck. But once he'd armed himself with an electric guitar, a gift from his uncle, in 1947, Waters went about inventing a new form, an urban blues, the Chicago blues, and this caught the attention of the Chess brothers. In 1950, Chess put out a Muddy Waters original, "Rollin' Stone," and sold tens of thousands of records. And look at him now. "I got enough salami for the two of us," he told his new protégé.

Guy still didn't see how he could compete in Chicago. But Muddy assured him that Ben Gold would give him gigs. Gold had seen how Guy's performance worked up the crowd, and, he said, when patrons get all "hot and bothered," they drink more, the owner gets paid, and, usually, so does the band.

"Funny, 'cause tonight was the night I almost called my daddy for a ticket home," Guy said.

"Tonight, you found a new home," Muddy Waters told him.

Over the next generation, Buddy Guy crossed paths with Muddy Waters countless times. He recorded with him, he performed with him, he went drinking with him and heard all the lore. Along with the other top blues performers in town—Junior Wells (who played harmonica alongside Buddy for years), Willie Dixon, Howlin' Wolf, Etta James, Mama Yancey, James Cotton, Otis Rush, Koko Taylor, and Magic Sam—they played the clubs. But never for much money. Well into his forties, Buddy Guy was often making just a few bucks a night.

In the seventies and eighties, Guy ran a club of his own on the South Side, the Checkerboard Lounge. After a stadium gig, in 1981, the Stones dropped by to play with Muddy Waters and Buddy. Guy remembered it as his one chance to make some money on the club, but the Stones entourage was so large, and the room so small, that there were almost no paying customers. He didn't make a dime.

In 1983, Ray Allison, Waters's drummer, came by to say, "Old man is kinda sick." Waters was dying of lung cancer, and was frightened of what lay ahead. "Don't let them goddam blues die on me, all right?" he told Guy. A few days later, he was gone.

———•———

Buddy Guy doesn't get back to Lettsworth much. In December, though, he flew down from Chicago to collect what he thought of as the honor of his life. The Louisiana legislature had voted unanimously to name a piece of Highway 418 in Pointe Coupee Parish "Buddy Guy Way." The celebration began on a Friday at Louisiana State University, where Guy had worked as a handyman and a driver. The next day, after a gumbo-and-catfish lunch at a place called Hot Tails, Guy and a small group of friends traveled the fifty miles from Baton Rouge to Lettsworth on a chartered bus.

It was cold and rainy. Very few people live in Lettsworth these days. "It's a ghost town now," Guy says. Some of the wooden shacks have long since been abandoned by sharecropper families who went north. But today people came out to wave from their porches. Guy looked sharp, in the Carlos Santana leather coat. The honors themselves weren't unusual—speeches, a plaque—but it all struck deep. Guy's mother never saw him perform. "Getting honored at the Kennedy Center and now this, it's hard to say which one is better," he told me. Guy invoked the words of a Big Maceo song: "You got a man in the East, and a man in the West / Just sittin' here wondering who you love the best."

Guy grew up in one of those shacks in Lettsworth. No electricity, no indoor plumbing, no glass windows. A white family, the Feduccias, owned the land and lived in a big house; Black sharecroppers, like the Guys, picked pecans and cotton. The Feduccias took half of the proceeds. Guy's parents had a third-grade education. His mother cooked in the big house. His father worked in the fields. As a child, Buddy went to a segregated school and early mornings and evenings he'd pick cotton, two dollars and fifty cents for a hundred pounds.

"My father worked all day cutting wood with a crosscut saw," Guy told me. "If that ain't exercise, I don't know what is. I look at those gyms with all those machines and I figure, fuck that. You can't sell me on that shit. If my father hadn't done all that 'exercise,' he'd still be living."

There were hardly any holidays. The reliable exception was Christmas. Someone would butcher a pig, and there were greens from the garden—a feast. "I never heard of other holidays," he says. "We didn't get no fuckin' Fourth of July. On Labor Day, we labored."

One friend who came around on Christmas was an odd cat named Henry (Coot) Smith. Coot carried a guitar, and, after playing a few songs and having a couple of drinks, he'd take a short nap before going on to the next house. While Coot slept, Buddy picked up that guitar and strummed it; it seemed like something magical, something he had to master. Much of the music he heard in those days was gospel music from church. On jukeboxes, he liked the bluesmen especially: Arthur Crudup, who wrote "That's All Right," Elvis Presley's first hit, and John Lee Hooker, a Mississippi plantation worker, who went north to work as a janitor in a Detroit Ford factory and, in 1948, recorded a droning, spooky hit called "Boogie Chillen." This was the first electrified blues Guy had ever heard, and he wanted to play just like that. He crafted his first instrument by stripping strands of wire out of the shack's mosquito screens and stringing them tightly between two cans.

At the general store, Guy played the jukebox, listening to other Black kids who had taken the train north and become stars. He started dreaming. Eventually, for two dollars, he got a less primitive instrument, and his favorite thing to do was to wander outside and play, all by himself. "There was nothing to stop that sound," he says. "I'd go sit on top of the levees and bang away with my guitar, and you could really hear it . . . That's just how country sound is. A little wind would carry it even better." As a teenager, Guy quit pumping gas and learned his craft in roadhouses around Baton Rouge. He never took a lesson. He listened. He watched. He had tremendous stage fright. Cheap wine, known as "schoolboy scotch," was the remedy.

"Nobody ever sat me down and said here's B-flat and here's F-sharp," he says. "I had to figure that out myself after I started playing with a band. I'm eighty-two years old. Most of the people above me—John Lee Hooker, Lightnin' Hopkins—I faced them, I watched their hands to see where they were going. They played by ear. And that's how I play now. I play by ear. I don't play by the rules."

On his valedictory trip to Lettsworth, people shyly approached him. As Guy got off the bus, a white man in his sixties said that his father had grown up with Guy. They couldn't play together or go to the same school, but they knew each other. He talked of how proud everyone was of Guy.

Guy was getting tired, but he hung in there. Some nights at Legends, when he's been posing for cell phone pictures for a little too long, he gets irritable and wonders how it can take so goddam long to push the button. But now he was ready to stay as long as anyone liked. "My mother told me, 'If you've got flowers to give me, give 'em to me now,'" he said. "'I won't smell them when I'm gone.' I was glad to get this honor now."

———•———

In the sixties, just as Guy was reaching a certain stature in the blues world, something curious began to happen. White people happened—white blues fans and white blues musicians. For its first half century, the blues was popular entertainment for, and of, Black people. Not completely, but almost. Guy told me that, when he played clubs in Chicago during the late fifties, "if you saw a white face, it was almost always a cop."

Soon, it was clear that some white kids, including Mike Bloomfield and Paul Butterfield, were in the audience, watching Guy the way he'd once watched Guitar Slim. At the same time, the best of the British Invasion expressed a kind of community awe toward the American urban blues. When Guy first toured Great Britain, in 1965, all the white English guitar heroes—Jeff Beck, Jimmy Page, and Eric Clapton—flocked backstage to ask him how he did this and how he did that. Guy had spent so much of his recording career backing up other musicians that he was shocked that people knew his name, much less the nuances of his work. But they did. As a young singer, Rod Stewart was so in thrall to Guy that he asked to carry his guitars.

"Our aim was to turn people on to the blues," Keith Richards said of the early days of the Rolling Stones. "If we could turn them on to Muddy and Jimmy Reed and Howlin' Wolf and John Lee Hooker, then our job was done." When the Stones were invited to play on the American television show *Shindig!*, they insisted on appearing alongside Howlin' Wolf, who had never received that kind of exposure. They invited Ike and Tina Turner, Buddy Guy, Junior Wells, and B.B. King to open for them.

And yet there was something unsettling about the spectacle of the Stones or Eric Clapton playing turbocharged versions of Robert Johnson, Mississippi Fred McDowell, and Muddy Waters to fifty thousand white kids a night, most of them oblivious of the Black origins of those songs. Clapton, for one, experienced a measure of guilt and, eventually, acted on it. "I felt like I was stealing music and got caught at it," he told the music critic Donald E. Wilcock. "It's one of the reasons Cream broke up, because I thought we were getting away with murder, and people were lapping it up. Doing those long, extended bullshit solos which would just go off into overindulgence. And people thought it was just marvelous." In 1976, Clapton went on a drunken, racist rant onstage, in Birmingham—an incident, he later said in an elaborate apology, that "sabotaged everything." Clapton never stopped playing the blues. In 2004, he put out an entire album covering Robert Johnson songs; it sold two million copies.

Some critics, notably the poet and playwright LeRoi Jones (Amiri Baraka), found the prospect of white blues players making a fortune enraging. In *Black Music*, he wrote, "They take from us all the way up the line. Finally, what is the difference between Beatles, Stones, etc., and Minstrelsy. Minstrels never convinced anyone they were Black either."

Black performers rarely allowed themselves to echo that sentiment publicly; Waters and Guy were usually quick to express friendship with the Stones, Clapton, and the rest. Yet hints of their disappointment came through. "It seems to me," Guy said in the nineteen-seventies to an interviewer for the magazine *Living Blues*, "all you have to do is be white and just play a guitar—you don't have to have the soul—you gets farther than the black man."

It also hurt that Black audiences, particularly younger Black audiences, were moving away from the Chicago blues. B.B. King told Guy that he cried after he was booed by such an audience. "He said that his own people looked on him like he was a farmer wearing overalls and smoking a corncob pipe," Guy recounted in his memoir. "They saw him as a grandfather playing their grandfather's music."

As late as 1967, Guy drove a tow truck during the day and played the clubs at night. The hours were punishing, and high blood pressure and divorce followed. (Guy married twice and divorced twice; he has eight adult children.) In Germany, he played at the American Folk Blues Festival, but he got booed, he said, because the audience thought he "looked too young, dressed too slick, and my hair was up in a do. Someone said he was also disappointed that I didn't carry no whiskey bottle with me onstage. They thought bluesmen needed to be raggedy, old, and drink."

Expectations placed constraints on his recordings, too. As sympathetic as the Chess brothers were to Black musicians, and as shrewd as they'd been in marketing their work, they had been reluctant to have Guy unleash the wildness, the originality, in his playing. As the singer-songwriter Dr. John said of Guy's early records, "You feel a guy in there trying to burst out, and he's jammed into a little bitty part of himself that ain't him."

Elijah Wald, a historian of the blues who has written biographies of Josh White and Robert Johnson, told me, "I feel like Buddy Guy is somebody who, due to American racism, never quite reached his potential. He could have been a major figure, but he was pigeonholed as a museum piece, even in 1965. Nobody from Warner Bros. was coming to Buddy Guy and saying, 'Here's a million dollars, what can you do?'" Bruce Iglauer, the owner of Alligator Records, a blues label in Chicago, agrees. Buddy Guy was one of a small handful of "giants," he said, who helped define the blues but never got the chance to become household names: "The door was never open to them at the time when they were most likely to walk through. By the time the doors were opened by Eric Clapton and the Stones, these guys were already in their thirties and forties."

In the late nineteen-sixties, Guy recounts, Leonard Chess called him into his office. "I've always thought that I knew what I was doing," he told Guy. "But when it came to you, I was wrong. I held you back. I said you were playing too much. I thought you were too wild in your style." Then Chess said, "I'm gonna bend over so you can kick my ass. Because you've been trying to play this ever since you got here, and I was too fucking dumb to listen."

Chess's failure could have stayed with Guy as a bitter memory. But he has turned the episode into a tidy, triumphant anecdote. He refuses any hint of resentment: "My mother always said, 'What's for you, you gonna get it. What's not for you, don't look for it.'"

———•———

There is no indisputable geography of the blues and its beginnings, but the best way to think of the story is as an accretion of influences. Robert Palmer, in his book *Deep Blues*, writes of griots in Senegambia, on the west coast of Africa, singing songs of praise, of Yoruba drumming, of the African origins of the "blue notes," the flatted thirds and sevenths, that are so distinctive in early southern work songs and later blues. There are countless studies on the influence of the Black church and whooping preachers; of field hollers and work songs sung under the lash in the cotton fields of Parchman Farm, the oldest penitentiary in Mississippi; of boogie-woogie piano players in the lumber and turpentine camps of Texas. The Delta blues, the kind of music that would one day galvanize Chicago, originated, at least in part, on Will Dockery's plantation, a cotton farm and sawmill on the Sunflower River, in Mississippi, where Black farmers lived in the old slave quarters. Charley Patton and Howlin' Wolf were residents. So was Roebuck (Pops) Staples, the paterfamilias of the Staple Singers. Accompanying themselves on guitar, they sang songs of work, heartbreak, the road, the rails, the fragility of everything.

"The blues contain multitudes," Kevin Young, the poet and essayist, writes. "Just when you say the blues are about one thing—lost love, say—here comes a song about death, or about work, about canned heat or loose women, hard men or harder times, to challenge your definitions. Urban and rural, tragic and comic, modern as African America and primal as America, the blues are as innovative in structure as they are in mood—they resurrect old feelings even as they describe them in new ways."

The richness of a form, however, does not guarantee its continued development or popularity. Guy didn't begin to make real money until the early nineteen-nineties, when he was nearing sixty. Like Sonny Rollins in jazz, Buddy Guy was now, at least in part, in the business of being a legend, an enduring giant in a dwindling realm. In 1991, *Damn Right I've Got the Blues*, an album on the British label Silvertone, sold well and won a Grammy; not long afterward, two more albums of his, *Feels Like Rain* and *Slippin' In*, also won Grammys. He began playing bigger halls around the world. His most recent album is titled, almost imploringly, *The Blues Is Alive and Well*, and one of the cuts is "A Few Good Years":

I been mighty lucky
I travel everywhere
Made a ton of money
Spent it like I don't care
A few good years
Is all I need right now
Please, please, lord
Send a few good years on down

Guy still performs at least a hundred and thirty nights a year, including a "residency" at his club every January.

Last spring, I called my eldest and asked them to go with me to see Guy at B.B. King Blues Club & Grill, in Times Square. The place opened in 2000, and a lot of great acts had performed there— James Brown, Chuck Berry, George Clinton, Aretha Franklin, Jay-Z—but the rents kept increasing, and now it was going out of business. Guy was there to close his old friend's club. I'd be lying if I said it was a transcendent night. It was a routine night. He opened with "Damn Right," which has become a kind of theme song, and then launched into a series of tributes. He played Muddy Waters ("Hoochie Coochie Man"), B.B. King ("Sweet Sixteen"), Eric Clapton ("Strange Brew"), Jimi Hendrix ("Voodoo Child"). He did his Guitar Slim thing, walking through the crowd while playing. He did his Charley Patton thing, cradling the guitar, playing with his teeth. He did his act, and we walked out happy to have been there.

A few weeks later I was talking to Bruce Iglauer, the Alligator Records man, who said that he, too, has seen many routine sets, but also some extraordinary ones. He walked into Legends not long ago and, by chance, Guy was onstage, singing "Drowning on Dry Land," an Albert King hit from 1969: *A cloud of dust just came over me, I think I'm drowning on dry land.* The music was fresh and spare. "And the singing!" Iglauer said. "He was singing like the high tenor of a gospel quartet. Guy has said he doesn't like his own voice, but when he immerses himself in his music his voice makes you cry, the pitch bending and the vibrato, and all at the top of his register, just about to crack. For ten minutes, he was the greatest blues singer on earth. People who can reach down and reach the depths of their soul and hand that to an audience—soul-to-soul communication? It's what you hope for."

———•———

Buddy Guy lives in Orland Park, a suburb twenty-five miles south of Chicago. His house, set way back from the main road, is vast and airy, and sits on fourteen wooded acres. There's a collection of vintage cars outside: a '58 Edsel, a '55 T-Bird, a Ferrari. The house became a possibility only after "Damn Right I've Got the Blues."

Guy gets up somewhere between 3 and 5 a.m., a lingering habit of country life. Mornings, he likes to putter around, shop, run errands. Then there is a long "siesta," from one to seven, before the evening begins at Legends or on tour. (Even on the road, the morning after a late gig, Guy expects the band to be on the bus by four or five—"ready to go or left behind.") He lives alone. There is an indoor pool, but, he said, "I ain't never been in it." He has reduced the failure of his two marriages to epigrammatic scale: "They weren't happy when I wasn't doing good, and when I was doing good they wasn't happy because I was on the road all the time."

Both of his ex-wives and his extended family came for Thanksgiving. Guy did all the cooking. He loves to cook. When I came by late on a Sunday morning, he was in the kitchen making a big pot of gumbo. Much of the animal and vegetable kingdoms simmered in his pot: crab, chicken, pork sausage, sun-dried shrimp, okra, bell pepper, onion, celery. Dressed in baggy jeans and a sweatshirt, Guy was hunched over the gumbo, adding just the right measure of hot sauce and, at the end, Tony Chachere's Famous Creole Cuisine gumbo filé. He did this with the concentration he might apply to a particularly tricky riff. A pot of Zatarain's New Orleans–style rice simmered nearby.

Guy took me around the house to give the flavors, as he said, time to "get acquainted." There were countless photographs on the walls: all the musicians one could imagine, family photographs from Louisiana, grip-and-grin pictures from when he was awarded the National Medal of Arts in the Bush White House and from the Kennedy Center tributes received during the Obama administration. (Obama has said that, after Air Force One, the greatest perk of office was that "Buddy Guy comes here all the time to my house with his guitar.")

An enormous jukebox in the den offered selections from pop, gospel, rock, soul. "I listen to everything," Guy said. "I'll hear a lick and it'll grab you—not even blues, necessarily. It might even be from a speaking voice or something from a gospel record, and then I hope I can get it on my guitar. No music is unsatisfying to me. It's all got something in it. It's like that gumbo that's in that kitchen there. You know how many tastes and meats are in there? I see my music as a gumbo. When you hear me play, there's everything in there, everything I ever heard and stole from."

As we looked at a row of black-and-white photographs, it was clear that the shadows of Guy's elders in the blues never leave his mind. "I hope to keep the blues alive and well as long as I am able to play a few notes," he told me. "I want to keep it so that if you accidentally walk in on me you say, 'Wow, I don't hear that on radio anymore.' I want to keep that alive, and hope it can get picked up and carry it on.

"But who knows?" he continued. "The blues might just fade away. Even jazz, which was so popular when I first got here—all of that disappeared."

We were sitting at the dining room table. When I returned to the subject of whether the blues would survive as a living form, Guy thought awhile. He recalled the nightly ritual at Legends, when the MC does a cheesy-seeming thing and asks audience members where they're from. The nightly census usually reveals tourists from out of town, new to Chicago and, often enough, new to this music. When Guy hears that, he said, "I can't help thinking: Somebody forgot us, forgot the blues."

Well, not entirely. There are still some extraordinary musicians around who play and sing the blues with the sort of richness that Guy admires: Robert Cray, Gary Clark Jr., Bonnie Raitt, Adia Victoria, Keb' Mo', Derek Trucks and Susan Tedeschi, Shemekia Copeland. Guy has even coached a couple of teenage guitar prodigies: Christone (Kingfish) Ingram, who comes from the Delta; and Quinn Sullivan, who first performed onstage with Guy when he was seven. But as Copeland, a singer and the daughter of the guitarist Johnny Copeland, told me, "The blues as Buddy knows it, as he does it, really will be gone when he is gone." In fact, she went on, "there are some artists now who think that if they call themselves blues artists it's like saying, 'I have herpes.' Like it's some terrible thing."

Among African American audiences, and for so many around the world, the dominant music has long been hip-hop. What's the link, if any, between the blues and hip-hop? Willie Dixon, who created some of the most famous blues songs in the Chess catalog, wrote in his memoir, "The blues are the roots and the other musics are the fruits." In some of the earliest proto-hip-hop performers, those roots were easy to hear. The Last Poets, the Watts Prophets, Gil Scott-Heron, and others called on blues lines and blues chord changes. Beyoncé is fluent in the blues, a musical and emotional strain that's especially pronounced on a song like "Don't Hurt Yourself," on *Lemonade,* or when she performs as Etta James in the film *Cadillac Records.* But as beats, electronics, and the like began to dominate the form, the connection between root and branch, between blues and hip-hop, became more attenuated.

Guy's daughter Rashawnna, born to his second wife, grew up in Chicago's hip-hop world. She knows Kanye West and Chance the Rapper. Performing as Shawnna, she was a featured presence on "What's Your Fantasy," a hit for Ludacris. She had a hit of her own called "Gettin' Some Head," which sampled Too Short's "Blowjob Betty."

"When I first started listening to it I was tapping my feet and my ex-wife said, 'You hear what she's saying?'" Guy recalled. When Guy admitted that he loved the beat but could not quite keep up with the pace of the lyrics, his ex-wife just said, "Sit down."

Guy recalls, "My daughter told me, 'This is your music and we just take it a step further.' It's like when the electric guitar came up on Lightnin' Hopkins. Leo Fender and Les Paul turned the old blues into folk music."

Rashawnna, who now works part-time at Legends, said that, if blues is often about the journey, hip-hop is about the conditions of the street. "I believe the connection is through the lyrics and the expression," she went on. "The blues came from being down and out, and making the best of it. Hip-hop is an explanation of growing up in the ghetto, telling our story, making the best of things." She worries that her father wears too heavily his sense of duty to the blues and to bluesmen lost: "We worry about him, but he's happy to keep his promise to Muddy Waters and B.B. King. That's why he won't stop touring."

Her father just smiles. Can't stop, won't stop. Every night onstage is in the service of what he loves best, and the rest was mapped out from the start. "Death is a part of life," Buddy Guy says. "My mother would tell us as children, 'If you don't want to leave here, you better not come here.' Sure as hell you come, sure as hell you go."

March 2019

GROOVIN' HIGH

In 1973, the editors of *New Musical Express* put Keith Richards, the principal guitarist and the musical soul of the Rolling Stones, at the top of their annual list of "rock stars most likely to die" within the year. Even by rock standards, Richards was a heroic consumer of heroin, cocaine, mescaline, LSD, peyote, Mandrax, Tuinal, marijuana, bourbon, and other refreshments, and it seemed to all observers that he was living on borrowed time. Rock's casualty list was already ominously long; Jimi Hendrix, Jim Morrison, and Janis Joplin merely headlined the necrology. In 1969, Richards and his fellow Stones had lost Brian Jones, who drowned in a pool just a few weeks after the band fired him. Richards did not so much guard his mortality as flaunt it. He memorialized his near-constant insensibility by giving open access to Robert Frank, Annie Leibovitz, and other image-makers, who captured him, backstage or in hotel rooms, half dressed and thoroughly zonked. You looked at those pictures of Richards, slumped, stoned, and stupid, and you figured it was only a matter of days before the wires would announce that he'd choked to death on his own vomit.

In fact, Richards went on and on, stumbling through concerts in a narcotic haze, sleeping through rehearsals, always on the edge of oblivion, and yet, together with Mick Jagger, producing some of the most vital pop music of the time. Between 1968 and 1972, the Stones recorded *Beggars Banquet, Let It Bleed, Sticky Fingers,* and *Exile on Main St.,* the core of their repertoire. They went on to perform those songs as long as Sinatra performed "Love and Marriage." Longer. The distinctiveness of the Stones was due less to Jagger's vocals than to Richards's capacity to ingest the blues-guitar styles of Chuck Berry and Jimmy Reed and create something new. There were far better technicians than Richards, far better soloists, but his sense of rhythm and riff and taste, his signature sustained chords and open spaces, gave the band its sound. And, through it all, the Grim Reaper was denied a backstage pass. *New Musical Express,* having kept Keith at Number One on its deathwatch for ten years, finally gave up and conceded his immortality.

The Stones have not written a song of consequence in thirty years, but they have survived four decades longer than their great contemporaries, the Beatles. And, even as their originality has waned to the vanishing point, their performing unit and corporate machine has been honed to perfection. Since 1989, the Stones have earned more than two billion dollars in gross revenues, helped along by sponsorship deals with Microsoft, Anheuser-Busch, and EPTrade. Promotour, Promopub, Promotone, and Musidor, firms based in Holland, for tax reasons, handle the various ends of the Stones' business concerns, and everything is watched over by teams of accountants, immigration lawyers, security experts, and, until very recently, an aristocratic business adviser named Prince Rupert zu Loewenstein-Wertheim-Freudenberg. Even in years without tours or albums, the Stones find a way. They licensed "Start Me Up" to Microsoft when the company rolled out Windows 95, and "She's a Rainbow" to Apple when a line of iMacs was in need of promotion. According to *Fortune,* the Stones are behind the merchandising of some fifty products, including underwear sold by Agent Provocateur. The Stones logo—a fat, lascivious tongue thrust through smiling, open lips—is as recognizable on the corporate landscape as the Golden Arches.

"The whole business thing is predicated a lot on the tax laws," Keith Richards told *Fortune*. "It's why we rehearse in Canada and not in the U.S. A lot of our astute moves have been basically keeping up with tax laws, where to go, where not to put it. Whether to sit on it or not. We left England because we'd be paying ninety-eight cents on the dollar. We left, and they lost out. No taxes at all. I don't want to screw anybody out of anything, least of all the governments that I work with. We put thirty percent in holding until we sort it out." Keith may fancy himself a symbol of '68, but he channels the fiscal policy of Grover Norquist.

The last time the Stones were out on the road, between 2005 and 2007, they took in more than half a billion dollars—the highest-grossing tour of all time. On Copacabana Beach, in Rio de Janeiro, they played to more than a million people. Few spectacles in modern life are more sublimely ridiculous than the geriatric members of the Stones playing the opening strains of "Street Fighting Man." The arena is typically jammed with middle-aged fans, who have donned après-office relaxed-sized jeans, paid the sitter, parked the minivan in the lot, and, for a few hundred dollars a seat, shimmy along with Mick, who, having trained for the tours as if for a championship bout, prances inexhaustibly through a two-hour set, at his best evoking the spawn of James Brown and Gumby, at his worst coming off like someone's liquored-up Aunt Gert, determined to trash her prettier sister's wedding with a gruesome performance on the dance floor. Ever since 1975, "the tour of the giant inflatable cock," as Richards calls it, the Stones have tried to outdo themselves with spectacle. Occasionally, they have gone too far. "There was a huge business of getting elephants onstage in Memphis," Richards says, "until they ended up crashing through ramps and shitting all over the stage in rehearsals and were abandoned." But, beyond the spectacle, we come to admire the unlikely persistence of the Stones,

an entity nearly half a century old, chugging comically, deter-
minedly on. The lads are approaching seventy. Pruney, dyed, and
bony, they storm through a set list that is by now as venerable and
unchanging as the Diabelli Variations. "You do, occasionally, just
look at your feet and think, 'This is the same old shit every night,'"
Richards has said, and yet he goes on playing and the crowds go on
paying, reluctant to give it up, the last link to glory days.

———•———

The newest artifact of the band's endurance is Keith Richards's
chipper new autobiography, called, defiantly, *Life*. Half book, half
brand extension, it's an entertaining, rambling monologue, a slurry
romp through the life of a man who knew every pleasure, denied
himself nothing, and never paid the price. Maybe *you* can't always
get what you want. The rule doesn't apply to Keith.

One obvious caveat: a memoir by a man whose memory is
fogged by countless years of narcotic obliteration is a memoir of a
particular kind. In 1978, when Richards was asked why the Stones
called their new album *Some Girls*, he replied, "Because we couldn't
remember their fucking names." Nevertheless, Little, Brown paid
Richards seven million dollars to produce the book. Richards, in
turn, selected a skilled ghost—James Fox, the author of *White Mis-
chief*, a well-told history of the murder of Josslyn Hay, the twenty-
second Earl of Erroll, who was one of the many dissipated expats
living in Happy Valley, outside Nairobi. For Fox, writing about the
drugs, sexual adventure, and exquisite boredom in Happy Valley
was good preparation for *Life*.

Richards and Fox know why the reader has put down his
money: the same reason that Keith staggers around the stage even
today, thirty years after kicking heroin, and, grinning maniacally,
tells the cheering crowd, "I'm glad to be here! I'm glad to be anywhere!" It's the titillation of hearing from someone who has never

seen the inside of a factory or an office, and has consumed what there is to consume and survived to crow about the fact. This is the man who invented the riff to "(I Can't Get No) Satisfaction" in his sleep and yet has known satisfactions beyond the imaginings of Giacomo Casanova. And so *Life* is in a hurry to enhance the Myth of Keef and give us what we want. It opens with an extended scene of the Stones touring the American South, in 1975, their cars packed with high-class narcotics—"pure Merck cocaine, the fluffy pharmaceutical blow." But in the town of Fordyce, Arkansas, population 4,237, Richards runs into trouble with the cops. An antic narrative of Stones misbehavior and southern justice ensues. Richards, who has just bragged to us of his possession and ingestion of vast quantities of dope, feigns incomprehension in the face of a possible prison sentence. Which, as usual, he dodges.

Richards boasts of his constitution. He not only recounts his "acid-fueled road trip with John Lennon" but also makes sure to tell us that Lennon "couldn't really keep up." Richards recalls, "He'd try and take anything I took, but without my good training. A little bit of this, a little bit of that, couple of downers, a couple of uppers, coke and smack, and then I'm going to work. I was freewheeling. And John would inevitably end up in my john, hugging the porcelain."

At times, the book sounds like a consequence-free version of William Burroughs's *Junky*. In one extended passage, Richard describes his daily diet:

> I would take a barbiturate to wake up, a recreational high
> compared to heroin, though just as dangerous in its own way.
> That was breakfast. A Tuinal, pin it, put a needle in it so it
> would come on quicker. And then take a hot cup of tea, and
> then consider getting up or not. And later maybe a Mandrax
> or quaalude. Otherwise I just had too much energy to burn. So
> you wake up slow, since you have the time. And when the effect

wears off after about two hours, you're feeling mellow, you've had a bit of breakfast and you're ready for work.

Richards is proud of many things, including his capacity to stay up for days at a time. His all-time record, he says, was a nine-day coke-assisted session of wakefulness, at the end of which he merely tipped over, slamming his head against a stereo speaker: "It was just a curtain of blood."

This aspect of the book, the addict's narrative, is the latest installment in a tradition that dates back to Romanticism and Thomas de Quincey's opium visions of crocodiles and other "unutterable monsters," to Crabbe, Coleridge, Byron, Baudelaire—where to stop? More specifically, *Life* follows the subcategory of the musician-addict memoir: Art Pepper's *Straight Life*, Anita O'Day's *High Times Hard Times*, Hampton Hawes's *Raise Up Off Me*, and Miles Davis's fabulously profane collaboration with Quincy Troupe.

After finishing Richards's book, I read a stack of these jazz memoirs, along with biographies of other addict geniuses, including Billie Holiday and Charlie Parker. In the wake of revisiting all the desperation, the bad dope, the prison terms, the lives cut short, I found something almost creepy about lucky Keith's ego and blithe spirits. Richards is full of cockeyed advice for the potential junkie and voyeur: no mainlining, take only the best and purest drugs, and, please, never overdo it. ("Well, I shouldn't say *never*; sometimes I was absolutely fucking comatose.")

Richards admires the music of his predecessors and betters, but he does not feel their pain. He is almost uniquely insulated from the junkie's predicaments by layers of money, attorneys, and privilege. Charlie Parker made "Relaxin' at Camarillo" after emerging from a mental hospital in California of the same name. Richards made *Exile on Main St.* as a tax exile living on an estate in Villefranche-sur-Mer. During breaks from shooting up and rehearsing, Richards would ply the Mediterranean in a speedboat in search of Eurotrash:

"We'd pull into Monte Carlo for lunch. Have a chat with either Onassis's lot or Niarchos's, who had big yachts there."

Another staple of the rock memoir or biography is the catalog of sexual conquests, and, on this subject, Richards is almost shy. He tells us that his colleagues Jagger and Bill Wyman bloodlessly tabulated their conquests. Keith is the passive sort. The ladies come to him. "I have never put the make on a girl in my life," he says. And yet he describes with delight how he stole the Teutonic model and artist Anita Pallenberg from Brian Jones as they motored down to Morocco in a Bentley:

> Anita and I looked at each other, and the tension was so high in the backseat, the next thing I know she's giving me a blow job. The tension broke then. Phew. And suddenly we're together . . . For a week or so, it's boinky boinky boinky, down in the Kasbah, and we're randy as rabbits but we're also wondering how we're going to deal with it.

Eventually, Richards and Pallenberg set out to make a life together. They are quite the pair, young junkies in love, constantly dodging jail terms. They cannot, however, dodge tragedy. In 1976, while Keith is on tour, his third child with Pallenberg, an infant named Tara, dies in his crib. This is Keith's considered expression of regret: "Never knew the son of a bitch or barely. I changed his nappy twice, I think . . . Anita and I, to this day, have never talked about it." This exceeds the limits of ordinary reticence.

Pallenberg's addiction and misbehavior are too much even for Richards. It's not so much that he's convinced she had an affair with Jagger—her third Stone!—as that she outstripped Keith's limits in the decadence department. "She was unstoppably self-destructive," he writes. "She was like Hitler; she wanted to take everything down with her." Finally, Keith finds happiness, and a far steadier existence, with an American model named Patti Hansen.

———•———

Richards is rough on many people in this book, as he has been in numerous interviews over the years. He thinks it's part of his roguish charm. He slags the punks as talentless. He has an occasional nice word for U2, but he is dismissive of everyone from Prince ("an overrated midget") to Elton John ("an old bitch") and Bruce Springsteen ("If there was anything better around, he'd still be working the bars of New Jersey"). The unschooled may be surprised to read in *Life* of how hard Richards can be on Mick Jagger, whom he sometimes refers to as "Brenda" or "His Majesty." He cannot bear Jagger's pretensions, his "calculation," his overattention to business affairs, his lust for establishment approval, and his occasional tendency to treat Richards and the other band members like the help. He portrays Jagger as fussy, joyless, and out for himself: "It's almost as if Mick was aspiring to be Mick Jagger, chasing his own phantom. And getting design consultants to help him do it . . . I used to love to hang with Mick, but I haven't gone to his dressing room in, I don't think, twenty years. Sometimes I miss my friend." Richards, who lives like a squire on gated estates in rural England and Connecticut, concedes that Jagger is his "brother," and he will always have his back, but he clearly thinks of himself as the more authentic man and musician.

Some readers may delight in Richards's sly have-it-all-ways self-regard, but for me the most winning sections of the book are the tales of his becoming, the way his close adolescent friendship with Jagger and their mutual love for their blues heroes rapidly led to the formation of the Greatest Rock-and-Roll Band in the World. It's a thrice-sung story, but Richards and Fox put the song over well.

Keith Richards and Mick Jagger were children of postwar London and schoolmates at the Wentworth Primary School, in Dartford. Keith was an only child of working-class parents. His father,

Bert, was a foreman at a General Electric plant. Raised on jazz, blues, and the emerging sounds of American pop music, Richards sang in the school choir. After his voice changed, he lost interest in school and started hanging around Dimashio's ice cream parlor, listening to the jukebox. "It was the one little bit of Americana in Dartford," he writes. "Life was black-and-white; the Technicolor was just around the corner, but it wasn't there yet in 1959." At night, he tuned in to Buddy Holly, Eddie Cochran, Little Richard, and his hero, Elvis Presley, on Radio Luxembourg. These were the years of "the Awakening," Britain's enthusiastic reception of American music. A budding musician, Richards became interested in side-men: Elvis's guitar player, Scotty Moore; Fats Domino's arranger and trumpet player, Dave Bartholomew. At Sidcup Art College, a feeder school to a job at J. Walter Thompson, Richards spent all his time goofing off and listening to blues records. Then, in 1961, at the Dartford train station, he ran into Jagger, who, he discovered, was a blues fanatic and a record collector. Jagger had all the latest disks from Chess: Muddy Waters, Chuck Berry, Howlin' Wolf, Wil-lie Dixon. The two boys listened to the records over and over again.

Jagger and Richards started a band and called it, at first, Little Boy Blue and the Blue Boys. By the spring of 1962, they had hooked up with another blues nut and guitar player, Brian Jones. The following January, they were joined by a drummer with a taste for jazz, Charlie Watts, and a bass player, Bill Wyman, whose main qualification was the ownership of a Vox amplifier. These were the Rolling Stones.

As the band took shape, Richards learned to copy B.B. King's single-note simplicity and T-Bone Walker's double-string solos—a technique that saved the band money, because it could "eliminate the need for a horn section." Richards and Jagger had a simple ambition: all they wanted was to be "the best blues band in Lon-don and show the fuckers what's what." Monkish in their devotion, they lived in cheap apartments and practiced through the night. "Anybody that strayed from the nest to get laid, or try to get laid, was a traitor," Richards recalls.

The band played clubs around London called the Flamingo, the Ealing, the Crawdaddy, the Marquee, and the Red Lion, and, in the fluid days of 1963—as the Beatles, a relatively veteran band, were in their ascendancy—the Stones released their first single, a cover of Chuck Berry's "Come On." The record shot onto the charts, and within a week the Stones were stars. That was all it took. "Suddenly they're dressing us up in dogtooth-check fucking suits and we're rushed along on the tide," Richards says, but the boys soon got rid of the pseudo-Beatles look. They did fine on their own terms. First as an opening act for Little Richard and Bo Diddley (from whom they learned countless lessons of pacing and showman-ship) and then as headliners, they caused riots wherever they went.

"In England, for eighteen months, I'd say, we never finished a show," Richards recalls. Their short set featured covers of "Not Fade Away," "I'm a King Bee," and "Around and Around," and yet the screaming was so intense that some nights the band just played "Popeye the Sailor Man" to see if anyone would notice. The boys threw bottle caps and coins; the girls were prepared to rip the Stones apart, so deep was their erotic frenzy. Even now Richards seems scared:

> The power of the teenage females of thirteen, fourteen, fifteen, when they're in a gang, has never left me. They nearly killed me. I was never more in fear for my life than I was from teenage girls. The ones that choked me, tore me to shreds, if you got caught in a frenzied crowd of them—it's hard to express how frightening they could be. You'd rather be in a trench fighting the enemy than be faced with this unstoppable, killer wave of lust and desire, or whatever it is—it's unknown even to them.

After one performance in the north of England, the band stayed behind in the theatre to wait for the crowds to clear. An old janitor who had helped clean up told Richards, "Very good show. Not a dry seat in the house."

When the Stones first came to America, in the summer of 1964, they played on bills behind Bobby Goldsboro and the Chiffons, and suffered the insults of Dean Martin, who mocked them as hairy primitives. They even shared a bill with a contortionist called the Amazing Rubber Man, who, come to think of it, may have been a formative influence on Jagger's evolving stage antics. It was only when, that same year, Jagger and Richards—the self-proclaimed Glimmer Twins—started writing songs that they pulled into a race with the Beatles. Nineteen sixty-five was the year of "Satisfaction." In a pattern that was typical of their collaboration in the following decades, Richards came up with the riff and Jagger filled out the lyrics.

In the teenage imagination, the virtue of being a member of the band is that you end the day in the sack with the partner, or partners, of your choice. Not so, Richards says: "You might be having a swim or screwing the old lady, but somewhere in the back of the mind, you're thinking about this chord sequence or something related to a song. No matter what the hell's going on."

Never does Richards show as much pleasure as when he is describing the feeling of playing his instrument, particularly the electric guitar, which, he says, is "like holding on to an electric eel." The come-to-Jesus moment in *Life* is purely musical, and it occurs "late in 1968 or early 1969," after Richards has discovered one of the secrets of the blues. The six strings of the guitar are ordinarily tuned E-A-D-G-B-E. After collaborating with the great instrumentalist and arranger Ry Cooder, Richards picked up "open G" tuning, in which the guitar is tuned to a G chord: D-G-D-G-B-D. Mississippi bluesmen like Robert Johnson, Son House, and Charley

Patton used this tuning; so did Don Everly on "Bye Bye Love." Richards removed the lowest string on a Fender Telecaster tuned G-D-G-B-D and came up with the riffs to "Tumbling Dice," "Brown Sugar," "Honky Tonk Women," "All Down the Line," "Can't You Hear Me Knocking," and many others. Anyone who played in a garage band in the sixties and seventies remembers the experience of trying to play these songs and discovering that they didn't quite have the droning, resonating sound that Keith Richards got on, say, *Get Yer Ya-Ya's Out!*, the best of the Stones' live albums. Now, of course, you can go on YouTube, punch in, say, "Brown Sugar, lesson," and some fourteen-year-old with a video camera and guitar is there instructing you on the way to use open G and "play like Keith." Keith himself says it best: "If you're working the right chord, you can hear this other chord going on behind it, which actually you're not playing. It's there. It defies logic. And it's just lying there saying, 'Fuck me.'"

———·———

Keith Richards is sixty-six. He's a grandfather. He's had emergency cranial surgery, albeit for a very Keith sort of reason: he fell out of a tree in Fiji. He says that he leads a "gentleman's life." He reads a lot of Patrick O'Brian's sea adventures and George MacDonald Fraser's Flashman novels. He has, it must be reported, also fallen off his library ladder. Where he used to have a wolfhound named Syphilis, he now has a golden Lab called Pumpkin. He and his wife pack Pumpkin onto a private jet and go to relax at their spread in Turks and Caicos. Gimme Shelter indeed. He lives like a private-equity pirate.

Age has provided Richards with a little insight into his own contradictions. He is thrilled with his life, but he is also aware of the hollow nature of his outlaw image: "I can't untie the threads of how much I played up to the part that was written for me. I mean the skull ring and the broken tooth and the kohl," he writes.

> Is it half and half? I think in a way your persona, your image, as it used to be known, is like a ball and chain. People think I'm still a goddamn junkie. It's thirty years since I gave up the dope! Image is like a long shadow. Even when the sun goes down, you can see it. I think some of it is that there is so much pressure to be that person that you become it, maybe, to a certain point that you can bear. It's impossible not to end up being a parody of what you thought you were.

One of the more touching moments in the book is when the very young Rolling Stones arrive at the Chess recording studios, in Chicago, a blues mecca. A workman is painting the ceiling. The workman's name is McKinley Morganfield, better known as Muddy Waters. The Stones were headed for a life of millions, and the least they could do over time was pay tribute to their heroes. They named the band for one of Morganfield's songs and sang his praises and the praises of all their best forebears. Richards had escaped the Reaper, but not his most essential debt, and he was true to it. "Me?" Keith once said. "I just want to be Muddy Waters. Even though I'll never be that good or that Black."

October 2010

LET THE RECORD SHOW

Early evening in late summer, the golden hour in the village of East Hampton. The surf is rough and pounds its regular measure on the shore. At the last driveway on a road ending at the beach, a cortège of cars—SUVs, jeeps, candy-colored roadsters—pull up to the gate, sand crunching pleasantly under the tires. And out they come, face after famous face, burnished, expensively moisturized: Jerry Seinfeld, Jimmy Buffett, Anjelica Huston, Julianne Moore, Stevie Van Zandt, Alec Baldwin, Jon Bon Jovi. They all wear expectant, delighted-to-be-invited expressions. Through the gate, they mount a flight of stairs to the front door and walk across a vaulted living room to a fragrant backyard, where a crowd is circulating under a tent in the familiar high-life way, regarding the territory, pausing now and then to accept refreshments from a tray.

Their hosts are Nancy Shevell, the scion of a New Jersey trucking family, and her husband, Paul McCartney, a bass player and singer-songwriter from Liverpool. A slender, regal woman in her early sixties, Shevell is talking in a confiding manner with Michael Bloomberg, who was the mayor of New York City when she served on the board of the Metropolitan Transportation Authority. Bloomberg nods gravely at whatever Shevell is saying, but he has his eyes fixed on a plate of exquisite little pizzas. Would he like one? He narrows his gaze, trying to decide; then, with executive dispatch, he declines.

McCartney greets his guests with the same twinkly smile and thumbs-up charm that once led him to be called "the cute Beatle." Even in a crowd of the accomplished and abundantly self-satisfied, he is invariably the focus of attention. His fan base is the general population. There are myriad ways in which people betray their pleasure in encountering him—describing their favorite songs, asking for selfies and autographs, or losing their composure entirely.

This effect extends to friends and peers. Billy Joel, who has sold out Madison Square Garden more than a hundred times, has spent Hamptons afternoons over the years with McCartney. Still, Joel told me, "he's a Beatle, so there's an intimidation factor. You encounter someone like Paul and you wonder how close you can be to someone like that."

In July 2008, when Joel closed Shea Stadium, as the final rock act before the place came under the wrecking ball, he invited McCartney to join him and perform "I Saw Her Standing There." Shea Stadium is, after all, where Beatlemania, in all its fainting, screaming madness, reached its apogee, in the sixties. For the encore, "Let It Be," Joel ceded his piano to McCartney. I asked him if he minded playing second fiddle to his guest. "I *am* second fiddle!" he said. "Everyone is second fiddle to Paul McCartney, aren't they?"

McCartney knows that, even in a gathering of film stars or prime ministers, he is surrounded by Beatles fans. "It's the strangest thing," he told me. "Even during the pandemic, when I'm wearing a mask, even sunglasses, people stop and say, 'Hey, Paul!'" He'll gamely try to level the interpersonal playing field by saying that, after so many years, "I'm a Beatles fan, too," often adding, "We were a good little band." But he also knows that fandom can curdle into malevolence. In 1980, Mark David Chapman, a Beatles fan, shot John Lennon to death outside the Dakota, on Central Park West. Nineteen years later, in Henley-on-Thames, west of London, another mentally troubled young man, Michael Abram, broke into George Harrison's estate and stabbed him repeatedly in the chest.

McCartney is a billionaire. A vast amount of that fortune can be ascribed to the songs that he wrote with Lennon before the first moon landing. Yet his audiences usually exceed those of his most esteemed peers. Bob Dylan's catalog of the past forty years is immensely richer than McCartney's, but Dylan generally plays midsize venues, like the Beacon, in Manhattan; McCartney sells out Dodger Stadium and the Tokyo Dome.

He continues to write and record, just as he continues to breathe—"It's what I do," he told me. Recently, *McCartney III Imagined*, a remix of his latest album, was at the top of *Billboard's* Top Rock Albums chart. Although he admits that he's "not very big" on hip-hop, he once holed up at the Beverly Hills Hotel with Kanye West to collaborate on a few songs. West's "Only One," inspired by his late mother, Donda, and his daughter North, came out of a session with McCartney. Another collaboration with West, "FourFiveSeconds," was a hit for Rihanna. When she ran into McCartney on a commercial airline flight a few years later, she took out her phone and posted a video on Instagram: "I'm about to put you on blast, Mr. McCartney!"

The party shifted into a new phase. A platform had been laid over the swimming pool, and rows of folding chairs were set up in front of a large screen. McCartney took his seat in the make-shift theatre flanked by his daughters Stella, who is fifty years old and a fashion designer, and Mary, who is fifty-two, a photographer, and the host of a vegetarian cooking show. It was time to screen a special hundred-minute version of *The Beatles: Get Back*, a three-part documentary series more than six hours in length made by the director Peter Jackson, and scheduled to stream on Disney+ during the Thanksgiving weekend.

The event had been billed as a sneak preview, but it was also an exercise in memory. *Get Back* is a remake of sorts. Nearly everyone at the party knew the story. In January 1969, the Beatles assembled at Twickenham Film Studios, in West London, to rehearse songs for their album *Let It Be*. The idea was to film their sessions there, perform somewhere in public—proposals ranged from an amphitheatre in Libya to Primrose Hill—and then release the edited result as a movie. By the time the eighty-minute documentary, also called *Let It Be*, appeared, in May 1970, the band had come to an end. Most fans have always thought of the documentary as "the breakup movie," a dour, dimly lit portrayal of bitter resentments and collapsing relationships. Jackson and his team combed through sixty hours of Beatles film and even more audiotape from more than half a century ago to tell the story anew.

The lights in the backyard went down. An audience of luminaries turned into dozens of anonymous silhouettes. First came a short, featuring Jackson, who made his name and fortune with the *Lord of the Rings* trilogy, speaking to us from his studio in New Zealand. He explained that he had relied on cutting-edge techniques to enhance the soundtrack and the imagery. And, even in the opening images of *Get Back*, Twickenham seemed less gloomy, the Beatles more antic and engaged. Gone was the funereal tone. "They put some joy in!" Ringo Starr told me later. "That was always my argument—we were laughing *and* angry." Jackson was clearly in synch with McCartney's hope that the new documentary would alter the narrative about his life and the final days of perhaps the biggest pop-cultural phenomenon of the twentieth century.

———•———

To retrieve the memories and sensations of the past, Proust relied mainly on the taste of crumbly cakes moistened with lime-blossom tea. The rest of humanity relies on songs. Songs are emotionally charged and brief, so we remember them whole: the melody, the hook, the lyrics, where we were, what we felt. And they are emotionally adhesive, especially when they're encountered in our youth. Even now I can remember riding in a van, at five, six years of age, headed to Yavneh Academy, in Paterson, New Jersey, and listening to "She Loves You" on someone's transistor radio. The older boys wore Beatle haircuts or acrylic Beatle wigs. Neither option looked particularly dashing with a yarmulke.

My father, an exceedingly quiet man, found his deepest connection with me through music. And, because he did me the honor of listening to the Beatles, I listened when he played records that he said figured into what seemed so new: Gilbert and Sullivan, English music hall tunes, Rodgers and Hammerstein, Rodgers and Hart, the jazz of the thirties and forties, Chuck Berry, Buddy Holly, Little Richard. In the same spirit of exchange, we watched Beatlemania take shape on television—news footage from Shea Stadium and airport press conferences. My father did not fail to mention that all the hysteria reminded him of a skinny Italian American singer from Hoboken. But this, he admitted, was much bigger.

Some years later, I began to see how music, and the stories of musicians, could play an uncanny role in our lives. One afternoon, I came home from my high school to report that a friend of mine was the son of a piano player. "He says his father is someone named Teddy Wilson," I added.

I might as well have told my father that my classmate's father was the Prince of Wales.

Wilson, my father explained, was the most elegant pianist in jazz. He had played with Billie Holiday, Louis Armstrong, Lester Young. In the mid-thirties, he joined Benny Goodman, Lionel Hampton, and Gene Krupa, forming a swing-era quartet that was as remarkable for its integration as it was for its syncopated wildness. In 1973, my classmate invited my father and me and some friends to the opening of the Newport Jazz Festival at Carnegie Hall, where

the old Goodman quartet was reuniting. We were allowed backstage beforehand, shyly watching as Teddy Wilson massaged his
hands and fingers and slowly rotated his wrists. "I ask my fingers to
do a lot," he said, "but these days they don't always answer in time."

———•———

One afternoon this summer, I went to meet McCartney at his
midtown office, a town house near the Ziegfeld Theatre. It was a
hot Saturday, and the Delta variant of COVID-19 had broomed away
most of the tourists and weekend wanderers. Although I was early,
he was there at the reception desk to greet me.

McCartney is seventy-nine, but—in the way we've grown to
expect of public performers with rigorous regimens of self-care—he
is a notably youthful version of it. There are now gray streaks in his
hair, though it's still cut in a fashion that is at least Beatle-adjacent.
In the elevator to the second floor, we went through the ritual
exchange of vaccine assurances and peeled off our masks. McCartney has slight pillows of jowl, but he remains trim. Most mornings,
he said, he works out while watching *American Pickers*, hosted for
more than twenty seasons by two guys, Mike and Frank, roaming
the country and searching for junk and treasure. He mimicked their
line: "How much are you going to want for that?"

No one in the public eye lacks vanity, but McCartney is knowing about it. We reached a large sitting room, and, as he plopped
down on the couch, a hearing aid sprang out of his right ear. He
rolled his eyes and, with a complicit smile, used his index finger to
push the wormy apparatus back in place. The space is decorated
with just a few mementos: a deluxe edition of *Ram*, his second solo
album; a brick from the rubble of Shea Stadium; a striking portrait
of Jimi Hendrix taken by McCartney's first wife, Linda, who died
of breast cancer in 1998.

In our conversations, McCartney struck me as charming and

shrewd, an entertainer eager to please but intent on setting the story straight. He has navigated a life with little precedent, one in which a few hometown friends played a pivotal role in the rise of rock and roll, the invention of the teenager, youth culture, and the sixties. Not everyone took part in global Beatlemania—there were not many Black fans in the Shea Stadium news footage—but the band was at the center of the closest thing we'd ever had to a pop monoculture after the Second World War. The rewards for this have been unimaginable, and yet, even at this late date, McCartney wants the history of the Beatles and his place in it to come out right. This is clearly part of the motivation for *Get Back*, and for the publication of *The Lyrics: 1956 to the Present*, a new two-volume compendium in which McCartney provides the personal and musical stories behind a hundred and fifty-four of his songs. Robert Weil, the editor in chief of Liveright, pursued McCartney for years to do the book and, in the end, helped put him together with the poet Paul Muldoon, who conducted dozens of interviews.

The resulting collection of essays is arranged alphabetically, as if to defy any obvious arc to McCartney's evolution, and to dissuade the reader from thinking that matters peaked in the summer of 1969, with "The End." The oldest song in the anthology is "I Lost My Little Girl," composed on a Zenith guitar, in 1956, when McCartney was fourteen. "You wouldn't have to be Sigmund Freud to recognize that the song is a very direct response to the death of my mother," he says. His mother, a midwife named Mary, had succumbed to breast cancer earlier that year. McCartney told me that he didn't have many pictures of his mother, although he recalls her approaching him with a red rubber tube and a bowl of soapy water telling him it was time for an enema. "I was crying and begging to not have this torture!" he said. But Mary—the "Mother Mary" of "Let It Be"—occupies a sainted place in his mind.

"One nice memory I have of her is her whistling in the kitchen," he said. And when she became ill, he went on, "I remember her sort of seeming a little bit tired, a little bit pale, but we were too young to make anything of it." The word *cancer* was never spoken. "There were all sorts of little euphemisms. But one thing I remember vividly was on the bedclothes there was some blood." It was a moment of realization: "Oh, God, this is worse than I'd been thinking."

His father, Jim, was a cotton salesman and an amateur jazz musician. Although Paul grew up in Liverpool on a working-class housing estate, he went to a good secondary school where he caught the bug for literature from his teacher Alan Durband, who had studied with F. R. Leavis at Cambridge. But, after a "pretty idyllic" childhood, his mother's death cast a pall over the house that lasted for many months. Paul could hear "this sort of muffled sobbing coming from the next room, and the only person in that room was your dad."

His own room was filling with music. In *The Lyrics*, McCartney talks about his delight early on in matching a descending chord progression (G to G7 to C) with an ascending melody and speculates that he might have picked up maneuvers like that from listening to his father, who had led Jim Mac's Jazz Band—and from his "aunties" singing at holiday parties at home. In those days, though, a kid playing his first chords on a guitar and furtively writing his first lyrics was unusual. To turn this lonely preoccupation into something bigger, he had to go out looking for a friend and a band.

On July 6, 1957, McCartney, now fifteen, rode his bike to a nearby fair to hear a local skiffle group called the Quarrymen. He paid the three-pence admission and watched them play "Come Go with Me," by the Del Vikings, as well as "Maggie Mae" and "Bring Me a Little Water, Silvy." He noticed that there was one kid onstage who had real presence and talent. After the set, McCartney got himself an introduction; the kid's name was John Lennon. McCartney nervily asked to have a go at his guitar, banging out a credible version of Eddie Cochran's "Twenty Flight Rock."

They had more in common than their talent and ambition.

Lennon's mother, Julia, died after being hit by a car, in 1958. (His father left the family when John was a child.) Lennon, more than a year older than McCartney, masked his wound with cocksure wit. And now he made a cunning, history-altering calculation. "It went through my head that I'd have to keep him in line if I let him join," Lennon said years later, "but he was good, so he was worth having." McCartney was now part of the band.

Not long afterward, McCartney brought in a school friend, George Harrison, a younger guitar player. "George was the baby," McCartney says. In 1960, the Quarry Men renamed themselves the Beatles and, two years later, nicked a crack drummer from Rory Storm and the Hurricanes named Richard Starkey, who went by Ringo Starr. All were working-class Liverpudlians (though John was posher, Ringo poorer). They had grown up listening to Frank Sinatra and Billy Cotton on the BBC. They heard their first rock-and-roll performers—Bill Haley, Elvis Presley, the Everly Brothers, Little Richard, Fats Domino, Ivory Joe Hunter—on Radio Luxembourg, a commercial station that broadcast American music. They liked what McCartney calls the "slim and elegant" shape of Chuck Berry's songwriting. Together, they figured out guitar chords as if they were ancient runes. When Paul and George heard that someone across town knew the fingering for the B7 chord—the essential chord to go with E and A for every blues-based song in the rock repertoire—they got on a bus to meet the guy and learn it.

First in Liverpool, and then for seven, eight hours a night in Hamburg, the Beatles cut their teeth, learning scores of covers and building a reputation. When they grew bored with singing other people's songs and wanted to avoid overlapping with the set lists of other bands on the bill, they became more serious about their own songwriting. At first, the songs were nothing special. McCartney heard Joey Dee's hit "Peppermint Twist" and answered it, writing "Pinwheel Twist." But the seeds of originality were there. Lennon had worked out "One After 909," which ended up on the *Let It Be* album, when he was about fifteen. "Fancy Me Chances with You," a comic song they slapped together in 1958, ended up on the *Get Back* tapes, complete with exaggerated Scouse accents. What was clear from the start was that writing would be a matter of Lennon and McCartney.

"I remember walking through Woolton, the village where John was from, and saying to John, 'Look, you know, it should just be you and me who are the writers,'" McCartney recalled. "We never said, 'Let's keep George out of it,' but it was implied."

———•———

As the Beatles gained a following, the sophistication of their songwriting deepened. McCartney, for instance, was taken with epistolary songs like Fats Waller's "I'm Gonna Sit Right Down and Write Myself a Letter." On a tour bus, he thought of the imperative phrase "Close your eyes" and went on from there. "We arrived at the venue, and with all the hustle and bustle around me—all the various bands and tour crews running about—I made my way to the piano and then somehow found the chords," he recalls in *The Lyrics*. At first, it was "a straight country-and-western love song," but then Lennon provided a unique swing to the verses by strumming his guitar in a tricky triplet rhythm. The result was "All My Loving." The Beatles recorded the song in 1963, and when they came to New York the following year they played it on *The Ed Sullivan Show*. More than seventy million people watched. Within two months, they had the top five songs on the *Billboard* charts and Beatlemania was under way.

The Beatles reveled not only in their music but in the fun, the just-us camaraderie, the inside jokes. "I don't actually *want* to be a living legend," McCartney once said. Fun had been the idea. "I came in this to get out of having a job. And to pull birds. And I

pulled quite a few birds, and got out of having a job." Lennon compared their tours to Fellini's *Satyricon*.

What was striking about the Beatles was the inventiveness of
their melodies and chord progressions. Every month, it seemed,
they became more distinct from everyone else. The development
from album to album—from three-chord teenage love songs to
intricate ballads to the tape loops and synthesizers of their psyche-
delic moment—both caught the zeitgeist and created it. And they
had a sense of style to match: the suits, the boots, the haircuts all
became era-defining. Even classical mavens were impressed. Leonard Bernstein went on television to analyze the structure of "Good
Day Sunshine." Ned Rorem, writing in *The New York Review of Books*,
compared a "minute harmonic shift" in "Here, There and Everywhere" to Monteverdi's madrigal "A un giro sol," and a deft key
change in "Michelle" to a moment in Poulenc.

McCartney waves away such high-flown talk, but he isn't above
suggesting that the Beatles worked from a broader range of musical languages than their peers—not least the Rolling Stones. "I'm
not sure I should say it, but they're a blues cover band, that's sort
of what the Stones are," he told me. "I think our net was cast a bit
wider than theirs."

The Beatles worked at a furious pace. Their producer, George
Martin, brought deep experience to the process, along with an
unerring ability to help the band translate their ideas into reality.
As McCartney recalls, "George would say, 'Be here at ten, tune
up, have a cup of tea.' At ten thirty you'd start." Two songs were
recorded by lunch, and often two more afterward. "Once you get
into that little routine, it's hard, but then you enjoy it. It's a very
good way to work. Because suddenly at the end of every day you've
got four songs."

By 1966, the Beatles had tired of the road. The fans nightly
screaming their hysterical adulation sounded to McCartney like "a

million seagulls." As the band came to think of themselves more as artists than as pop stars, they saw performing in stadiums as an indignity. "It had been sort of brewing, you know, this distaste for schlepping around and playing in the rain with the danger of electricity killing you," McCartney told me. "You kind of just look at yourself and go, 'Wait a minute, I'm a musician, you know. I'm not a rag doll for children to scream at.'"

On August 29, 1966, the Beatles played Candlestick Park, in San Francisco. The band stood on a stage at second base, far removed from their fans, and ended their half-hour set with Little Richard's "Long Tall Sally." "It was just a dispiriting show, we just went through the motions," McCartney told me. They came off the stage, he said, and "we got loaded into a kind of meat wagon, just a chrome box with nothing in it, except doors. We were the meat." The Beatles never played for a paying audience again.

———•———

The divorce rate among musical collaborators is high, and the breaking point is hard to predict. In 1881, Richard D'Oyly Carte, a leading impresario of the West End, built the Savoy Theatre, on the Strand, to showcase the comic operas that made W. S. Gilbert and Arthur Sullivan famous. Nine years and many triumphant openings later, Gilbert, the librettist, took umbrage at the extravagance of the rug that Carte had installed in the Savoy's lobby, and wound up in an intense dispute with Sullivan, the composer. After the inevitable unearthing of other resentments, Gilbert wrote to Sullivan, "The time for putting an end to our collaboration has at last arrived." They soldiered miserably on for a little longer, petering out with a mediocrity, *The Grand Duke.*

The Beatles never sank to mediocre work; they went out on the mastery of *Let It Be* and *Abbey Road.* Nor did the band's dissolution have any singular trigger—any carpet. But perhaps the problems started when in August 1967, their manager, Brian Epstein, died of a drug overdose. Although Epstein was only thirty-two, the band saw him as a unifying, even paternal, figure. Eventually, Lennon, Harrison, and Starr hired the Stones' manager, Allen Klein, to run the group's affairs; McCartney sensed that Klein wasn't to be trusted, and insisted on doing business with Lee and John Eastman, the father and the brother of Linda Eastman, his soon-to-be wife.

The band's creative core was also drifting apart. Lennon-McCartney was no longer an "eyeball to eyeball" collaboration. Once, they had worked in constant proximity—on tour buses or in shared hotel rooms. Now Lennon wrote at his estate in the suburbs, McCartney at his house in North London. They still got together to give each other's most recent songs a polish, or to suggest a different line, or a bridge—the "middle eight." The results could be sublime, as when McCartney added "woke up, fell out of bed, dragged a comb across my head . . ." to Lennon's "A Day in the Life." But the process had changed. And Harrison, who was developing as a songwriter, was growing frustrated with his modest quota of songs per album. After hanging out in upstate New York with members of the Band, he believed he had glimpsed a more communal and equitable version of musical life.

All these stress fractures could be felt in 1969 when the Beatles gathered at Twickenham after the New Year's holiday. Usually, they came to the studio with fourteen or so songs that were more or less ready to be recorded. Not this time. "John had no songs, and Paul had no songs," Ringo Starr told me from his home in Los Angeles. "It's the first time ever we went into the studio like that." McCartney's song "Get Back," for instance, was so skeletal that at one point it took shape as an attack on Enoch Powell's anti-immigrant politics. "We never learned so many new numbers at once," Lennon said.

In the documentary *Let It Be*, we see intervals of careful, creative work, ebullient playing, and purposeful noodling, but they are interrupted by long passages of chilly tension and joyless boredom.

Then, there was the presence of Yoko Ono, who freely offered her thoughts. Like the "dramatic" possibility of having the Beatles perform to "twenty thousand empty chairs." At one point at Twickenham, McCartney says, "It's going to be such an incredible sort of comical thing, like, in fifty years' time, you know: 'They broke up 'cause Yoko sat on an amp.'" Feminism was not a powerful strain in the Beatles, and Lennon's bandmates struggled with the constant presence of a girlfriend in the sacred space of the studio.

One of the more memorable moments in the film—it also appears, with less emphasis, in *Get Back*—is an exchange in which Harrison bristles at McCartney for telling him what to play. McCartney takes pains not to come on too bossy, but he wants what he wants:

> McCartney: I'm trying to help, you know. But I always hear
>   myself annoying you, and I'm trying to—
> Harrison: No, you're not annoying me.
> McCartney: I get so I can't say—
> Harrison: You don't annoy me anymore.

Harrison was increasingly brittle. After a week of rehearsing, Lennon was derisive of Harrison's "I Me Mine," a song that broadly hinted at the egos at work in the Beatles:

> Harrison: I'm leaving . . .
> Lennon: What?
> Harrison: . . . the band now.
> Lennon: When?
> Harrison: Now.

After another sour moment, Harrison made good on his threat, heading home to his estate in Surrey. "See you around the clubs," he said by way of farewell. That afternoon, he wrote "Wah-Wah," lamenting his bandmates' failure to "hear me crying." Lennon seems unfazed. "I think if George doesn't come back by Monday or Tuesday, we ask Eric Clapton to play," he says.

When I asked Starr about Harrison's walkout, he laughed and said, "It wasn't that huge in our eyes. We thought he'd gone for lunch like the rest of us. Then I got on the drums, Paul got on his bass, John on the guitar, and we were like a heavy-metal band . . . That's how we got that emotion out." Although Lennon, Starr, and McCartney initially drew on their wit and the catharsis of playing to cope, their inability to get through to Harrison, who decamped for a couple of days to Liverpool, weighed heavily on them. "So, cats and kittens," Lennon says, "what are we going to do?" The end now seemed a little more real.

At Twickenham, Lennon could be unfocused and petulant; he "was on H," as he put it, sporadically using heroin—not injecting it but probably sniffing it. And he was clearly defensive about Ono. "I mean, I'm not going to lie," he tells McCartney one day. "I would sacrifice you all for her."

Eventually, Harrison got over his snit and returned to the fold. After the Beatles moved from Twickenham to more familiar studio space at Apple headquarters, at 3 Savile Row, the situation calmed considerably; Billy Preston, a keyboard player from Ray Charles's and Little Richard's bands, joined them and lifted up the band's sound and its collective spirit. The Beatles were having fun again. Now, amid yellow teacups and overflowing ashtrays, there was progress and even greater collaboration. When Harrison looked for help with the lyrics to "Something," Lennon told him to play *Mad Libs*: "Just say whatever comes into your head each time: 'Attracts me like a cauliflower,' until you get the word."

No matter what troubled them, the Beatles thrived when they were making music together. "Musically, we never let each other down," Starr says. They also recognized that McCartney had become the band's insistent engine, the one pushing them to get the work done. "We'd make a record, and then we'd usually be in my garden, John and I, hanging out," Starr recalls. "It's a summer's day—you get three a year in Britain—and we'd be relaxing and the phone would ring and we would know by the ring: it was Paul. And he'd say, 'Hey, lads, you want to go into the studio?' If it hadn't been for him, we'd probably have made three albums, because we all got involved in substance abuse, and we wanted to relax." And yet when they put down their instruments their problems were hard to ignore. To recall a moment from Twickenham:

> Harrison: I think we should have a divorce.
> McCartney: Well, I said that at the meeting. But it's getting near it, you know.
> Lennon: Who'd have the children?

———•———

The Beatles finished recording *Abbey Road* in August 1969. At a business meeting a few weeks later, Lennon told McCartney that his idea of playing small gigs and returning to their roots was "daft." "The group is over," he declared. "I'm leaving."

"That was sad for all of us," McCartney told me. "Except John didn't give a shit, because he was clearing the decks and about to depart on the next ferry with Yoko." McCartney made the breakup public when he included a short interview with the release of his first solo album.

Lennon was now fully engaged with a new outfit, the Plastic Ono Band. Starr recorded an album of standards and then one of country tunes. Harrison, who promptly made *All Things Must Pass*, the best work of his career, was especially glad to get on with his post-Beatles life. The band, he said, "meant a lot to a lot of people, but, you know, it didn't really matter *that* much."

It mattered plenty to McCartney. He and Linda went off to

a farm in Campbeltown, Scotland, where McCartney drank too much, slept late into the afternoons, and then drank some more. He'd always enjoyed a drink or a joint. And when he took acid, he told me, he had visions of bejewelled horses and the DNA helix. But now, he said, "there was no reason to stop." He was depressed. "The job was gone, and it was more than the job, obviously—it was the Beatles, the music, my musical life, my collaborator," he told me. "It was this idea of 'What do I do now?'" In McCartney's absence, a rumor that he'd died began on a Detroit radio show and spread across the world. Jimi Hendrix and Miles Davis sent a telegram inviting McCartney to record with them; a Beatles aide replied that McCartney was out of town. When a reporter and a photographer from *Life* showed up on the farm, McCartney threw a bucket of water at them. "The Beatles thing is over," he told them after settling down. "Can you spread it around that I am just an ordinary person and want to live in peace?"

The crackup was raw and public. Lennon, who was undergoing Arthur Janov's primal-scream therapy, was not prepared to muffle his pent-up grievances. Seven months after the *Let It Be* documentary was released, he gave a long and acrid interview to Jann Wenner, the editor and cofounder of *Rolling Stone*. The Beatles, Lennon said, "were the biggest bastards on earth." McCartney and Harrison, especially, had shown nothing but contempt for Ono. He took aim at journalists who wrote about her looking miserable in the documentary: "You sit through sixty sessions with the most big-headed, uptight people on earth and see what it's fuckin' like."

Lennon went after McCartney in particular. "We got fed up with being sidemen for Paul," he said. The documentary itself was evidence of McCartney's self-serving manipulations, he thought. "The camera work was set up to show Paul and not to show anybody else. That's how I felt about it. And on top of that, the people that cut it, cut it as 'Paul is God' and we're just lying around there . . . There was some shots of Yoko and me that had been just chopped out of the film for no other reason than the people were oriented towards Engelbert Humperdinck." Lennon was so disaffected that when Wenner asked him if he would do it all over again he said, "If I could be a fuckin' fisherman, I would!"

That period was intensely painful for McCartney, but he had to laugh when I read him that last line. "John talked a lot of bullshit," he said.

———•———

As a showman, McCartney likes to "please the average punter." He plays the hits and plays them precisely as recorded. But in the first few years after the breakup of the Beatles he avoided the songs he'd written with Lennon. You didn't get "Day Tripper"; you got "Mary Had a Little Lamb." You didn't get "Ticket to Ride"; you got "Hi, Hi, Hi." No matter. He sold tickets. He sold records. Mixed in with the music, however, were gestures of mockery—or, in Liverpudlian terms, taking the piss. Long before the hip-hop diss-track era, McCartney put out "Too Many People," a song from the *Ram* album that scowled at Lennon: "You took your lucky break and broke it in two." Not long afterward, Lennon lambasted McCartney on the *Imagine* album in a far more scathing song called "How Do You Sleep?" "The only thing you done was yesterday," he sang at his old friend. "The sound you make is Muzak to my ears." Lennon's son Sean told me that his father eventually came to recognize that he was as upset with himself as he was with his friend. "Those were crabby moments, but people made too big a deal of it," he added. "It didn't reach the level of Tupac telling Biggie Smalls that he'd slept with his wife" in "Hit 'Em Up."

With time, relations improved, and McCartney, who guards his sunny public image carefully, allowed that neither man was his cartoon image. "I could be a total prick, and he could be a softie," as he put it to me. There were phone calls between the two and some visits to the Dakota, where Lennon and Ono had an apartment. When Lennon separated from Ono, in 1973, and went on an eighteen-month bender with May Pang, the couple's assistant— Beatles Studies scholars refer to this as the "lost weekend" period— McCartney went to Los Angeles to see his friend, and encouraged him to go home. They even played some music in a studio with Stevie Wonder and Harry Nilsson. Here and there, rumors spread of a Beatles reunion. Starr told me a story about a promoter who offered them a fortune to play a concert but also mentioned an opening act that would feature a man wrestling a shark. "We called each other and said no," Starr said. "We were taking our own roads now." By the late seventies, Lennon and McCartney talked from time to time about domestic matters—raising children and baking bread. When Lorne Michaels, the producer of *Saturday Night Live*, went on the air in 1976 and jokingly offered the Beatles three thousand dollars to come on the show, McCartney happened to be visiting Lennon at the Dakota and they were watching the program. They were tempted to go to the studio, at Rockefeller Center. "It was only a few blocks away," McCartney told me, "but we couldn't be bothered, so we didn't do it."

Then, on December 8, 1980, Lennon was murdered. Four months later, Philip Norman published *Shout!*, a best-selling biography of the band built around the idea that Lennon was "three-quarters of the Beatles" and McCartney little more than a cloying songwriter and a great manipulator. And Ono did not relent, remarking that Lennon had told her that McCartney had hurt him more than any other person had. McCartney was hamstrung; how could he respond? Lennon was now a martyr. People gathered outside the Dakota to sing "Imagine" and leave behind flowers or a burning candle.

McCartney kept his counsel for a while. Otherwise, he told me, "I'd be walking on a dead man's grave." But in May 1981, he called Hunter Davies, who had once published an authorized Beatles biography, and unloaded about Lennon and Ono: "No one ever goes on about the times John hurt me. When he called my music Muzak. People keep on saying I hurt him, but where's the examples, when did I do it?" McCartney went on like this for more than an hour. "I don't like being the careful one," he said. "I'd rather be immediate like John. He was all action . . . He could be a maneuvering swine, which no one ever realized. Now since the death he's become Martin Luther Lennon." Then, there was the issue of who wrote what: "I saw somewhere that he says he helped on 'Eleanor Rigby.' Yeah. About half a line. He also forgot completely that I wrote the tune for 'In My Life.' That was my tune. But perhaps he just made a mistake on that."

He wavered for years, savoring his partnership with Lennon and declaring his love and his sense of loss, but also relitigating old resentments, to the point of challenging the order of their trademark: "Lennon-McCartney." (Indeed, in *The Lyrics* McCartney has the credit lines for "his" Beatles songs read "Paul McCartney and John Lennon.") It was a struggle for reputation, for the narrative of their lives together and apart. And yet, even in his rant to Davies, McCartney made plain that he could see the absurdity of it all: "People said to me when he said those things on his record about me, you must hate him, but I didn't. I don't. We were once having a right slagging session and I remember how he took off his granny glasses. I can still see him. He put them down and said, 'It's only me, Paul.' Then he put them back on again and we continued slagging . . . That phrase keeps coming back to me all the time. 'It's only me.'"

———•———

For years, McCartney thought about writing a memoir but, he told me, it seemed like "too much work." Instead, he authorized an old friend, Barry Miles, to write a biography, which appeared in 1997 as *Paul McCartney: Many Years from Now*. Miles took pains to counter the notion of McCartney as a soapy balladeer and, by inference, of Lennon as the group's sole intellectual and artistic radical. The book provides accounts of McCartney hanging out with William Burroughs, Harold Pinter, Kenneth Tynan, and Michelangelo Antonioni; discussing the war in Vietnam with Bertrand Russell; and listening to Sun Ra, John Coltrane, Albert Ayler, and John Cage. There is also a tender account of McCartney's marriage to Linda Eastman and the grief he felt at her loss.

Popular music is an arena of partisanship and posturing; your identity is wrapped up in both what you love and what you can't stand. But the Beatles historian Mark Lewisohn, who in 2013 published the first of a planned three-volume biography, *The Beatles: All These Years*, has established a reputation for Robert Caro–like research and a disinclination to judge. Having listened to more than ninety hours of audiotapes of the sessions at Twickenham, Lewisohn, like Peter Jackson, takes the view that the *Let It Be* documentary exaggerated the discord at the studio; and that collaboration, exuberant and vital, was at the heart of things. I called Lewisohn, who lives just outside London, and has managed to sustain a generous view of all the Beatles. He speaks respectfully of the McCartney songbook of recent decades. There are ups and downs, he allows, but McCartney "has been dropping diamond gifts into the world for sixty years now, and that work will endure."

The rock-critic establishment has not been so generous. Jann Wenner was a Lennon partisan and, for years, *Rolling Stone* reflected that view. The *Village Voice* critic Robert Christgau, sometimes known as the dean of the guild, once called *Red Rose Speedway*, McCartney's 1973 album with his new band Wings, "quite possibly the worst album ever made by a rock and roller of the first rank." In truth, McCartney often seems inclined to issue everything that he has had occasion to record, and much of it is undercooked and sentimental. He sometimes joins in the criticism. The song "Bip Bop," on *Wild Life*, the first Wings album, from 1971, "just goes nowhere," he once said. "I cringe every time I hear it." In some cases, though, the critical reception has been revised upward over the years, as with the album *Ram* or the single "Arrow Through Me."

Not a few peers will speak up for McCartney, including his post-Beatles work. "He can do it all," Bob Dylan told *Rolling Stone*, in 2007. "And he's never let up. He's got the gift for melody, he's got the rhythm, and he can play any instrument. He can scream and shout as good as anybody . . . He's just so damn effortless. I just wish he'd quit!" Taylor Swift has also noted the "seemingly effortless" quality of McCartney's work. "His melodies both confound you and also feel like the most natural sounds you've ever heard," she told me. "Mostly, what I've learned from Paul is that he never fell out of love with music because he never stopped creating it."

When I asked Elvis Costello, who has collaborated with McCartney, about the highlights of the post-Beatles catalog, he reeled off "Jenny Wren"—"That's just one melody that could stand next to the greatest songs written while Paul was in the Beatles"—as well as "Every Night," "Let Me Roll It," and "That Day Is Done." He also cited "If I Take You Home Tonight," which McCartney wrote for Costello's wife, Diana Krall. "Take a listen to that melody and you will hear an indelible harmonic signature," Costello said. And his own memories of working with McCartney speak to an undimmed penchant for collaborative creativity. "We were pulling words and notes out of the air, finishing songs, and recording them in his studio, downstairs, minutes later," he told me, describing their work on the songs that ended up on the album *Flowers in the Dirt*.

As a young man, Costello had a Lennonesque edge, and I wondered if that informed their collaboration. "Paul McCartney and John Lennon were teenage friends who went to outer space together," Costello told me. "Nobody could imagine themselves in that place . . . If he got the innocent line and I got the sarcastic line in a duet dialogue, it would be, like, 'Hold on a minute, I've seen this movie before,' and we'd laugh and change it around."

The desire to change things around has sometimes led McCartney to make curious decisions; and critics have, at times, suggested that he stay in his lane. When McCartney's classical foray *Liverpool Oratorio* made its American debut, in 1991, Edward Rothstein, of *The New York Times*, ended his review by recalling the story of George Gershwin approaching Arnold Schoenberg for lessons in composition. "Why do you want to be an Arnold Schoenberg?" Schoenberg supposedly asked. "You're such a good Gershwin already." Yet McCartney, while being a well-compensated conservationist and traveling performer of the Beatle past, is intent on exploring whatever moves him. When he's living in the English countryside, as he often is, he will work out in the morning and then head for his studio to write and record.

As a musician and a performer onstage, McCartney remains phenomenal, playing three-hour concerts—five or six times longer than the Beatles' shows in their heyday—to enormous crowds. He sings Beatles songs in their original keys and at the top of his register: "I can't be bothered to transpose them." He seems eager never to disappoint. As his daughter Mary told me, "Look, he's an entertainer! You'll see him play 'Live and Let Die' and he's surrounded at the piano by all these pyrotechnics, all these flames, and I'm, like, 'Dad, I can feel the heat from those flames! Do you have to do that?' But he says the audience loves it. I say, 'Don't do that to yourself, it's a huge risk!' But he won't be told."

———•———

When I watch McCartney perform, I can't help thinking about that Newport Jazz concert my father and I attended in 1973. When we were backstage, Gene Krupa, the drummer for Benny Goodman's band, sat slumped in a chair, silent, staring at a space in the carpet between his shoes. He seemed racked with dread and very old. Then, onstage, he shook off whatever weighed on him and came alive to the sound of his old friends: Goodman's sinuous clarinet, Hampton's glowing vibes, Wilson's liquid runs on the piano. Just before "Avalon," the customary closer, Krupa had his moment, beating his mother-of-pearl tom-tom to open "Sing, Sing, Sing," a standard that Goodman and Krupa had made into an extended improvisational set piece. Krupa was a runaway train. The hall throbbed to his foot at the bass drum. There was something ominous, even frightening, about the spectacle of this sickly man, now come dangerously alive, at the edge of abandon. When Krupa was done, and the applause rained over him, you could see that his shirt was drenched.

After the show, we waited by the stage door on Fifty-sixth Street, hoping to see Teddy Wilson and thank him. The door banged open and an immense security guard burst onto the sidewalk. He was carrying an old man, seemingly unconscious, in his arms. It was Krupa, wrapped in towels. A cab pulled up, and the guard funneled him into the back seat. Less than four months later, we read in the paper that Krupa had died, after struggling for years with leukemia. He was sixty-four.

For a time, the melodies just seemed to pour forth from McCartney, as if he were a vessel for something unearthly. He is still able to locate the magic occasionally. *McCartney III* is not the White Album, but there is a homemade, easygoing quality to his music, the work of a contented family man, a grandfather many times over. On songs like "Long Tailed Winter Bird" and "Find My Way," he is a craftsman who comes across with infectious, play-all-the-instruments zest. He knows as well as any critic that the essential songs were almost all done with the Beatles. But why bang on about "Bip Bop"? Who among the living has brought more delight into the world?

Paul Muldoon, McCartney's collaborator on *The Lyrics,*

observes, "For every Yeats, who did pretty well into old age, there are a hundred Wordsworths. Most poets and songwriters fade as they continue. Look at the Stones or the Kinks or Pink Floyd. It's very hard to keep on doing it. But Paul is kind of engineered to do it, to keep going."

And maybe there are other factors. Stevie Van Zandt, who has been playing guitar in Springsteen's E Street Band since the early seventies, said, "The rock generation has changed the concept of chronological time. I personally know seven artists in their eighties still working. And the entire British Invasion is turning eighty in the next few years. Nobody's grandparents made it past their sixties when we grew up." He sees "the birth of something I call 'wisdom art'—art that the artist could not have created when they were young . . . so there is a legitimate justification for continuing to create. You perform as much of your latest work as you feel like. Then you play 'Hey Jude' so everyone goes home happy."

It's a good deal: McCartney continues to explore his creativity in the studio, but, when it comes time to perform, he knows that his magic trick is to reach across time and put the coin into the juke-box. The melancholy of age and the power of memory have always been central themes for McCartney. He wrote the tune for "When I'm Sixty-four" at the age of sixteen. "Yesterday," one of the most covered songs of all time, is a melody that came to him almost six decades ago, in a dream.

————•————

The morning after the party, I returned to McCartney's house on the beach. He'd been up late. Once the film was over, there was dancing to a string of boomer hits—"Hey Jude," "We Will Rock You," "Miss You"—and he occupied the center of the floor, shimmying for all he was worth. Also, he'd had a few drinks.

"I'm a bit knackered," he admitted, greeting me at the door.

His complexion was pale, his eyes droopy. As we walked into the kitchen, he said in a comic stage whisper, "Coffee! Coffee!"

Nancy Shevell came by, dressed in a bathrobe and reading texts on her phone. For a few minutes, they did a post-party rundown, assessing the thank-yous from their guests. Outside, workers were loading up the glassware and the folding chairs. Shevell went to inspect their progress. McCartney smiled. "Nancy loves it," he said. "She's a little sad that it's over, I think."

Stella McCartney was in tears when she watched the film with her father. "It did occur to me, watching it, that we spent a lot of our childhood with Dad recovering from the turmoil and the breakup," she told me. "Can you imagine being such a critical part of that creation and then having it crumble? And, as children, we were part of a process in which our dad was mourning. It was not an easy thing for Dad, and it lasted for a lot longer than we probably knew."

Sean Lennon, who was five when his father was killed and who now, with Yoko Ono's having withdrawn from public life, represents the family's interests in the Beatles business, told me, "Time has sort of made us all grow to soften our edges and appreciate each other much more. Paul is a hero to me, on the same shelf as my dad. My mom loves Paul, too, she really appreciates him. They've had tensions in the past, and no one is trying to deny it. But all the tension we ever had, hyperbolized or not, makes it a real story about real human beings."

McCartney sat down to talk on a screened porch. Projects lay ahead, some of which he'd be completing as he hit eighty. There's a new children's book just out: *Grandude's Green Submarine*. He's collaborating with the scriptwriter Lee Hall, known for *Billy Elliot*, on a musical version of *It's a Wonderful Life*. There's even a quasi-Beatles song to finish. After Lennon died, Ono gave the surviving members demos that he'd recorded at home. McCartney, Starr, and Harrison worked on three, but added tracks only to "Free as a Bird" and "Real Love." Now McCartney wants to fill out the last of them,

"Now and Then," even though Harrison had declared the song "fucking rubbish." McCartney also wants to go back on the road, a life that he finds invigorating. "I've been doing this for a long time," he said. "So another me takes over: Professional Performing Paul—the triple 'P'!" If the question is "Why do you keep at it?," the answer is plain: "I plan to continue living. That's the central idea."

But the pandemic has been persistent, and McCartney was immersed in the business of the past, with getting the narrative right. The screening had been emotional. He watched images of Linda as a beautiful young woman, pregnant with Mary, who was now sitting beside him. And he saw himself with his friends, at the end of the film, performing not at a Libyan amphitheatre or in a London park but on the roof of the Apple building, running through sublime takes of songs they'd been working on, nailing them at last. Forty-odd minutes of music that ended with Lennon's immortal announcement: "I'd like to say thank you on behalf of the group and ourselves, and I hope we've passed the audition." Down on the street, people heading out to lunch stared up in wonder, unaware that they were hearing the Beatles play together in public for the last time.

The performer was now the spectator, the observer of his younger self and his "fallen heroes." Amid that footage of the Beatles, dressed in woolly winter getups, playing with pace and precision, all the bad stuff seemed to melt away. Even for McCartney, there's been a shift in perspective—in part, a literal one. "Whenever I was in the band, playing live, I'd be facing out," he said. "John was to the left or to the right of me, so I never got to sort of see him perform so much. Except in the film. And there he is in massive closeup. I can study everything about him."

Here and there, as McCartney watched, he got a flash of the "old feeling"—Why is Yoko sitting on that amp!—but time, coupled with a new framing of the past, has allowed him, and the audience, a more benign view of things. They were a gang, a unit, even a family, and happy families are a bore, if they exist at all. "The elder brother does shout at the younger brother, and then they have fisticuffs, or whatever," McCartney said. "It's all very natural." He raised his voice above the sound of workmen outside packing up the tents. "Buying into this myth that I was the bad one, it bothered me for years. But I sort of feel like it doesn't bother me now, because I feel like a lot of people sort of get it." If he's not entirely over it, it's because he's still in it.

October 2021

THE GOSPEL LIFE

Mavis Staples has been a gospel singer longer than Queen Elizabeth II wore the crown. During concerts, sometimes, she might take a seat and rest while someone in her band bangs out a solo for a chorus or two. No one minds. Her stage presence is so unfailingly joyful—her nickname is Bubbles—that you never take your eyes off her. Staples sings from her depths, with low moans and ragged, seductive growls that cut through even the most pious lyric. She is sanctified, not sanctimonious. In her voice, "Help Me Jesus" is as suggestive as "Let's Do It Again." When she was a girl, singing with her family ensemble, the Staple Singers, churchgoers across the South Side of Chicago would wonder how a contralto so smoky and profound could issue from somebody so young.

She is eighty-two. While singers a fraction of her age go to great lengths to preserve their voices, drinking magical potions and warming up with the obsessive care of a gymnast, she doesn't hold back. Time, polyps, and a casual disdain for preservation have conspired to narrow her range and sand down her old shimmer, but she is not about to hum lightly through a rehearsal. A little ginger tea and onward she goes. Singing is what connects her to the world.

Sly, sociable, and funny, Staples reminds you of your mother's most reliable and cheerful friend, the one who comes around with good gossip and a strawberry pie. Her cheeks are round and smooth; her hair is done in a copper bob; her resting expression is one of delight. "She is a ray of sunshine," Bonnie Raitt, her frequent touring companion, said. "She's never cranky. She has an abiding belief in God and His plan and believes the world is moving toward a higher and more loving world." Staples has spent the past few decades lending her voice to a startling range of collaborators: Prince, Arcade Fire, Nona Hendryx, Ry Cooder, David Byrne. Anyone who has something to say, she'll help them say it, in an inimitable gospel voice. One collaborator, Jeff Tweedy, of Wilco, said, "All day long, Mavis is having a good time. She's excited about making music and just being alive. I hope I have that energy when I'm her age, but the truth is I don't even have it now."

And yet life has its way of wearing down even the most radiant spirit. For two years, during the worst of the pandemic, Staples stayed home in Chicago—she lives in a modern high-rise overlooking Lake Michigan—and was, like just about everyone else in the music business, unable to perform or record. She watched cable news and saw the ravaging effect that COVID-19 was having on folks her age. She didn't go out, and she let no one in. For company, she'd pick up her phone and check in with "the Twitter people." The empty days went on and on. "Oh, man, I hated it," she said. There was only one thing left to do. "I'd start singing around the house. Mostly our old stuff, the songs we started singing when I was a kid: 'Didn't It Rain,' 'Help Me Jesus.'"

The pandemic was the least of it. The passage of time has relentlessly winnowed the comforts of her old life. For decades, she performed in the cocoon of a family that was remarkably warm, loving, and cooperative. Compared with the Jacksons, the Turners, or the Beach Boys, the Staple Singers is a story free of dark drama. But now the other members of Mavis Staples's family—her father, Roebuck; her mother, Oceola; her brother, Pervis; her sisters, Cleotha,

Cynthia, and Yvonne—are gone. "It's just me now," she said. She's left with memories of a bygone world: backyard barbecues at the Staples place, with Redd Foxx, Aretha Franklin, and Mahalia Jackson piling their plates with ribs and creamed corn; starlit rides in the family Cadillac, touring the gospel capitals of the Deep South; singing "Why? (Am I Treated So Bad)" at rallies before Martin Luther King Jr. delivered an oration. "Ghosts," as Staples put it to me one day. "So many ghosts."

We were having lunch at a restaurant downstairs from her apartment, and Staples was saying that even now she dreams about her family. Like anyone of a certain age, she has a quarry of stories she mines to explain the shape of her life. She tells these stories expertly, as if each time were the first. She is an entertainer, after all. But, when the matter of loss comes up, there is no sense of performance. She takes a deep breath and lets herself settle, as if to say, *This is the important thing about me.* Her father—everyone called him Pops—died in 2000, just after the Staple Singers were inducted into the Rock & Roll Hall of Fame. She still misses him, she says, so much that he shows up in her dreams to give her advice: "And, when I wake up, I be so mad that it was just a dream!" Pops, a son of the Mississippi Delta, was the paterfamilias, soft-spoken and kind. He sang, wrote songs, assembled the set lists, booked the dates, ran the business. The sole instrumentalist in the group, he played a bluesy Fender guitar, surrounding the vocal lines with a spare, tremolo sound. For years, his absence onstage left Staples feeling adrift. "I was having a hard time," she said. "I didn't hear Daddy's guitar."

Staples tried singing alone for a while, with a hired band of musicians, and she let her sister Yvonne, who never liked being in front of a crowd, focus on business matters. But, when the loneliness got to be too much, Staples persuaded her to come back onstage. "Yvonne was with us on tour for about ten years," Rick Holmstrom, Staples's guitar player, said. "They had adjoining rooms. They were constantly talking and bickering. That kept Mavis from being lonely."

Then it became evident that Yvonne, like Cleotha before her, was developing Alzheimer's. "When Yvonne got to the point where she had a hard time knowing where she was, or started wandering away from the microphone, it distracted Mavis onstage," Holmstrom said. "Finally, Yvonne stayed home and her friend Penny took care of her. Mavis couldn't imagine being on the road without family. I was worried about her. When Yvonne started to fade, I thought Mavis might retire." Yvonne died in 2018.

Staples no longer goes to church on Sundays. She hasn't lost her faith; she's lost the habit. She still sends her tithe to Trinity United Church of Christ, in Chicago—Jeremiah Wright's old church—but she hasn't been there for years. "I can go in my closet and pray," Staples said. "I don't have to go to church. The church is a building. I'm the church." She works out her deepest dilemmas at home, but with a little help. "The other day, I was talking about retiring, but then I thought, 'What would I do?'" she said. "I just felt like, why is this eighty-two-year-old woman going up onstage with these kids? I don't want to burden nobody. Speedy, my road manager, has to help me get in the van. I use a wheelchair in the airport. Some beds are too high and I have to take a running leap! I talked to the Lord. I asked him, 'Why am I still here? My whole family is gone. What do you want of me? What am I supposed to do? Have you kept me up for a reason?' And the only reason I could see is to sing my songs."

———•———

It's impossible to locate the precise birthplace of something as various as the blues, but one of its most effective incubators was a ten-thousand-acre plantation in Sunflower County, Mississippi, founded in 1895 by an eccentric white businessman named Will Dockery. At its peak, as many as four hundred Black families lived and worked on Dockery Farms. Most were sharecroppers who harvested cotton and a variety of other crops. Dockery was of Scottish descent, wore a dark suit every day, abstained from drinking and smoking, and believed in modesty and moral uplift. His plantation was a self-enclosed agrarian universe, with its own cotton gin, a sawmill, a commissary, a post office, and two churches (Methodist and Baptist). It even had its own currency. The sharecroppers lived in old boxcars and rough-hewn cabins.

The Staples family was among the Dockery farmers. Roebuck Staples (his parents had great esteem for the mail order giant of the day, Sears, Roebuck & Co.) was the youngest of fourteen children. He was raised singing praise songs, but the blues was in the air—in juke joints and general stores, on street corners and in barrelhouses. Dockery Farms and the surrounding towns produced an astonishing crop of blues players, including Robert Johnson, Son House, McKinley Morganfield (aka Muddy Waters), and Chester Arthur Burnett (aka Howlin' Wolf). Roebuck listened to them all. But the crucial progenitor was Charley Patton, a boastful, lusty, sometimes violent man who played guitar and sang with alarming ferocity. Long before Magic Slim or Jimi Hendrix came along, Patton entertained listeners by playing his guitar between his legs and behind his back. Roebuck heard him at the Holly Ridge Store and thought, "If I ever get to be a man, I'm gonna get me a guitar and play the blues." As a teenager, Roebuck made ten cents a day feeding hogs and chickens. He put those coins together to buy his first guitar, a Stella acoustic, and soon developed a fingerpicking style that drew on all he was hearing around him. The blues, he once said, "got into me, and into my sound, and into my fingers."

When Roebuck was eighteen, he married Oceola Ware, who was two years younger. In 1936, they joined the Black migration north, ending up on the South Side of Chicago. Early on, Oceola was a hotel maid. Roebuck worked as a bricklayer, in a steel mill, and in a vast and fragrant slaughterhouse that was known in town as the House of Blood.

Roebuck had moved from one musical mecca to another. Chicago was the locus of urban blues and the center of the burgeoning gospel scene. "I don't care where anybody else comes from or what anybody else does, Chicago is the capital of gospel and always will be," the singer Albertina Walker once said. Gospel music has sources in both English revival hymns and the spirituals sung in America since the arrival of Black men and women, but the godfather of Chicago's particular brand of gospel—a genre both sanctified and blues-inflected—was Thomas A. Dorsey. Born in rural Georgia in 1899, Dorsey was a prodigy, a pianist who got his education in church pews and revival tents and his early work experience in brothels and bars. After moving to Chicago, around 1919, he built a reputation playing behind Ma Rainey. But he was intent on bringing the energy of the juke joint to more hallowed ground. In Sunday services, Dorsey encouraged hand clapping, foot stomping, and improvisation. He was determined to defy the conventions of the more conservative churches and provide some uplift in miserable economic times. He'd had a hit, in the nineteen-twenties, with "It's Tight Like That"; now, as the Depression settled in, he was writing songs in the mode of "If You See My Saviour." In 1932, while Dorsey was on the road, his wife, Nettie Harper, died in childbirth; their child died a day later. In the wake of that tragedy, Dorsey wrote "Take My Hand, Precious Lord," a song that became so central to the gospel canon that Mahalia Jackson sang it at Dr. King's funeral.

Dorsey helped construct the musical world in which Roebuck Staples and his family took up residence. Even while working exhausting days at the slaughterhouse, Roebuck made extra money performing at parties and churches: "I'd do the gospel on Sunday. Pick up three dollars at the joint, five dollars from the offering plate at church, and make eight dollars for the weekend and live high on the hog when my peers were happy just to get the three dollars. But I wanted to be playing only gospel even then." For a time, he sang with a group called the Trumpet Jubilees. But he grew dismayed by the group's indiscipline and decided to try something new, closer to home. One day in 1948, he gathered his children in a circle to teach them the church harmonies he had learned in Mississippi. The first song they worked on was "Will the Circle Be Unbroken," a tune taken up by country ensembles like the Carter Family. In their living room, Pops drilled his children on that song for days. "Mavis was headstrong and stubborn," he told Greg Kot, Mavis's biographer. "It took her almost two years before she could catch on to her part."

Staples acknowledges that she was a resistant pupil at first. "I didn't like to rehearse," she told me. "Pops said, 'Mavis, your voice is a gift that God gave you. If you don't use it, he'll take it back.' I was the first one in rehearsal after that."

———•———

One afternoon, Staples and I drove around the South Side, passing through her old neighborhood, "the Dirty Thirties," and beyond. She pointed out her school, the churches where she prayed and performed, the site of the Regal Theatre—the Apollo of Chicago, now long gone. But it was only when we drove past the place where she lived and sang in those first rehearsals that she really came to life. "When my aunt Katie came and heard us rehearsing one time, she said, 'Shucks, y'all sound pretty good. I believe I want y'all to come sing in my church Sunday,'" Staples recalled. "We were glad to have somewhere to sing that wasn't the living room floor." The next Sunday, the Staples family sang at a Baptist church in the neighborhood. The shouts from the pews—the ultimate currency of approval—were startling, but they also posed a problem. "We didn't know about encores," Staples said. "We just had the one song. So we sang it three times."

Staples knew from an early age that if she was going to sing in public it could only be gospel music. Sometimes, when Pops was struggling to support the family, Mavis and Yvonne were sent to live with Oceola's mother, in Mound Bayou, Mississippi, and one day Mavis took part in a school talent show there. Without thinking much, she sang "Since I Fell for You," a jukebox hit by Ella and Buddy Johnson. When Grandma Ware found out, she was furious: "Oh, you was singing the blues, huh?" Out came the switch.

"I got the worst whipping in my life!" Staples said. "She sent me back to school with my little short dress on, my legs had pink welts. I started printing letters to my mother. I said, 'Mama, I want to come home. Grandma won't let me sing!'"

Pops was a stickler, too. Forget about the kids singing the blues: in those days, he wouldn't even let them play cards. But he was excited about the offers they were getting after that one-song premiere. He taught the kids to sing "Tell Heaven," "Too Close," and what became, in 1956, their first recorded hit, "Uncloudy Day." From the start, the Staple Singers were a distinctively old-fashioned group in the quartet tradition. Their haunting, down-home church harmonies reminded listeners of earlier times. "When we first went on the road, people thought we were old people because we were singing such old songs," Staples said. The one departure from tradition was Pops's guitar—a rarity in those days, and a "devilish" instrument to some. It was only later that many other gospel groups, like the Mighty Clouds of Joy and the Dixie Hummingbirds, hired guitar players to accompany them.

The old neighborhood was rich in musical talent. Staples developed a crush on Sam Cooke, who lived nearby, and routinely encountered the stars of the gospel world, including her role model, Mahalia Jackson. "My name is Mavis," she shyly told the singer on their first meeting. "I sing, too."

"Oh, you do?"

"Yes, ma'am. With my father and my brother and my sisters."

"I want to hear you."

"Well, you'll hear me, because I sing *loud*."

In the early nineteen-fifties, Roebuck decided that the Staple Singers were a business. While Mavis was still in school, they would set out touring for long weekends on the "gospel highway," a circuit of southern churches, school gymnasiums, and VFW halls. They crossed paths with the Soul Stirrers, Lou Rawls and the Pilgrim Travelers, the Reverend C. L. Franklin and his daughter Aretha. Mavis got used to finishing homework assignments in boarding-houses and modest hotel rooms across the Jim Crow South.

At the start of their touring days, she said, "Pops sat us down and said, 'Now listen, y'all, we're going down south. It's a different place. Everybody don't like you. And there's certain things that you'll see that's going to be different. If you want to drink water, if you see a sign that say 'Colored,' that's the water fountain that you drink from. And, when you go in the store, you have to be very careful.'"

Many Black touring acts carried a copy of the Green Book, an annual compendium published by Victor Hugo Green. The Green Book informed them where they could find gas, food, and lodging, and warned them which places had been designated "sundown towns"—dangerous for Black people after dark. Even so, trouble was always around the corner: random arrests, overnight stays in some dank drunk tank, white kids trying to run your car off the road. No one who'd grown up on a gospel lyric like "Were you there when they nailed Him to the tree?" failed to make the connection between a crucifixion in the ancient world and the lynchings in modern America. Staples, young as she was, knew the score. In 1955, when she was sixteen, she read about the murder of Emmett Till, in Mississippi—not far from where Pops grew up—and tried sending a message of condolence to Till's grieving mother.

When Staples finished high school, in 1957, Pops quit his job and declared it possible for the Staple Singers to focus completely on their music. Staples resisted, telling him that she wanted to study to be a nurse. "He said, 'Mavis, baby, don't you know you're already a nurse?'" she recalled. "'Don't you know that when you be singing, and those people come around crying and want to touch your hand, you're making them feel better?'" Staples was not the rebellious sort. The Staple Singers were now a full-time concern. "Uncloudy Day," which the group had recorded with Vee-Jay Records the previous year, was getting a lot of radio play; they were performing before bigger audiences, on longer, multistate tours. (The Staple Singers later expanded into gospel-inflected soul and pop, on Riverside, Epic, Stax, and other labels.) They even made guest appearances on network television.

Pops did not think of his family, at first, as a political enterprise, but he'd been listening intently to Dr. King's sermons on the radio, and, while the Staple Singers were in Montgomery, Alabama, they went one Sunday to a service at Dr. King's church on Dexter Avenue. In a meeting afterward, King made it plain to Pops that the Staple Singers had a role to play in the movement. Enslaved people sang "Steal Away" on the plantations and abolitionists sang "John Brown's Body" during the Civil War, King once reminded a reporter. "For the same reasons the slaves sang, Negroes today sing freedom songs, for we, too, are in bondage." That was the case he made to Pops.

The family went back to their hotel, and Pops called his children to his room. "I like this man's message," he said. "And I think that if he can preach it, we can sing it." In the early nineteen-sixties, the Staple Singers started releasing "message songs": "I've Been Scorned," "Freedom Highway," "Long Walk to D.C.," "Respect Yourself," "When Will We Be Paid?," and Dr. King's favorite, "Why? (Am I Treated So Bad)." Although they maintained their restrained sound, their lyrics grew more insistently political: "The whole wide world is wonderin' what's wrong with the United States," they sang in "Freedom Highway." Those songs became as important to the movement as Sam Cooke's "A Change Is Gonna Come" or the Impressions' "Keep on Pushing." This was a commitment that Mavis Staples would go on upholding. She admires the current crop of rappers whose music is saturated with both politics and gospel influence—Chance the Rapper and Kendrick Lamar among them—and doesn't want to sing only the songs of the civil rights era. Disgusted by the election of Donald Trump and the bigotry it enabled, she teamed up with her friend Jeff Tweedy on an album of assertively political new material, *If All I Was Was Black*.

On those early southern tours, stardom did not shield the Staples family from the cruelties that they were singing about. One night in November 1964, the group wrapped up a concert in Jackson, Mississippi, packed into Pops's Cadillac, and headed north toward home. It was Mavis's turn at the wheel, and around 1 a.m. she pulled in to a gas station, in Memphis, and politely asked the attendant if he would fill the tank and clean the bug-specked windshield. She also asked for a receipt. The attendant, a tall, skinny white boy, ignored her request. As Staples told me the story: "He said, 'If you want a receipt, N-word, you come over to the office.'"

Pops, furious, told Mavis to pull the car up to the service station office and wait. He followed the attendant into the office, where they quickly got into a shouting match.

"Let me tell you something," the white boy yelled, again using the N-word. Before the boy could continue his disquisition, Pops clocked him with a right hand. "Pops had this pinkie ring on his finger," Staples recalled, "and blood spattered." Pops, who was wearing slippers, slid on the greasy floor. Mavis saw that the attendant had grabbed a crowbar and was coming toward him. She woke Pervis, who'd been asleep, and he sprang up—"Pervis came from under those coats and out of that car like Superman!"—and hustled his father to safety. Mavis hit the gas, driving across the Mississippi into Arkansas. But soon they were pulled over by three police cars, lights flashing. The station attendant had called the police and claimed that he'd been beaten and robbed.

"They had shotguns on us, dogs were barking, big old German shepherds," Staples told me. "They had us standing on the highway with our hands up over our heads. Then they handcuffed us and one of them said, 'This boy here looks like he wants to run.' They kept calling my father 'boy.'"

In the trunk, the cops found a cigar box full of cash—more than a thousand dollars—and a gun. The cash was from their earnings on the road, and the pistol was legally registered. But the cops seemed convinced that this was evidence of a felony.

The officers shoved the Staples family into the squad cars and brought them to the local police station. "Pops walked in, hands cuffed behind his back, and this Black man is there mopping the floor," Staples recounted. "He said, 'Papa Staples, what you doing here?' And we laughed about that way later—but we couldn't laugh then." The police captain, a white man named Bobby Keen, thought he recognized Pops from television—*The Tonight Show, Hootenanny*, he couldn't remember which—and said, "My wife loves you! Is that you?"

"Yes," Pops said. "In person."

"Get them handcuffs off them people," Captain Keen told his officers. Before heading back to the interstate, Pops autographed a few of their record albums they kept in the trunk for Captain Keen.

Six weeks later, the Staple Singers were performing at the Mason Temple, in Memphis, a major stop on the gospel highway. Mavis looked over to the VIP area, and there were Keen and some of his officers. Pops said, "Well, Chief, it's mighty nice of y'all to come out here to see us, but who's minding the town?"

———•———

Earlier this year, I went to see Staples and her band at the Barns, a small indoor venue on the grounds of Wolf Trap, the performing arts center in Vienna, Virginia. The fans who lined up to show their immunization records and take their seats were almost entirely white, and of a certain vintage. That's typical of Staples's crowds these days. If I had to guess, I'd say that most people at Wolf Trap first encountered the Staple Singers in *The Last Waltz*, Martin Scorsese's film of the Band's final concert, an all-star farewell held on Thanksgiving Day, 1976, at the Winterland Ballroom, in San Francisco. The Band's guests included Muddy Waters, Van Morrison, Joni Mitchell, and Bob Dylan, and yet the Staple Singers stole the movie, without even appearing at the concert itself. They were touring in Europe. Weeks later, Scorsese filmed them on an MGM soundstage playing "The Weight" together with the Band. Gospel had been an essential spice in the Band's musical stew. "We worshipped the Staple Singers, plain and simple," Levon Helm, the Band's drummer, told Greg Kot. "We tried to sing with the same kind of delivery in our harmonies. They were who we looked to." During a break in the filming, Helm tried to pass a joint to Pops, but Pops demurred. "Man, I don't want none of that mess," he said.

In the movie, Cleotha, Yvonne, and Pops are in good form, and Mavis is at her best, giving "The Weight"—a surreal, country gallop—a spiritual lift. After Helm takes the first verse, Mavis takes the second and brings the whole affair to church. Pops sings the third verse in his sweet, whispery tone, the narrative oozing out of him like a slow, thick stream of Bosco. But it's at the end, as everyone sings the verse and Mavis lags on the beat, with her signature grunts and moans and claps, that your scalp tingles and you think about the Staples family, at their start, singing in their living room on the South Side.

Dylan had heard that sound at a formative age. Growing up in the Iron Range of Minnesota, he tuned in to the high-wattage radio stations from Nashville and Memphis, Shreveport and Atlanta, that blanketed the country each night with music that was far from the jukebox mainstream. "At midnight, the gospel stuff would start," Dylan later told a documentary filmmaker. "I got to be acquainted with the Swan Silvertones and the Dixie Hummingbirds, the Highway Q.C.'s and all that. But the Staple Singers came on . . . and they were so different." What shook him was the shivery sound of "Sit Down Servant," a spooky, almost medieval-seeming song that Pops and his children had recorded in 1953. "Mavis was singing stuff like 'Yonder come little David with a rock and sling, I don't want to meet him, he's a dangerous man' . . . I thought, 'Oh, my goodness!' That made my hair stand up. I thought, 'That's how the world is.'"

You can see black-and-white video of Staples singing that song in the early sixties. Pops is dressed in a dark suit, the kids in dark choir gowns. Mavis, a startlingly beautiful young woman, stands in the foreground. Her hands are lifted, her expression glowing, and then comes that heavy voice, a great rumbling from her deepest self: "I don't want to meet him . . . He's a daaayn-*jus* man!" And, from a hushed chant, the singing picks up volume and pace, propelled by that warbly guitar, the slinky licks up the fretboard, a cross-play of hand clapping on the beat and after the beat, until Mavis achieves a kind of scary, wheels-off propulsion:

> God spoke to Joshua to do thy will
> He said if you fight the battle, the sun'll stand still
> He give me a lantern and he told me to go
> He give me a harp and he told me to blow

Something otherworldly is going on; the voices grow as swift and strange as some kind of celestial railroad. If you were a kid listening to that song in the dark, on the Iron Range or anywhere else, you, too, might hide under the covers until daybreak.

Dylan arrived in New York in January 1961, when he was nineteen. As he was building a reputation on the folk scene in Greenwich Village, he ran into the Staple Singers at a music festival in the city, and an acquaintance introduced them. "Bob said, 'I know the Staple Singers!'" Staples recalled. "He said, 'Pops, he has a velvety voice, but Mavis gets *rough* sometimes.' And then he quoted that verse in 'Sit Down Servant.'"

"I didn't know no white boy knew our stuff!" Pops said.

As the sixties wore on, the Staple Singers broadened their repertoire. Pops, who was in equal measure idealistic and shrewd, saw a growing appetite, among white listeners as well as Black, for his message songs. He even had the group record some of Dylan's songs, including "Masters of War" and "A Hard Rain's A-Gonna Fall." Dylan developed what Staples calls a case of "puppy love." On a cafeteria line before a performance, Dylan turned to Pops and said, "Pops, I want to marry Mavis."

"Well, don't you tell me, tell Mavis," Pops said.

Staples delights in talking about it: "He was a cute little boy, little blue eyes, curly hair. He and Pervis got to be tight. They'd sit out on the stoop, drink wine."

She describes their relationship as "courting," with some "smooching" here and there. But, when I asked if they almost got married, she smiled and said, "Nobody *almost* gets married.

"I still have letters that we would write to each other. And the only time we would see each other was when we happened to be on the same show." She went on, "I was the one that dodged a bullet. I wouldn't have been able to keep up with him." But, she added, "if I stayed with him in his life, I don't think he would have turned to drugs like he did."

Many years later, in 2016, Staples and her band toured as an opening act for Dylan. As a matter of self-preservation, Dylan makes a habit of keeping to himself on the road, rarely consorting with the opening act when he's got one. This time was different.

"The first show, someone knocked on my door and said someone wants to see you," she told me. "In comes Bobby. And I said, 'Bobby, I'm so glad to see you. I been wanting to see you for so long.'"

"You should have married me," Dylan said. "You would've seen me every day."

———•———

Staples did marry once, and miserably. In 1964, she met a Chicago mortician named Spencer Leak. The Leak family was prominent on the South Side, and their wedding was a major social event. But Leak wasn't happy about his wife's stardom, and it didn't help that they could not have children, a grave disappointment to Staples. The end came six years later, with Staples changing the locks on her door and Leak sleeping in the funeral parlor. Her next album, a solo effort, was called *Only for the Lonely*. Years later, she told Prince about her marriage, inspiring him to write a song for her called "The Undertaker."

Staples is a canny retailer of her own story. She's not going to get into a funk over lost loves and ancient disappointments—not now, not in front of you or me. Instead, she'll tell you about when the Staple Singers went to Ghana, and a bureaucrat showed up at her hotel door with a note from a Ghanaian chief. "Chief Nana wanted me to be Wife No. 4," she said. "We had all gone to his palace one night. All this marble!" The chief, she said, was "good-looking, but not good-looking enough for me to say, 'Oh, yes, I'll be Wife No. 4.' I mean, what's Wife Nos. 2 and 3 gonna do? Probably tear me apart."

That ability to deflect, to find humor in complicated experience, indicates not a lack of depth but a self-knowing soul. "I'm always struck by how Mavis, no matter what she sings, no matter what the decade is, is always leading you back to the sound of the church," Braxton Shelley, a scholar of music and the Black church at Yale, told me. "At the same time, Mavis always *seems* like Mavis. She tells that terrible story about the gas station and getting arrested, and she is talking about white supremacy, about painful things. But, at the same time, you always sense that she has woven whatever emotional pain she's experienced into the fabric of her life. I don't pretend to deep knowledge of her inner life, but there is a deep sense of *pleasantness* about Mavis Staples, which is a kind of miracle, you know?"

Because Staples is not eager to tell unhappy stories or engage in trash talk, you're taken aback in the rare moment when she heads into scratchy territory—as when she discusses her relationship with Aretha Franklin. Staples knew the Franklin family for much of her life. When she was a teenager, Aretha's father, C. L. Franklin, one of the country's leading Black preachers, came to Chicago from Detroit to deliver his famous sermon "The Eagle Stirreth Her Nest." "I ran all around and around the church," Staples told me. "The Holy Spirit had me." It was, she said, like a "fire hitting you from the bottom of your feet."

She became good friends with Aretha Franklin and her siblings. There's no question that Franklin had a more powerful and versatile vocal instrument, and Staples, despite her ability to put over a song with an uncommon depth of feeling, has never pretended otherwise. But she always felt somewhat diminished by Franklin, and, after they teamed up to record a live church performance of Edwin Hawkins's "Oh Happy Day," in 1987, she felt outright disrespected. When the recording was released, it became clear that Franklin had turned down the volume on Staples's vocal track. Staples said she just shrugged and let it go. "I should've told her, 'No, just don't put the record out,'" she said. "But you know me: goody-goody Mavis."

Franklin, she admits, put her temperament to the test. "I put up with her for a long time till I got tired, you know?" Staples told me. "She was very insecure. I tried my best to be her friend. She would call me and ask me to call her back. When I called her back, the number was changed. So, you know, she was weird like that."

Still, Staples said, "I'm just a happy-go-lucky, you know? I can get over anything." Except deaths in the family. Through the years, Pops and Mavis were the constants in the Staple Singers. Yvonne, Pervis, and Cleotha moved in and out of the group; Oceola stayed home. The one sibling who never performed was Cynthia, the youngest. Cynthia suffered from depression. Kids had bullied her in school and pestered her, asking why she wasn't singing with her famous family. Sometimes, when Mavis was in Chicago, she let Cynthia come stay with her and tried to cheer her up. "I pushed Pops to have Cynthia play tambourine or something for us," Staples said, but that never worked out.

One day in 1973, when Cynthia was twenty-one, she was at home with Oceola, who was in the kitchen making supper. The rest of the family was on the road, performing in Las Vegas. Cynthia mentioned to Oceola that she'd received a check in the mail from Pops and wanted to write a thank-you note. Instead, she went into the living room and shot herself with a .38 caliber revolver. "We just never knew how bad she was suffering," Staples said.

———•———

Backstage at Wolf Trap, Staples and her band prepared for the show as they often do, by singing a gospel tune, "Wonderful Savior." Sometimes, particularly in the South, Staples might get a crowd that is racially mixed, but not often. It's been a long time since she could measure her performance by the number of shouts and "amen"s from an audience; no one at Wolf Trap was likely to require a deacon to fan them back into consciousness. Those gospel theatrics and emotions belong to a different world. And modern gospel—whether it is Kirk Franklin's hip-hop-inflected music or the vast number of choirs in churches across the country or Kanye West's Sunday Service Choir—is not a presence for most of these listeners. All the same, Staples will sometimes have her guitar player, Rick Holmstrom, sneak a look at the audience. "I can sense a difference in her when we get an amen corner with even some pockets of African Americans—it changes the vibe," he told me. "I'll peek, and she'll say, 'How does it look? Slim and his brother None?' I'll say, 'I don't think it's a "Weight" night.' That means there's some Black folks. We can lean on soul and gospel. A 'Weight' night would be when it's a white crowd."

The Staple Singers, like their leading Black brethren in the blues, have always had a reverent audience of white musicians. One of the first singles the Rolling Stones recorded was "The Last Time," a hit in 1965, which is credited to Mick Jagger and Keith Richards but was inspired by a Staple Singers recording from a decade before. Pops Staples didn't mind; the tune is from a traditional gospel song. Then the Stones' management asked the Staple Singers to open for them on their 1972 tour. By now, Pops had shifted the group into more popular material. Singles like "I'll Take You There" might have displeased some gospel purists, but they widened the group's appeal and made them wealthy. No matter. The Stones offered the Staple Singers a paltry five hundred dollars a night. Pops turned them down. "I'd like to think Mick Jagger doesn't know about this," he told a reporter for *Variety*.

Mavis Staples has no patience for segregation, in politics or in music. She is at once sure-minded about the essential place of Black composers and performers in American music and open to singing with anyone who can keep up. Over and over in recent years, she has been a presence in that gumbo genre known as Americana. Among her albums in that vein is a sentimental one called *Carry Me Home*, recordings that she did in 2011 with Levon Helm, at his barn in Woodstock. Helm, who died in 2012, was suffering from throat cancer; he was terribly thin, his voice raspy and weak, and yet together they rise to the occasion, collaborating on Curtis Mayfield's protest anthem "This Is My Country," Dylan's gospel song "Gotta Serve Somebody," "The Weight," and, yes, "This May Be the Last Time."

Onstage at Wolf Trap, Staples was energetic. She put together a set that mixed Staple Singers hits ("If You're Ready," "I'll Take You There"), a Delta blues (Mississippi Fred McDowell's "You Got to Move"), and covers of songs by Talking Heads, Buffalo Springfield, and Funkadelic. She also did a ribald version of "Let's Do It Again," a song that Curtis Mayfield had to talk Pops into performing. "I'm a church man, I'm not singing that," Pops had protested. "Oh, Pops, the Lord won't mind," Mayfield said. "It's just a love song." Commerce prevailed. Besides, how many hours are there, really, between Saturday night and Sunday morning? As if to deepen the sin, Staples got into a kind of squatting, hip-bumping thing with Holmstrom, and, at one point, he even used the head of his guitar to lift her skirt. Afterward, she scolded him, laughing, "Rick, you took that sin song too serious! You can't be doing that!"

For the most part, the band stands back and lets Staples sing, giving her the space to move within the song and have her way with it. Holmstrom said, "Pops would tell her, 'Sing it plain. Put it out there.' She was once screaming a little, getting a little too much, and Pops said, 'Just stand there and sing it nice and plain and you'll get your point across.'" These days, she finishes her set with "I'll Take You There." She has performed that song as often as Dylan has performed "Like a Rolling Stone," but she does it with such lightness and conviction that, as the audience sings along, you get the sense that she wouldn't mind singing all the night through. At the end, Holmstrom touches her gently on the elbow and leads her into the wings.

When we talked later, Staples returned, as always, to the weight that bears down on her: the loneliness she feels when she is not singing, all the missing—Oceola, Cynthia, Pervis, Cleotha, Pops, Yvonne. I asked her if she thinks about the end.

"You know, I do," she said. "I do quite often. And I wonder how I'm going to go. Where will I be? I've prepared everything. I have a will—because I have a lot of nieces and nephews, Pervis's children, and charities. But I seem to think about that more now than ever. And I tell myself, 'I gotta stop thinking.' Speedy, he tells me maybe I should talk to a therapist. I said, 'Don't need no therapist. The Lord is my therapist. That's who I talk to when I need help.'"

I asked her if she gets an answer.

"Yes, indeed. That's why I'm still here. He lets me know when I'm right and when I'm wrong, but he ain't letting me know about when my time is coming. But, see, I just have to be ready. If it comes tomorrow, I'm ready. I have done all that I'm supposed to do. I've been good. I've kept my father's legacy alive. Pops started this, and I'm not just going to squander it. I'm going to sing every time I get on the stage—I'm gonna sing with all my heart and all I can put out."

June 2022

THE BIRD WATCHER

Every weekday for the past twenty-seven years, a long-in-the-tooth history major named Phil Schaap has hosted a morning program on WKCR, Columbia University's radio station, called *Bird Flight*, which places a degree of attention on the music of the bebop saxophonist Charlie Parker that is so obsessive, so ardent and detailed, that Schaap frequently sounds like a mad Talmudic scholar who has decided that the laws of humankind reside not in the ancient Babylonian tractates but in alternate takes of "Moose the Mooche" and "Swedish Schnapps."

For Schaap, Bird not only lives; he is the singular genius of mid-century American music, a dynamo of virtuosity, improvisation, harmony, velocity, and feeling, and no aspect of his brief career is beneath consideration. Schaap's discursive monologues on a single home recording—say, "the Bob Redcross acetate" of Parker playing in the early nineteen-forties over the Benny Goodman Quartet's 1937 hit "Avalon"—can go on for an entire program or more, blurring the line between exhaustive and exhausting. There is no getting to the end of Charlie Parker, and sometimes there is no getting to the end of *Bird Flight*. The program is the anchor of WKCR's daily schedule and begins at 8:20. It is supposed to conclude at 9:40. In the many years that I've been listening, I've rarely heard it end precisely as scheduled. Generations of Columbia DJs whose programs followed Schaap's have learned to stand clutching an album of the early Baroque or nineteenth-century Austrian yodeling and wait patiently for the final chorus of "I'll Always Love You Just the Same."

Schaap's unapologetic passion for a form of music half a century out of the mainstream is, at least for his listeners, a precious sign of the city's vitality; here is one obstinate holdout against the encroaching homogeneity of Clear Channel and all the other culprits of American sameness. There is no exaggerating the relentlessness of Schaap's approach. Not long ago, I listened to him play a recording of "Okiedoke," a tune that Parker recorded in 1949 with Machito and His Afro-Cuban Orchestra. Schaap, in his pontifical baritone, first provided routine detail on the session and Parker's interest (via Dizzy Gillespie) in Latin jazz, and then, like a car hitting a patch of black ice, he veered off into a riff of many minutes' duration on the pronunciation and meaning of the title—of "Okiedoke." Was it "okey-doke" or was it, rather, "'okey-dokey,' as it is sometimes articulated"? What meaning did this innocent-seeming entry in the American lexicon have for Bird? And how precisely was the phrase used and understood in the Black precincts of Kansas City, where Parker grew up? Declaring a "great interest in this issue," Schaap then informed us that Arthur Taylor, a drummer of distinction "and a Bird associate," had "stated that Parker used 'okeydokey' as an affirmative and 'okeydoke' as a negative." And yet one of Parker's ex-wives had averred otherwise, saying that Parker used "okeydoke" and "okeydokey" interchangeably. (At this point, I wondered, not for the first time, where, if anywhere, Schaap was going with this.) Then Schaap introduced into evidence a "rare recording of Bird's voice," in which Parker is captured joshing around onstage with a disk jockey of the forties and fifties named Sid Torin, better known as Symphony Sid. After a bit of chatter, Sid instructs Parker to play another number: "Blow, dad, go!"

Okeydoke, says Bird.

Like an assassination buff looping the Zapruder film, Schaap repeated the snippet several times and then concluded that Charlie Parker did not use "okeydoke" as a negative. "This," Schaap said solemnly, "tends to revise our understanding of the matter." The matter was evidently unexhausted, however, as he launched a rumination on the cowboy origins of the phrase and the Hopalong Cassidy movies that Parker *might well have seen*, and perhaps it was at this point that listeners all over the metropolitan area, what few remained, either shut off their radios, grew weirdly fascinated, or called an ambulance on Schaap's behalf. At last, Schaap moved on to other issues of the Parker discography, which begins in 1940, with an unaccompanied home recording of "Honeysuckle Rose" and "Body and Soul," and ends with two Cole Porter tunes, "Love for Sale" and "I Love Paris," played three months before his death, in 1955.

Schaap is not a musician, a critic, or, properly speaking, an academic, though he has held teaching positions at Columbia, Princeton, and Juilliard. And yet through *Bird Flight* and a Saturday-evening program he hosts called *Traditions in Swing*, through his live soliloquies and his illustrative recordings, commercial and bootlegged, he has provided an invaluable service to a dwindling form: in the capital of jazz, he is its most passionate and voluble fan. He is the Bill James of his field, a master of history, hierarchies, personalities, anecdote, relics, dates, and events; but he is also a guardian, for, unlike baseball, jazz and the musicians who play it are endangered. Jazz today is responsible for only around three percent of music sales in the United States, and what even that small slice contains is highly questionable. Among the current top sellers on Amazon in the jazz category are easy-listening acts like Kenny G and Michael Bublé.

For decades, jazz musicians have joked about Schaap's adhesive memory, but countless performers have known the feeling that Schaap remembered more about their musical pasts than they did and was always willing to let them in on the forgotten secrets. "Phil is a walking history book about jazz," Frank Foster, a tenor sax player for the Basie Orchestra, told me. Wynton Marsalis says that Schaap is "an American classic."

In the eyes of his critics, Schaap's attention to detail and authenticity is irritating and extreme. He has won six Grammy Awards for his liner notes and producing efforts, but his encyclopedic sensibility is a matter of taste. When Schaap was put in charge of reissuing Benny Goodman's landmark 1938 concert at Carnegie Hall for Columbia, he not only included lost cuts and Goodman's long-winded introductions but also provided prolonged original applause tracks, and even the sounds of the stage crew dragging chairs and music stands across the Carnegie stage to set up for the larger band. His production work on a ten-disk set of Billie Holiday for Verve was similarly inclusive. Schaap wants us to know and hear *everything*. He seems to believe that the singer's in-studio musings about what key to sing "Nice Work If You Can Get It" in are as worthy of preservation as a bootleg of Lincoln's Second Inaugural. Reviewing the Holiday set for the *Village Voice*, Gary Giddins called Schaap "that most obsessive of anal obsessives."

That's one way of looking at the matter. Another is that Schaap puts his frenzied memory and his obsessive attention to the arcane in the service of something important: the struggle of memory against forgetting—not just the forgetting of a sublime music but forgetting in general. Schaap is always apologizing, acknowledging his long-windedness, his nudnik tendencies. "The examination may be tedium to you," he said on the air recently as he ran through the days, between 1940 and 1944, when Parker might have overdubbed Goodman's "Chinaboy" in Bob Redcross's room at the Savoy Hotel in Chicago. ("His home was Room 305.") Nevertheless, he said, "my bent here is that I want to know when it happened because I believe in listening to the music of a genius chronologically where possible, particularly an improvising artist." The stringing together of facts is the Schaapian process, a monologuist's way of painting a picture of "events of the past" happening "in real time."

"I just hope the concept speaks to some," he said as his soliloquy unspooled. "It's two before nine. I'm speaking to you at length. I'm Phil Schaap."

———•———

On a recent Sunday morning, I met Schaap at the WKCR studios, at Broadway and 114th Street. (The station is at 89.9 on the FM dial; it also streams live online at wkcr.org.) Schaap is tall and lumbering and has a thick shock of reddish hair. It was March 9th, Ornette Coleman's seventy-eighth birthday. Schaap, his meaty arms loaded up with highlights and rarities in the Coleman discography, had come prepared for celebration. Nearly everything in his grasp was from his home collection. He does not consider collecting to be at the center of his life, but allowed that he does own five thousand 78s, ten thousand LPs, five thousand tapes, a few thousand hours of his own interviews with jazz musicians, "and, well, *countless* CDs." Schaap, who was married once, and briefly, in the nineties, lives alone in Hollis, Queens, in the house where he grew up. He admits that his collection, and his living quarters, could use some straightening.

"I've got to get things in order," he said. "I'm determined to do it. This is the year. If I didn't have a memory, I wouldn't know where anything is."

The WKCR studios are a couple of blocks south of the main entrance to the Columbia campus, and they tend to look as though there'd been a post-exam party the previous night and someone tried, but not hard, to clean up. The carpets are unvacuumed, the garbage cans stuffed with pizza boxes and crushed cans. Taped to the wall are some long-forgotten schedules and posters of John Coltrane and Charles Mingus. The visitor's perch—a red Naugahyde armchair—was long ago dubbed the "Dizzy Gillespie chair," after Gillespie, Parker's closest collaborator, sat there for hours of conversation with Schaap. Usually, the only person around at WKCR is the student host on the air. Schaap is Class of '73. He is fifty-seven. "Financially, I live, at best, like a twenty-five-year-old," he said. He has been broadcasting on WKCR, pro bono, since he was a freshman. The Parker–Tiny Grimes collaboration "Romance Without Finance" could be the theme for his income tax form.

"Take a seat," he said, plopping his records down near his microphone. "I gotta get busy."

Conversation with Schaap in the studio, especially when the program features the breakneck tunes of early jazz or swing music—the soprano saxophonist Sidney Bechet playing "The Sheik of Araby" followed by Benny Carter and His Orchestra on "Babalu"—does not allow for Schaapian reflection. "Deadlines every three minutes!" he'll shout, throwing up his hands. "So many records!"

When he's working, Schaap concentrates hard, and not merely on his own solos. He takes pride in the art of the segue, paying particular attention to the "sizzling sonic decay" of a last cymbal stroke. ("You won't hear that again in your lifetime!" he boasted after one particularly felicitous transition.) But with Ornette Coleman, an avatar of extended improvisation, Schaap had more time. The first number he broadcast was "Free Jazz," Coleman's 1960 breakthrough, played with two quartets; "Free Jazz" is the Action painting of American music and lasts thirty-seven minutes and three seconds. The sound started to build, the quartets began their dissonant duel. Schaap smiled off into the distance. "Eddie Blackwell's right foot, man!" he said, then he remembered himself and turned the volume down. "So?" he said.

When I asked Schaap about his childhood, he turned morose, saying, "I may have gotten all my blessings in life up front." His parents, and nearly all his teachers and the scores of musicians he befriended from school age, were dead. "Everyone that raised me is gone."

Schaap was born to jazz. His mother, Marjorie, was a librarian, a classically trained pianist, and an insistent bohemian. At Radcliffe, she listened to Louis Armstrong records and smoked a corncob pipe. His father, Walter, was one of a group of jazz-obsessed Columbia undergraduates in the thirties who became professional critics and producers. In 1937, he went to France to study at the Sorbonne and work on an encyclopedia of the French Revolution. While he was there, he collaborated with the leading jazz critics of Paris, Hugues Panassié and Charles Delaunay, on a bilingual edition of their pioneering magazine, *Jazz Hot*. He helped Django Reinhardt with his English and Dizzy Gillespie with his French. Back in New York, he earned his living making educational filmstrips, in partnership with the jazz photographer William P. Gottlieb.

"They lived for music, and the rest was making a check," Phil said. "Jazz was always playing in the house." By the time he was five, Schaap could sing Lester Young's tenor solo on the Count Basie standard "Taxi War Dance." When he was six, his babysitter rewarded him for doing her geometry homework by taking him to Triboro Records, in Jamaica, to buy his first 45s: Ruth Brown's "Mama, He Treats Your Daughter Mean" and Ray Charles's "(Night Time Is) The Right Time." Phil soon started buying discarded jazz 78s by the pound.

In his parents' living room and then on his own pushy initiative, Schaap met many first-rank jazz musicians and came to consider them his "grandfathers." Some, like the bassist Milt Hinton and the trumpet player Buck Clayton, lived around Hollis, which had become a bedroom community for musicians. Others came into his life, he said, "as if by magic."

"In August 1956, I went to the Randall's Island Jazz Festival with my mother, and we saw Billie Holiday, Dizzy Gillespie, and a lot of others," he said. "At one point, we went backstage after the Basie band played. Remember, this is through the hazy recollections of a five-year-old, but I do recall someone trying to hit on my mother, and he asked her about Joe Williams, who was singing then for Basie. To brush the guy off, she said she preferred the earlier singer for the Basie band, Jimmy Rushing, and at that point another man, who turned out to be Basie's drummer, Jo Jones, said, 'Madame, I heard that—that was wonderful.' The two of them got to talking, and Jo asked me if I knew who Prince Robinson was. I said that he was a tenor player for McKinney's Cotton Pickers. I'd heard a Bluebird 78 that my father owned. Jo Jones was impressed. So he said, 'Madame, you've got yourself a new babysitter.'"

Jo Jones was arguably the greatest drummer of the swing era. When Jones was in New York, Walter Schaap would drop off his son at Jones's apartment and Phil and "Papa Jo" watched cartoons and played records. Inevitably, other musicians came over and took an interest in the kid with the unusual immersion in jazz. "That was when Jo was living at 401 East Sixty-fourth Street," Schaap said. "Later, he lived at 333 East Fifty-fourth Street and also at the Hotel Markwell, on Forty-ninth Street—lots of musicians lived there. He played a Basie record for me once in order to teach me about Herschel Evans, the great tenor player. It must have been 'Blue and Sentimental.' Jo called me 'Mister.' 'Mister, what does that sound like to you?' I blurted out, 'It sounds friendly to me.' And Jo said, 'That's right. The first thing to know is, Herschel Evans is your friend.'"

In first grade, Schaap pestered his schoolmate Carole Eldridge (and, when that failed, her mother) until he got an introduction to her father, the trumpeter Roy Eldridge. When he was fourteen, he hitched a ride into Manhattan with Basie during the 1966 subway strike. "When I started hearing that Phil was going around meeting all the jazz greats at the age of six, I wondered if it was all fantasy," his father told *The New York Times*.

The family became accustomed to their son's range of friend-ships. Phil once brought home the saxophonist Rahsaan Roland Kirk, who was known for his ability to play three horns at once and for his heroic capacities at the dinner table. Schaap challenged Kirk to an eating contest. The event came to a halt when they had eaten, in Schaap's recollection, "one mince pie each baked by Her-bie Hall's wife. You know Herbie? A major clarinet player."

The capacity of Schaap's memory was almost immediately evi-dent. He claims that at the age of two he recited the names of the American presidents, in order, "while standing on a rocking chair." He was the kind of kid who knew the names and numbers of all the New York Rangers of the nineteen-sixties and, whether you liked it or not, recited them. He was the kind of kid, too, who wrote to the manager of the Baltimore Orioles to give him advice backed up by statistical evidence. He routinely beat all comers, including his older cousin the late sportswriter Dick Schaap, in the board game Con-centration. At school, this was not a quality universally admired. "I guess some kids may have found it annoying," he allows. But musicians were generally fascinated by young Schaap. Count Basie was one of many who discovered that Schaap knew the facts of his life almost better than he did. "I think that kind of freaked Basie out," Schaap said. "I'd talk to him about a record date he did in the thirties, and he looked at me, like, 'Who . . . is . . . this . . . child?'"

By the time Schaap was established on the radio, nearly every musician who passed through New York was aware of his mental tape recorder. Twenty-five years ago, the bandleader, pianist, and self-styled space cadet Herman (Sonny) Poole Blount, better known as Sun Ra, swept by a nightclub and, before having to give a speech at Harvard, "kidnapped" Schaap. Sun Ra claimed that as a young man he had been "transmolecularized" to Saturn, and thereafter he expounded a cosmic philosophy influenced by ancient Egyptian cosmology, Afro-American folklore, and Madame Blavatsky. In order to prepare for his audience in Cambridge, Sun Ra insisted that Schaap fill him in on the details of his existence on Earth. Schaap obliged, telling Sun Ra that, according to his musicians' union forms, he was born in Birmingham, Alabama, in 1914. "I could tell him things like what 78s by Fletcher Henderson he was listening to in the thirties and about his time playing piano for the Henderson Orchestra later on," Schaap said. "He was vague about it all, but what I said made sense to him. I also knew that his favorite flavor of ice cream was the Bananas 'n Strawberry at Baskin-Robbins. It was a hot summer night, so I went up the block and bought him a quart, and we ate sitting in the car."

———•———

The urge to preserve, to collect, to keep time at bay, to hold on to the past is a common one. In this Schaap is kin to Henri Langlois, who tried to find and preserve every known film for the French Cinémathèque, kin to the classical music fanatics who drift through thrift shops looking for rereleases of Mengelberg and Furtwängler acetates, kin even to Felix Mendelssohn, who helped revive the music of Bach for Germans. He is one with all the bibliophiles, cinephiles, audiophiles, oenophiles, butterfly hunters, fern and flower pressers, stamp and coin collectors, concert tapers, and opera buffs who put an obsession at the center of their lives. "There is no person in America more dedicated to any art form than Phil is to jazz," his friend Stanley Crouch, who is writing a biography of Charlie Parker, said. "He is the Mr. Memory of jazz, and, as with the Mr. Memory character in *The 39 Steps*, the Hitchcock movie, there are those who think he ought to be shot. He can get on your nerves, but, then, you can get on his."

The day after Ornette Coleman's birthday was the birthday—
the hundred and fifth—of the cornet player Bix Beiderbecke, and
Schaap returned to the studios for another marathon of close attention. Along with Louis Armstrong and Sidney Bechet, Beiderbecke
was a pioneer of jazz as it moved from the all-in polyphony of the
earliest bands to a form of ensemble playing that allowed for solo
improvisation. The broadcast was a strange time-tunnel transition,
from Ornette's self-invented "harmolodic" experiments to Bix's
short solo flights on "Goose Pimples" and "Three Blind Mice," but
Schaap's taste is broad. As he queued up his records, he said to me,
"I remember March 10, 1985. I did 5 a.m. to 5 p.m. It was some
birthday for Bix." Schaap was unshaved, sleepy, complaining, as
usual, of overwork. He felt as if he, too, were a hundred and five.

Schaap is perpetually weary. He works hard: there are the
radio shows, the classes he's teaching now at Juilliard and at Jazz
at Lincoln Center, and various producing projects. But it's not the
work, exactly. Schaap carries with him a burden of loss and a dis-
interest in the contemporary world. He is theatrically, adamantly,
old: "I haven't seen more than six movies since 1972. Three baseball
games, maybe five. I think the last novel I read was *Invisible Man*,
when I was at Columbia. I haven't seen any television after the first
husband in *Bewitched*." He never bothered to see *Bird*, Clint East-
wood's Charlie Parker biopic. He does not own an iPod. And unless
you have a spare afternoon it is best not to ask him what he thinks
of digital downloads.

Before long, he was off on a Schaapian riff sparked by the playing of "Wringin' an' Twistin'," recorded, as Schaap said, "eighty-one
years ago by Okeh records with Frankie Trumbauer on C-melody
saxophone and Eddie Lang on guitar." Eventually, through the surface scratches, one could hear a voice say, "Yeah, that's it!" Schaap
assured his listeners that there was "no doubt of the voice's identity."
It was Trumbauer. But that was not enough to cool his curiosity.
"Someone is also humming the passage," he went on. "Is it Eddie

Lang or is it Trumbauer? I *wonder* about it. It's a test cut on the metal part before the passage begins. And then there's another voice that you can hear say, 'Yeah.' That 'yeah' is not Eddie Lang. It *could* be unidentified. Or it could be Bix's voice."

Schaap played the sequence again.

Yeah.

And again.

Yeah.

One more time.

Yeah.

Meanwhile, the Earth warmed imperceptibly; glaciers plunged into the sea.

Yeah.

"There," Schaap said. "*There!* That's it! September 17, 1927. Not that it's the most important thing that ever happened to you. But, still. I'd like to know, if possible, what Bix's speaking voice was like."

These questions were of no less moment to Schaap than the Confederate maneuvers at Shiloh were to Shelby Foote. Such is the flypaper of his mind and the didactic turn of his personality. When, finally, Schaap played another Beiderbecke record—a twenty-minute string of tunes, to be fair—I asked him what possible interest he could have in the provenance of the ghostly "yeah"s of yesteryear.

"What can I say? I make no apologies. I'm interested," he said. "Did Bix have a southern accent? A German accent? A midwestern accent? Did he sound shy or did he speak with authority? I really do think it's him, that it's Bix who says, 'Yeah.'"

Schaap paused and listened to a passage in "Goose Pimples."

"Okay," he said, "it may not be a *great* mystery. But it's a mystery, all the same. I do these things that are a turnoff, but it's my dime. I try very hard to make sure that everyone gets something out of all this. I guess for the first twenty years I was on the radio I was concerned about telling you absolutely everything about every tune. Then, in the nineties, I started concentrating on small issues, one at a time. Like that 'Okiedoke' thing. These days, I'm going for a little balance."

As a broadcaster, Schaap is unpoetic. He does not have the evocative middle-of-the-night gifts of a radio forebear like Jean Shepherd. Or take Jonathan Schwartz, whose specialty for both XM satellite radio and WNYC, in New York, is American singers. Schwartz is as obsessed with Frank Sinatra as Schaap is with Parker, but Schwartz, a storyteller with a café-society voice as smooth as hot buttered rum, conjures Sinatra's world: the stage of the Paramount, the bar at Jilly Rizzo's. Schaap is an empiricist, an old-fashioned historicist. Facts are what he has. His capacity to evoke Charlie Parker's world—Kansas City in the Pendergast era; the Savoy Ballroom scene uptown; Minton's, the Three Deuces, and Birdland; Bird's dissolution and early death—is limited to the accumulation of dates, bare anecdotes, obscure names. The emotional side of his broadcasts comes from his relationships with the musicians. His mental life can be spooky even to him. "Sometimes," he said, "I think I know more about what Dizzy Gillespie was thinking in 1945 than I do what I was thinking in 1967 or last week."

———•———

The precocious obsessive is a familiar high school type, but the object of Schaap's obsession was a peculiar one among his classmates. "The lonely days were adolescence," he admitted. "My peer group thought I was out of my mind. But, even then, kids knew basic things about jazz. Teddy Goldstein knew 'Take the A Train.' But he kept telling me, 'Don't you know what the Beatles are doing? Your world is doomed!'"

When he was in his teens, Schaap played the trumpet. He took theory classes at Columbia. "I even got a lesson in high notes from

Roy Eldridge," he said. But his playing, especially his intonation, was mediocre. "I put my trumpet in its case and that was it," he said. "March 11, 1974."

Schaap learned to serve the music anyway. In the wake of the Columbia campus strikes in 1968, a group of students set out to get rid of WKCR's "classroom of the air" gentility. "All of us were listening to the Grateful Dead and Jimi Hendrix, but we knew that all of that stuff was available elsewhere," Schaap told me over a burger near Lincoln Center. "Jimi Hendrix didn't need WKCR." And so the station began broadcasting jazz, including multiday festivals on Albert Ayler (1970), John Coltrane (1971), Charles Mingus (1972), Archie Shepp (1972), and Charlie Parker (1973). During the 1973 Parker festival, Schaap did two forty-eight-hour work shifts, splitting his time between WKCR and his paying job, at the university's identification card office. "On Friday, August 31, 1973, I had to get to the ID card office," he recalled. "The last record I played was 'Scrapple from the Apple.' Recorded November 4, 1947. The C take. On Dial. But I think I played the English Spotlite label. Anyway, I entered the back stairwell and the record was still playing in my head"—Schaap interrupted himself to hum Parker's solo—"and then I was out on 114th Street and I could hear it playing from the buildings, from the open windows. That was a turning point in the station's history. The insight was that Charlie Parker was at least tolerable to all people who liked jazz. If you idolized King Oliver, you could tolerate Charlie Parker, and if you think jazz begins with John Coltrane playing 'Ascension' you can still listen to Bird, too."

Musicians were beginning to tune in. During a Thelonious Monk festival, one of the DJs went on about how Monk created art out of "wrong notes." Monk, who rarely spoke to anyone, much less a college student, called the station and, on the air, declared, "The piano ain't got no wrong notes." In 1979, Schaap was at the center of a Miles Davis festival at a time when Davis was a near recluse living off Riverside Drive. Davis started calling the station, dozens and dozens of calls—"mad, foul, strange calls," Schaap recalled. Davis's inimitable voice, low and sandpapery, was unnerving for Schaap. But then one day—"Friday, July 6, 1979"—his tone changed, and for nearly three hours the two men went over the details of *Agharta*, one of his later albums. Finally, after Schaap had clarified every spelling, every detail, Davis said, "You got it? Good. Now forget it. Play 'Sketches of Spain'! Right now!"

Just after starting as a DJ, Schaap began organizing musical programs, mainly at the West End, on Broadway at 113th Street. He managed the Countsmen—former sidemen for Count Basie— along with other groups made up of refugees from other big bands, and got them work. Older musicians, such as Jo Jones, Sonny Greer, Sammy Price, Russell Procope, and Earle Warren, who had known Schaap as an eccentric teenager now welcomed him as a meal ticket.

"When I was a child, I lived under the illusion that these performers, who put on such an excellent front, dressed to the nines and acting like kings, made real money," Schaap said. He lost that innocence decades ago, when he happened to glance at a check made out to Benny Morton, a trombonist who had been with the Fletcher Henderson and Basie bands. "It was for fifty-eight dollars, and it was for a gig at Carnegie Hall," Schaap recalled. Jazz reached its commercial peak in the mid-nineteen-forties, but by nineteen-fifty the ballrooms had closed down. The postwar middle class no longer went out dancing; they were watching television and listening to records at home. The clubs on Fifty-second Street—the Onyx, the Famous Door, the Three Deuces—disappeared. Eventually, rock and roll displaced jazz as America's popular music. World-class musicians were scrounging for work. Performers who had enjoyed steady employment took second jobs as messengers on Wall Street, bus drivers, and bank guards. For comradeship, they were hanging out at the Chock Full o' Nuts at Fiftieth and Broadway and at a few bars around town.

"Phil took these guys out of the Chock Full o' Nuts and put

them on the stage of the West End," Loren Schoenberg, the executive director of the National Jazz Museum in Harlem, told me. "So for the young people who idolized them, and guys who'd never heard of them, Phil brought them to us." Screamin' Jay Hawkins, an early rhythm-and-blues star, used to call Phil Schaap's mother at home and beg her to get her son to do for him what he'd done for the horn players of the Basie band.

As *Bird Flight* became a fixture of the jazz world, Schaap began to get jobs teaching, but, even with the rise of academic jazz programs, no one has offered him a professorship. Some of his students—including Ben Ratliff, who is now the main jazz critic for *The New York Times*, and Jerome Jennings, a drummer for, among others, Sonny Rollins—swear by Schaap as a teacher, but some complain that his displays of memory can be tiresome and aimed at underscoring his students' cluelessness. This spring, I took Schaap's Charlie Parker course at Swing University, the educational wing of Jazz at Lincoln Center, and could see both sides. In four two-hour evening sessions, he provided an incisive, moving narrative of Parker's incandescent career, but he could also be oppressive, not least with his pointless occasional class "surveys." "Who knows 'Yardbird Suite'?" he'd ask. Then, moving from desk to desk, he'd poll the students, embarrassing those honest enough to confess their ignorance.

As a teacher, Schaap is less concerned about the tender sensibilities of his students than with developing knowledgeable and passionate listeners. "The school system is creating six thousand unemployable musicians a year—from the Berklee College of Music, Rutgers, Mannes, Manhattan, Juilliard, plus all the high schools," he said. "There are more and more musicians, and no gigs, no one to listen. So what happens to these kids? They work their way back to the educational system and help create more unemployable musicians. My rant is this: I'm not trying to teach you to play the alto sax. No. I'm trying to get you to learn how to listen to Charlie Parker. Louis Armstrong is the greatest musician of the twentieth century. But name twenty musicians today who really listen to Louis Armstrong. Go ahead: I'll give you a week."

There are many excellent young (and youngish) jazz musicians around, including the pianist Jason Moran and the sax player Joshua Redman, the singer Cécile McLorin Salvant, to say nothing of the extended family of players around Wynton Marsalis. There are isolated, limited, moments of popularity. In February, Herbie Hancock won an Album of the Year Grammy for his arrangements of Joni Mitchell songs. But, generally, a hit album in jazz means sales of ten thousand. Ornette Coleman, Sonny Rollins, and a few other giants of an earlier time still roam the earth, but even they cannot reliably sell out a major hall. Coleman's concert at Town Hall in March was as thrilling a musical event as has taken place this year in New York. The theatre was at least a quarter empty.

"In the fall of 1976, when Woody Herman was rehearsing for a forty-year-anniversary concert at Carnegie Hall, I was invited to watch," Schaap told me. "A saxophonist wasn't paying attention, and at one point Woody Herman crept up on him, put his face next to the musician's, and said, 'Son, what do you want to be?' And the guy said, 'I want to be the next Stan Getz.' And Woody Herman said, 'Son, there's not gonna be another Stan Getz!' In other words, people like Stan Getz and Woody Herman were pop stars! That's not going to happen again."

———•———

In the spring of 1947, around the same time that Charlie Parker was playing the Hi-De-Ho club, in Los Angeles, a young Bedouin herding goats along the northwest shore of the Dead Sea discovered several tall clay jars that contained manuscripts written in ancient

Hebrew and Aramaic. Wrapped in linen, the manuscripts were part of a much larger cache of ancient texts, which came to be known as the Dead Sea Scrolls.

"For decades, there were rumors that jazz had its own Dead Sea Scrolls," Schaap told me more than once. "One was a cylinder recording of Buddy Bolden"—the New Orleans cornetist and early jazz pioneer who was committed to a mental institution before the rise of 78s. "But this will probably never be found. The second, of course, is called 'the Benedetti recordings.'"

All of Schaap's listeners have grown accustomed to his close attention to the "crucial" obscurities of the Parker discography: "the unaccompanied 1940 alto recording in Kansas City," "the paper disk of 'Cherokee,'" "the Wichita transcriptions," and "the little-known Clyde Bernhardt glass-based acetate demo disks." These recordings can be revelatory, but they also try the patience. Recently on *Bird Flight*, Schaap showcased a home recording of Parker in February 1943—important because he was playing tenor saxophone, not his customary alto—and the sound was so bad that you couldn't quite tell if you were hearing "Sweet Georgia Brown" or radio waves from the surface of the planet Uranus.

The Benedetti recordings, however, occupy a privileged place not only in Schaap's mental Bird cage but also in musical history. And Schaap helped bring them out of their urns.

For decades, stories circulated in the jazz world that Dean Benedetti, a saxophonist of modest distinction, upon hearing Parker play in the mid-forties, threw his own horn into the sea and pledged himself to follow Parker everywhere he went, recording his hero's performances. Benedetti was said to have obtained, through Army connections, a Nazi-era German wire recorder, and he carried out his mission at clubs, concert halls, and private apartments all over the world. In the meantime, he was rumored to be a drug dealer who supplied Bird, a longtime addict, with heroin. Many of the legends of Benedetti's devotions came from *Bird Lives!*, an entertaining but iffy biography published in 1973 by a Los Angeles–based record producer, Ross Russell. Through the decades, no recordings surfaced. Ornithologists could not help but wonder: Had they been lost? Had they sunk, as rumored, along with a freighter in the Atlantic? Eventually, only the most committed, with their collections of 78s and back issues of *Down Beat*, spoke much of the matter. Like "the Bolden cylinder," the Benedetti recordings seemed to have taken their eternal rest in the watery grave of jazz legend.

But then, in 1988, Benedetti's surviving brother, Rigoletto (Rick), got in touch with Mosaic, a small jazz outfit in Stamford, Connecticut, that specializes in reissues from the vaults of the major labels. It was true, Rick Benedetti informed the owner, Michael Cuscuna: there really were recordings. Was Mosaic interested?

"The real backstory was incredible," Cuscuna told me.

On July 29, 1946, Parker was in desperate shape: depressed, drinking, strung out, broke, and lonely in Los Angeles, he had struggled through an afternoon recording session with the trumpeter Howard McGhee. His recording that day of "Lover Man" was a technical mess—Parker was barely able to make it through the song—but it is a painful howl, as devastating to hear as Billie Holiday's last sessions. That night, at the Civic Hotel, Parker twice wandered into the lobby naked. Later on, he fell asleep while smoking, setting his mattress on fire. The police arrested him and a judge had him committed to the Camarillo State Hospital, a psychiatric facility. When he was released, six months later, he was off heroin for the first time since he was a teenager in Kansas City. His musician friends threw a jam session party for him on February 1, 1947, at the home of a trumpet player named Chuck Copely. One of the guests was a handsome young man—pencil mustache, dark eyes, hipster clothes—named Dean Benedetti.

Benedetti went out and bought a Wells-Gardner 78 rpm portable disk-cutter at Sears, Roebuck and, in March, recorded Parker playing with Howard McGhee's band at the Hi-De-Ho. (The his-

torical bonus here is that Parker plays tunes from McGhee's reper-
tory, and so we hear him soloing, for the first and last time, on Gus
Arnheim's "Sweet and Lovely" and Al Dubin and Harry Warren's
"September in the Rain.") Later that year, in New York, Parker was
back on drugs but still at the height of his musical powers. He formed
what is now considered his "golden era" quintet: Parker on alto sax,
the twenty-one-year-old Miles Davis on trumpet, Max Roach on
drums, Duke Jordan on piano, and Tommy Potter on bass. Benedetti recorded the quintet on March 31, 1948, at the Three Deuces,
on Fifty-second Street, Parker's primary base of operations. By this
time, Benedetti was using heroin and had no means of support;
when the management realized that he didn't plan to spend any
money, it provided him with what Schaap would call "the ultimate
New York discourtesy"—it threw him out. In Schaap's terms, it is
a "tragedy" that Benedetti was unable to record the rest of Parker's
nights at the Three Deuces. And it is true that, of all the Benedetti
recordings, these are the most significant. On "Dizzy Atmosphere,"
Parker plays with dangerous abandon, a runaway truck speeding
down the highway into oncoming traffic, never quite crashing;
and even the twenty-six-second passage from the ballad "My Old
Flame" is memorable, a flash of human longing in sound.

Finally, in July 1948, Benedetti recorded the Parker quintet
for six nights at the Onyx, a rival club on Fifty-second Street. The
sound from the Onyx sessions is the worst of all, mainly because
Benedetti was forced by the club's management to place his microphone near Max Roach's drum kit. The effect is often like trying to
hear a lullaby in a thunderstorm.

The recordings are not for casual listeners. Disks and tape
were expensive commodities, and to save money Benedetti usually
turned on the machine only when Parker was soloing. Many recordings are no more than a minute long. One morsel lasts precisely
three seconds. There are no fewer than nineteen versions of "52nd
St. Theme." But to the aficionado this is like complaining that the

Dead Sea Scrolls were torn and discolored. One hears Parker on Coleman Hawkins tunes like "Bean Soup" and quoting H. Klosé's *25 Daily Exercises for Saxophone.*

Cuscuna said that, faced with stacks of cracking forty-year-old tapes and ten-inch acetate disks, he realized that "only Phil Schaap was brilliant enough—and insane enough—to do the job."

Schaap took the materials to the apartment where he was living at the time—a record-and-disk-strewn place in Chelsea—and "just stared" at them for "many, many hours." He felt an enormous sense of responsibility. "This increased the volume of live improvisations of a great artist by a third," he told me one morning after signing off from *Bird Flight.* "Imagine if someone were to find a third more Bach, a third more Shakespeare plays, a third more prime Picasso."

When Schaap first tried to play a tape, it snapped. He tried hand-spinning the tape. It broke again. He realized that the tapes were backed with paper, not plastic. The paper had dried out, making the tape extremely fragile. The solution, Schaap decided, was to secure the most delicate spots with Wite-Out. And so he went through every inch of the Benedetti tapes—all eight miles—and did the job, the tape in his left hand, a tiny Wite-Out brush in his right.

"I guess the only thing I've ever done in jazz that was harder was when we did an eleven-day Louis Armstrong festival on WKCR, in July 1980," he said. Schaap worked for more than two years on the Benedetti project. He and Cuscuna once figured out his remuneration. "I think it was approximately .0003 cents an hour," Schaap said. "But who's complaining?"

Mosaic has so far sold five thousand copies of *The Complete Dean Benedetti Recordings of Charlie Parker.*

"That's triple platinum for us," Cuscuna said.

For Schaap, the fascinations and mysteries of the discography are unending, even though Parker's career lasted less than fifteen years. Parker died on March 12, 1955, at the Stanhope Hotel, while watching jugglers on Tommy Dorsey's television variety show. A doctor who examined the body estimated that Parker was in his mid-fifties. He was thirty-four.

———•———

On Easter Sunday, I met Schaap in the lobby of the Kateri Residence, a nursing home on Riverside Drive. He was there to visit one of the last of "the grandfathers who helped raise him."

We went to the twelfth floor and headed for a small room at the end of the hall. From the doorway, we could see a round old man slumped in a wheelchair, sleeping, a wool scarf over his shoulders and a blanket on his lap. It was Lawrence Lucie. "I met Larry fifty-one years ago," Schaap said. He was six. Lucie played guitar for almost anyone worth playing for: from Jelly Roll Morton to Joe Turner. He played in the big bands of Fletcher Henderson, Benny Goodman, Lucky Millinder, Duke Ellington, and Benny Carter. When Coleman Hawkins recorded "Body and Soul," Lucie was in the band. Lucie not only played with Louis Armstrong; he was the best man at Armstrong's wedding. He is the last person alive to have played with Ellington at the Cotton Club. Lucie's father was a barber in Emporia, Virginia; he was also a musician, and Lawrence joined his father's band as a banjo player when he was eight. Now he is a hundred years old. No one alive is as intimately connected to the origins of jazz music as Lucie. His last gig, which he quit only recently, was playing standards at Arturo's, a coal-oven-pizza joint on Houston Street in the Village.

"Larry, it's me, Phil."

Schaap gently shook the old man's shoulder.

Lucie opened his eyes and, very slowly, looked up at his visitor. As he brought Schaap into focus, he smiled and his eyes brightened.

"Phil! How nice!"

Not many people are still around to visit. A grandnephew is the closest relative that Schaap knows of, and he lives in California.

Schaap and Lucie were clearly thrilled to see each other. Nearly all of Schaap's jazz grandfathers—Jo Jones, Roy Eldridge, Buck Clayton, Doc Cheatham, Max Roach—are gone. Lucie had not lost his elegance. Although he had no reason to expect a visit, he was wearing a tie, a smart silk one with an abstract blue-and-red pattern. On the other side of his bed was a guitar in a battered case and, above it, a poster of the Lucy Luciennaires, a quartet that featured his late wife, the singer Nora Lee King. In the seventies and eighties, Lucie and King used to perform weekly on a Manhattan public-access cable channel.

Lucie, who celebrated his centennial in December, was glad to hear Schaap talk about his days with Fletcher Henderson. And when Schaap asked him if he remembered the name of the song that Benny Carter opened with at the Apollo seventy-four years ago, Lucie said, "I know, Phil, but do you?"

"Sure, it was 'I May Be Wrong (But I Think You're Wonderful).'"

"That's right." Both men laughed.

"And you played the first notes," Schaap said. Indeed, they were the first notes played in the Apollo when, in 1934, the theatre opened under that name and began admitting African American audiences.

Schaap wheeled Lucie to the elevator and up to a solarium on the penthouse floor, where they could look out over the Hudson River and reminisce, a conversation that was more a matter of Schaap recalling highlights of Lucie's career and Lucie saying, over and over, "Phil Schaap knows me better than I know me. Phil Schaap knows his jazz."

Finally, Lucie asked to go down to the fifteenth floor, where a volunteer was playing piano and singing show tunes.

"You coax the blues right out of my heart."

Arrayed in front of the piano were fifty or sixty residents, some of them nearly as old as Lucie and many a great deal less healthy. A nurse passed out Easter cookies. Lawrence Lucie had heard better music in his time, but he was happy to stay and listen. "There's always something going on here," he said dryly. "The action never stops."

Schaap bent over and told his friend that he was off.

"What a delight," Lucie said. "It's always so good to see you."

"I'll be back soon," Schaap said. "You know I will."

May 2008

Phil Schaap died on September 7, 2021.

WE ARE ALIVE

Nearly half a century ago, when Elvis Presley was filming *Harum Scarum* and "Help!" was on the charts, a moody, father-haunted, yet uncannily charismatic Shore rat named Bruce Springsteen was building a small reputation around central Jersey as a guitar player in a band called the Castiles. The band was named for the lead singer's favorite brand of soap. Its members were from Freehold, an industrial town half an hour inland from the boardwalk carnies and the sea. The Castiles performed at sweet sixteens and Elks-club dances, at drive-in movie theatres and ShopRite ribbon cuttings, at a mobile-home park in Farmingdale, at the Matawan-Keyport Rollerdrome. Once, they played for the patients at a psychiatric hospital, in Marlboro. A gentleman dressed in a suit came to the stage and, in an introductory speech that ran some twenty minutes, declared the Castiles "greater than the Beatles." At which point a doctor intervened and escorted him back to his room.

One spring afternoon in 1966, the Castiles, with dreams of making it big and making it quick, drove to a studio at the Brick Mall Shopping Center and recorded two original songs, "Baby I" and "That's What You Get." Mainly, though, they played an array of covers, from Glenn Miller's "In the Mood" to the G-Clefs' "I Understand." They did Sonny and Cher, Sam and Dave, Don & Juan, the Who, the Kinks, the Stones, the Animals.

Many musicians in their grizzled late maturity have an uncertain grasp on their earliest days on the bandstand. (Not a few have an uncertain grasp on last week.) But Springsteen, who is sixty-two and among the most durable musicians since B.B. King and Om Kalthoum, seems to remember every gaudy night, from the moment, in 1957, when he and his mother watched Elvis on *The Ed Sullivan Show*—"I looked at her and I said, 'I wanna be *just . . . like . . . that*'"—to his most recent exploits as a multimillionaire populist rock star crowd-surfing the adoring masses. These days, he is the subject of historical exhibitions; at the Rock and Roll Hall of Fame Museum, in Cleveland, and at the National Constitution Center, in Philadelphia, his lyric sheets, old cars, and faded performing duds have been displayed like snippets of the Shroud. But, unlike the Rolling Stones, say, who have not written a great song since the disco era and come together only to pad their fortunes as their own cover band, Springsteen refuses to be a mercenary curator of his past. He continues to evolve as an artist, filling one spiral notebook after another with ideas, quotations, questions, clippings, and, ultimately, new songs. His latest album, *Wrecking Ball*, is a melodic indictment of the recessionary moment, of income disparity and what he calls "the distance between the American reality and the American dream." The work is remote from his early operettas of humid summer interludes and abandon out on the Turnpike. In his desire to extend a countertradition of political progressivism, Springsteen quotes from Irish rebel songs, Dust Bowl ballads, Civil War tunes, and chain-gang chants.

Early this year, Springsteen was leading rehearsals for a world tour at Fort Monmouth, an Army base that was shut down last year; it had been an outpost since the First World War of military communications and intelligence, and once employed Julius Rosenberg and thousands of militarized carrier pigeons. The twelve-hundred-acre property is now a ghost town inhabited only by steel dummies meant to scare off the ubiquitous Canada geese that squirt a carpet of green across middle Jersey. Driving to the far end of the base, I reached an unlovely theatre that Springsteen and Jon Landau, his longtime manager, had rented for the rehearsals. Springsteen had performed for officers' children at the Fort Monmouth "teen club" (dancing, no liquor) with the Castiles, forty-seven years earlier.

The atmosphere inside was purposeful but easygoing. Musicians stood onstage noodling on their instruments with the languid air of outfielders warming up in the sun. Max Weinberg, the band's volcanic drummer, wore the sort of generous jeans favored by dads at weekend barbecues. Steve Van Zandt, Springsteen's childhood friend and guitarist-wingman, keeps up a brutal schedule as an actor and a DJ, and he seemed weary, his eyes drooping under a piratical purple headscarf. The bass player Garry Tallent, the organist Charlie Giordano, and the pianist Roy Bittan horsed around on a roller-rink tune while they waited. The guitarist Nils Lofgren was on the phone, trying to figure out flights to get back to his home, in Scottsdale, for the weekend.

Springsteen arrived and greeted everyone with a quick hello and his distinctive cackle. He is five-nine and walks with a rolling rodeo gait. When he takes in something new—a visitor, a thought, a passing car in the distance—his eyes narrow, as if in hard light, and his lower jaw protrudes a bit. His hairline is receding, and, if one had to guess, he has, over the years, in the face of high-def scrutiny and the fight against time, enjoined the expensive attentions of cosmetic and dental practitioners. He remains dispiritingly handsome, preposterously fit. ("He has practically the same waist size as when I met him, when we were fifteen," says Steve Van Zandt, who does not.) Some of this has to do with his abstemious inclinations; Van

Zandt says Springsteen is "the only guy I know—I think the only guy I know at *all*—who never did drugs." He's followed the same exercise regimen for thirty years: he runs on a treadmill and, with a trainer, works out with weights. It has paid off. His muscle tone approximates a fresh tennis ball. And yet, with the tour a month away, he laughed at the idea that he was ready. "I'm not remotely close," he said, slumping into a chair twenty rows back from the stage.

Preparing for a tour is a process far more involved than middle-aged workouts designed to stave off premature infarction. "Think of it this way: performing is like sprinting while screaming for three, four minutes," Springsteen said. "And then you do it again. And then you do it again. And then you walk a little, shouting the whole time. And so on. Your adrenaline quickly overwhelms your conditioning." His style in performance is joyously demonic, as close as a white man of Social Security age can get to James Brown circa 1962 without risking a herniated disk or a shattered pelvis. Concerts last in excess of three hours, without a break, and he is constantly dancing, screaming, imploring, mugging, kicking, windmilling, crowd-surfing, climbing a drum riser, jumping on an amp, leaping off Roy Bittan's piano. The display of energy and its depletion is part of what is expected of him. In return, the crowd participates in a display of communal adoration. Like pilgrims at a gigantic outdoor Mass—think John Paul II at Gdansk—they know their role: when to raise their hands, when to sway, when to sing, when to scream his name, when to bear his body, hand over hand, from the rear of the orchestra to the stage. (Van Zandt: "Messianic? Is that the word you're looking for?")

Springsteen came to glory in the age of Letterman, but he is anti-ironical. Keith Richards works at seeming not to give a shit. He makes you wonder if it is harder to play the riffs for "Street Fighting Man" or to dangle a cigarette from his lips by a single thread of spit. Springsteen is the opposite. He is all about flagrant exertion. There always comes a moment in a Springsteen concert, as there always did with James Brown, when he plays out a dumb show of the conflict between exhaustion and the urge to go on. Brown enacted it by dropping to his knees, awash in sweat, unable to dance another step, yet shooing away his cape bearer, the aide who would enrobe him and hustle him offstage. Springsteen slumps against the mike stand, spent and still, then, regaining consciousness, shakes off the sweat—*No! It can't be!*—and calls on the band for another verse, another song. He leaves the stage soaked, as if he had swum around the arena in his clothes while being chased by barracudas. "I want an *extreme* experience," he says. He wants his audience to leave the arena, as he commands them, "with your hands hurting, your feet hurting, your back hurting, your voice sore, and your sexual organs *stimulated*!"

So the display of exuberance is critical. "For an adult, the world is constantly trying to clamp down on itself," he says. "Routine, responsibility, decay of institutions, corruption: this is all the world closing in. Music, when it's really great, pries that shit back open and lets people back in, it lets light in, and air in, and energy in, and sends people home with that and sends me back to the hotel with it. People carry that with them sometimes for a very long period of time."

The band rehearses not so much to learn how to play particular songs as to see what songs work with other songs, to figure out a basic set list (with countless alternatives) that will fill all of Springsteen's demands: to air the new work and his latest themes; to play the expected hits for the casual fans; to work up enough surprises and rarities for fans who have seen him hundreds of times; and, especially, to pace the show from frenzy to calm and back again. In the past several years, Springsteen has been taking requests from the crowd. He has never been stumped. "You can take the band out of the bar, but you can't take the bar out of the band," Van Zandt says.

The E Street Band members are not Springsteen's equals. "This is not the Beatles," as Weinberg puts it. They are salaried musicians; in 1989, they were fired en masse. They await his call to record, to tour, to rehearse. And so when Springsteen sprang out of his chair and said, "Okay, time to work," they straightened up and watched for his cue.

Huh . . . two . . . three . . . four.

As the anthemic opener, "We Take Care of Our Own," washed over the empty seats, I stood at the back of the hall next to the sound engineer, John Cooper, a rangy, unflappable Hoosier, who was monitoring a vast soundboard and a series of laptops. One hard drive contains the lyrics and keys for hundreds of songs, so that when Springsteen calls for something off the cuff the song quickly appears on teleprompters within sight of him and his bandmates. (The crutch is hardly unique—Sinatra, in late career, used a tele-prompter, and so do the Stones and many other bands.) Although more than half the show will be the same from night to night, the rest is up for grabs.

"This is about the only live music left, with a few exceptions," Cooper said. Lip-synchers are legion. Coldplay thickens its sound with heaps of pre-taped instruments and synthesizers. The one arti-ficial sound in Springsteen's act is a snare drum sound in "We Take Care of Our Own" that seemed to elude easy reproduction.

That afternoon at Fort Monmouth, Springsteen was intent on nailing "the opening four," the first songs, which come rapid fire. The band and the crew gave particular attention to those lingering seconds between songs when the keys modulate and the guitar techs pass different instruments to the musicians. It is intricate work; the technicians have to move with the precision of a Daytona pit crew.

Before the tour officially began, in Atlanta, there were a few smaller venues to play, including the Apollo Theatre, in Harlem.

At Springsteen's shows there are usually more African Americans onstage than in the seats, but he is steeped in Black music and he was especially eager to play the date in Harlem. "All of our teachers stood on those boards at the Apollo," he said. "The essence of the way this band moves is one of soul. It's *supposed* to be overwhelming. You shouldn't be able to catch your breath. That's what being a front man is all about—the idea of having something supple underneath you, that machine that roars and can turn on a dime."

———•———

Rock tours generally have a theme: a band's coltish arrival, a new style or look, a reunion, a new set of songs, a political moment. Springsteen was salting the show with the political material from *Wrecking Ball*, but the most vivid theme on this tour was to be time passing, age, death, and, if Springsteen could manage it, a sense of renewal. The surviving core of the band—Van Zandt, Tallent, Weinberg, Bittan, and Springsteen—had been playing together since the Ford administration; Lofgren and Patti Scialfa, Springsteen's wife, who is a singer and guitar player, joined in the eighties.

The run of tragedy, debility, and erosion has seemed relentless in recent years. Nils Lofgren has had both hips replaced, and both his shoulders are a wreck. Max Weinberg has endured open-heart surgery, prostate cancer treatment, two failed back operations, and seven hand operations. The morning after a concert, he told me, he feels like the Nick Nolte character in the football movie *North Dallas Forty*: bruised and barely able to move. Lofgren has compared the backstage area to "a MASH unit," with ice packs, heating pads, Bengay tubes, and masseuses on call. More alarmingly, Jon Landau, Springsteen's manager and closest friend, was recovering from brain surgery.

There have been deeper, permanent losses. In 2008, Danny Federici, who played organ and accordion with Springsteen for forty years, died of melanoma. Springsteen's body man on tour, a Special Forces veteran named Terry Magovern, died the year before. Springsteen's trainer died at the age of forty.

The most shocking loss came last year, when Clarence Clemons, Springsteen's saxophone player and onstage foil and protector, died of a stroke. Clemons was a colossus—six-four, a former football player. As a musician, he possessed a raspy tone reminiscent of King Curtis. He was not a great improviser, but his solos, painstakingly scripted over long hours in the studio with Springsteen, were set pieces in every show. Then, there was his sheer stage presence. Clemons gave Springsteen a mythic companion who embodied the fraternal spirit of the band. "Standing next to Clarence was like standing next to the baddest ass on the planet," Springsteen said of him in tribute. "You felt like no matter what the day or the night brought, nothing was going to touch you."

Clemons's lifestyle was considerably less disciplined than Springsteen's, and, in recent years, his body had been breaking down, requiring hip replacements, knee replacements, back surgery. On the last tour, Clemons was driven around the arena tunnels in a golf cart. Onstage, he was spending less time exerting himself on the horn and more time resting on a stool and banging on a tambourine. When he did play, it was clear that he was losing the high notes. After one of his last concerts, he told a friend, "I deserve a God-damned Academy Award." He said that he felt like Mickey Rourke's character in *The Wrestler*; he was portraying a powerful figure onstage even as he was falling apart physically.

At the funeral, held in a chapel in Palm Beach, Springsteen paid passionate homage to Clemons, recalling that he had put up with a "world where it still wasn't so easy to be big and Black." He recalled his friend's "raunchy mysticism," his appetites, even his dressing room, which was draped in exotic scarves and dubbed "the Temple of Soul": "A visit there was like a trip to a sovereign nation

that had just struck huge oil reserves." At the same time, Springsteen gestured toward Clemons's erratic family life (he was married
five times) and the occasional tensions in their relationship. Speaking to Clemons's sons, he said, "C lived a life where he did what he
wanted to do, and he let the chips, human and otherwise, fall where
they may. Like a lot of us, your pop was capable of great magic and
also of making quite an amazing mess."

Months later, Springsteen was still feeling the loss. He was
twenty-two when he met Clemons, on the Asbury Park music circuit. Losing Clemons was like losing "the sea and the stars," and it
was clear that Springsteen was anxious about performing without
him. "How do we continue? I think we discussed this more than
anything in our history," Van Zandt told me. "The basic concept
was, we need to reinvent ourselves here a little bit. You can't just
replace a guy." Clemons was replaced not by a musician but by a
contingent—a five-man horn section.

Rehearsals were partly a matter of figuring out how to acknowledge the losses without turning the concert into a lugubrious memorial service. "The band is a little community up there," Springsteen
said, "and it gathers together, and we try to heal the parts that God
broke and honor the parts that are no longer with us."

During the breaks, I noticed that one of the horn players, a
young tenor player wearing a considerable Afro, oblong eyewear,
and an intent expression, was wandering around, nervously playing snatches of familiar solos on his horn: "Tenth Avenue Freeze
Out," "Jungleland," "Badlands," "Thunder Road." This was Jake
Clemons, Clarence's thirty-two-year-old nephew. For years, Jake
had been touring halls and clubs with his own band. Now he had
the assignment of filling his uncle's shoes in front of audiences of
fifty thousand. He would do so literally. Jake wore his uncle's size 16
shoes—snakeskin boots, slick loafers, whatever was left to him.
Nearly all of his horns, too, had been gifts from Uncle Clarence.

In January, Springsteen invited Jake to his house, and they played long into the night. Bruce introduced the idea of his joining the band. "But you have to understand," Springsteen told him. "When you blow that sax onstage with us, people won't compare you to Clarence on the last tour. They'll compare you to their *memory* of Clarence, to their *idea* of Clarence." That gave Jake Clemons pause. Raised on gospel in a family led by a Marine band officer, he knew Springsteen's catalog only casually. The audience would know the songs, not to mention the history of the band, much more intimately than he did. After Clarence died, Jake did a few tribute shows, and he could sense the audience making comparisons.

"I don't know if anyone can perform in the shadow of a legend," Jake said. "To me, Clarence is still on that stage, and I don't want to step on his toes."

Springsteen believed that these worries, and the larger sense of loss and injury, might provide an energy that the tour could draw on. After all these years onstage, he can stand back from his performances with an analytic remove. "You're the shaman, a little bit, you're leading the congregation," he told me. "But you are the same as everybody else in the sense that your troubles are the same, your problems are the same, you've got your blessings, you've got your sins, you've got the things you can do well, you've got the things you fuck up all the time. And so you're a conduit. There was a series of elements in your life—some that were blessings, and some that were just chaotic curses—that set fire to you in a certain way."

———·———

When Springsteen was touring behind the *Born to Run* album, in the mid-seventies, he would stand at the lip of the stage in a spotlight, vamping on a chord, and tell the story of growing up in a dingy two-family house next to a gas station in a working-class section of Freehold known as Texas, because it was first populated by hillbilly migrants from the South. I was in the balcony at a show, in November 1976, at the Palladium, on Fourteenth Street, when Springsteen laid things out in the starkest terms:

> My mom, she was a secretary, and she worked downtown . . . And my father, he worked a lot of different places. He worked in a rug mill for a while, he drove a cab for a while, and he was a guard down at the jail for a while. I can remember when he worked down there, he used to always come home real pissed off, drunk, sit in the kitchen. At night, nine o'clock, he used to shut off all the lights, every light in the house, and he used to get real pissed off if me or my sister turned any of them on. And he'd sit in the kitchen with a six-pack, a cigarette . . .
>
> He'd make me sit down at that table in the dark. In the wintertime, he used to turn on the gas stove and close all the doors, so it got real hot in there. And I remember just sitting in the dark . . . No matter how long I sat there, I could never ever see his face. We'd start talking about nothing much, how I was doing. Pretty soon, he asked me what I thought I was doing with myself. And we'd always end up screaming at each other. My mother, she'd always end up running in from the front room crying, and trying to pull him off me, try to keep us from fighting with each other . . . I'd always end up running out the back door and pulling away from him. Pulling away from him, running down the driveway screaming at him, telling him, telling him, telling him, how it was my life and I was going to do what I wanted to do.

At the end of the story, an entirely accurate one, Springsteen would segue into "It's My Life," by the Animals, a spine-jangling declaration of independence. In Springsteen's voice, it was a declaration of independence from a household in which threats were shouted, telephones were ripped off the wall, and the police were summoned.

Doug Springsteen was an Army driver in Europe during the Second World War who came home and seethed at his crabbed circumstances. Van Zandt told me that Springsteen's father was "scary" and best avoided. In those days, "*all* fathers were scary," Van Zandt said. "The torture we put these poor guys through, when you think of it now. My father, Bruce's father—these poor guys, they never had a chance. There was no precedent for us, none, in history, for their sons to become these long-haired freaks who didn't want to participate in the world they built for them. Can you imagine? It was the World War Two generation. They built the suburbs. What gratitude did we have? We're, like, 'Fuck you! We're gonna look like girls, and we're gonna do drugs, and we're gonna play crazy rock and roll!' And they're, like, 'What the fuck did we do wrong?' They were scared of what we were becoming, so they felt they had to be more authoritarian. They *hated* us, you know?"

Doug Springsteen grew up shadowed by the death of his five-year-old sister, Virginia, who was hit by a truck while riding a tricycle, in Freehold in 1927. His parents, according to a biography of Springsteen by Peter Ames Carlin, were ravaged by grief. Doug dropped out of school after ninth grade. In 1948, he married Adele Zerilli. Bruce was born the next year. For long stretches of Bruce's childhood, his grandparents lived with his family, and, as Springsteen told Carlin, he always sensed that much of the affection he received from them was a way "to replace the lost child," which was confusing: "The dead daughter was a big presence. Her portrait was on the wall, always front and center." Decades after the event, the whole family—the grandparents, Doug and Adele, Bruce and his sister Ginny—went to the cemetery every weekend to visit Virginia's grave.

In biographies and clippings, Doug Springsteen is described

with adjectives like "taciturn" and "disappointed." In fact, he seems to have been bipolar, and he was capable of terrible rages, often aimed at his son. Doctors prescribed drugs for his illness, but Doug didn't always take them. The mediator in the house, the source of optimism and survival, and the steadiest earner, was Bruce's mother, Adele, who worked as a legal secretary. Still, Bruce was deeply affected by his father's paralyzing depressions, and worried that he would not escape the thread of mental instability that ran through his family. That fear, he says, is why he never did drugs. Doug Springsteen lives in his son's songs. In "Independence Day," the son must escape his father's house because "we were just too much of the same kind." In the ferocious "Adam Raised a Cain," the father "walks these empty rooms / looking for something to blame / You inherit the sins / You inherit the flames." The songs were a way of talking to the silent father. "My dad was very nonverbal—you couldn't really have a conversation with him," Springsteen told me. "I had to make my peace with that, but I had to have a conversation with him, because I needed to have one. It ain't the best way to go about it, but that was the only way I could, so I did, and eventually he did respond. He might not have liked the songs, but I think he liked that they existed. It meant that he mattered. He'd get asked, 'What are your favorite songs?' And he'd say, 'The ones that are about me.'"

The past, though, is anything but past. "My parents' struggles, it's the *subject* of my life," Springsteen told me at rehearsal. "It's the thing that eats at me and always will. My life took a very different course, but my life is an anomaly. Those wounds stay with you, and you turn them into a language and a purpose." Gesturing toward the band onstage, he said, "We're repairmen—repairmen with a toolbox. If I repair a little of myself, I'll repair a little of you. That's the job." The songs of escape on *Born to Run*, the portrait of post-industrial struggle on *Darkness on the Edge of Town*, were part of that job of early repair.

Doug and Adele Springsteen left Freehold for northern California when Bruce was nineteen, and they were puzzled when, several years later, their son, a long-haired misfit in their eyes, came visiting, as he puts it, "lugging a treasure chest behind" and telling them to buy the biggest house around. "The one satisfaction you get is that you do get your 'See, I told you so' moment," Springsteen said. "Of course, all the deeper things go unsaid, that it all could have been a little different."

Doug Springsteen died in 1998, at seventy-three, after years of illness, including a stroke and heart disease. "I was lucky that modern medicine gave him another ten years of life," Springsteen said. "T Bone Burnett said that rock and roll is all about 'Daaaaddy!' It's one embarrassing scream of 'Daaaaddy!' It's just fathers and sons, and you're out there proving something to somebody in the most intense way possible. It's, like, 'Hey, I was worth a little more attention than I got! You blew that one, big guy!'"

———•———

The redemptive moments in Springsteen's youth were musical: the songs coming out of the transistor radio and the television set; his mother taking out a bank loan for sixty dollars to buy him a Kent guitar when he was fifteen. Springsteen became one of those kids who escape into an obsession. He believed, as he sings in "No Surrender," "We learned more from a three-minute record, baby, than we ever learned in school." At St. Rose of Lima, the Catholic school in Freehold, he was a screwup, disdained by the nuns. The hip, literary kids were far away. ("I didn't hang around with no crowd that was talking about William Burroughs," he told Dave Marsh, an early biographer.) After graduating from high school, Springsteen attended classes at Ocean County Community College, where he started reading novels and writing poems, but he quit after a nervous administrator, on the lookout for hippies and other undesirables, made it plain to Springsteen that there had been "complaints" that he was strange. "Remember, we didn't go into this life because we were courageous or brilliant," Van Zandt said. "We were the last guys standing. Anyone with a choice to do something else—be a dentist, get a real job, *whatever*—took it!"

The place where Springsteen went looking for his future was just a short drive east of Freehold—the Asbury Park music scene. In the sixties and seventies, there were dozens of bands that played in the bars along the boardwalk.

On a spring afternoon, I stood out in front of the best-known club in Asbury Park, the Stone Pony, and waited for an aging drummer named Vini (Mad Dog) Lopez, the unluckiest man in the E Street saga. Lopez was thrown out of the Springsteen band just before they hit it big. Springsteen's bandmates may be employees, but they have been handsomely paid and are worth many millions of dollars each. The drummer who made it for the long haul, Max Weinberg, owns houses in the New Jersey countryside and Tuscany. Lopez works as a caddy. On weekends, he plays in a band called License to Chill. The band's mascot is Tippy the Banana. "We're at the bottom of the food chain," Lopez told me. "We like to say that we're exclusive but inexpensive."

Lopez pulled up to the Pony in a beat-up Saturn. He climbed out of the car creakily, as if out of a space capsule after an interplanetary voyage. He squinted in the ocean light and limped toward me. He'd been in a car wreck on the way home from a memorial concert for Clarence Clemons. His knee was shot, and so was his back. Also, someone had dropped an amplifier on his foot at a gig a couple of nights before. "That didn't help," he said.

We walked along the boardwalk for a while and settled on a place to eat. On the way, and throughout lunch, people stopped him to say hello, to get an autograph.

In 1969, Lopez invited Springsteen to jam at an after-hours loft, called the Upstage, above a Thom McAn shoe store in Asbury

Park. Eventually, Springsteen and Lopez formed a band called Child, which they soon renamed Steel Mill. It featured Lopez on drums, Danny Federici on organ and accordion, and Steve Van Zandt on bass. The boys lived for a while in a surfboard factory run by their manager. "Bruce lived in the front office, and Danny and I had daybeds in the bathrooms," Lopez said. They made around fifty dollars a week. Some of the band members held manual jobs to make ends meet: Van Zandt worked construction, Lopez put in time at a boatyard and on commercial fishing boats. Springsteen declined. The future working-class clarion never really worked.

Lopez took a long sip of his Bloody Mary and stared out at the ocean, where a surfer bobbed on a wave and fell. Springsteen still throws some extra royalties his way from the first two albums—"He does it out of the goodness of his heart," Lopez said—but it's not a living.

The Springsteen Lopez describes was a young man of uncommon ambition who was also prone to bouts of withdrawal. For all the girls around, for all the late-night Monopoly games and pinball marathons, Springsteen wasn't easily distracted. "Bruce would come to a party where people were doing all kinds of things, and he would just go off with his guitar," Lopez said.

For Van Zandt, that intensity was a lure. He recognized in Springsteen a drive to create original work. In those days, he said, you were judged by how well you could copy songs off the radio and play them, chord for chord, note for note: "Bruce was never good at it. He had a weird ear. He would hear different chords, but he could never hear the *right* chords. When you have that ability or inability, you immediately become more original. Well, in the long run, guess what: in the long run, original wins."

Asbury Park, for all its brassy bar bands and boardwalk barkers, was not immune to the times. On the July 4th weekend in 1970, race riots broke out. Young Black men and women in town were especially angry that most of the summer jobs in the restaurants and stores along the boardwalk were going to white kids. Springsteen and his bandmates watched the flames on Springwood Avenue from a water tower near their surfboard factory home. Nevertheless, Bruce's crowd remained almost completely apolitical. "The riots just meant that certain clubs didn't open and certain ones did," Van Zandt said.

As Steel Mill dissolved, Springsteen dreamed up a temporary lark: Dr. Zoom and the Sonic Boom, a kind of Noah's ark carnival act, with two of everything—guitarists, drummers, singers— plus Garry Tallent on tuba, a baton twirler, and two guys from the Upstage who played Monopoly onstage. Then Springsteen got serious. He formed his own band. He called it the Bruce Springsteen Band.

———·———

A week after closing down rehearsals at Fort Monmouth, Springsteen and the band start rehearsing at the Sun National Bank Center, the home of the Trenton Titans, a minor-league hockey team. The theatre at Fort Monmouth was secluded and cheap, but not nearly large enough for the crew to set up the full traveling stage, with all the proper lights, risers, ramps, and sound system.

Inside the arena, Springsteen is walking around the empty seats, a microphone in his hand, giving stage directions. "We can't see the singers from this angle," he says. "One step to the right, Cindy!" The crew moves the riser. Cindy Mizelle, the most soulful voice in the new, seventeen-piece version of the E Street Band, takes one step to the right.

Springsteen lopes to another corner, and, as he sets his gaze on the horn section, a thought occurs to him. "Do we have some chairs for those guys when they aren't playing?" he says. His voice ricochets around the empty seats. Chairs appear.

The band gets in position and starts to rip through the basic set list in preparation for the Apollo show. Lofgren plays the slippery opening riff of "We Take Care of Our Own"—a recession anthem in the key of G—and the band is off. Springsteen rehearses deliberately, working out all the spontaneous-seeming moves and postures: the solemn lowered head and raised fist, the hoisted talismanic Fender, the between-songs patter, the look of exultation in a single spotlight that he will enact in front of an audience. ("It's theatre, you know," he tells me later. "I'm a theatrical performer. I'm whispering in your ear, and you're dreaming my dreams, and then I'm getting a feeling for yours. I've been doing that for forty years.") Springsteen has to do so much—lead the band, pace the show, sing, play guitar, command the audience, project to every corner of the hall, including the seats behind the stage—that to wing it completely is asking for disaster.

In the midst of the fifth song in the set, he introduces the band. As they run through a vamp of "People Get Ready," the old Curtis Mayfield tune, Springsteen grabs a mike and strolls across the stage. "Good evening, ladies and gentlemen," he says to the empty arena. "I'm so glad to be here in your beautiful city tonight. The E Street Band has come back to bring the power, hour after hour, to put a whoop-ass session on the recession. We got some old friends, and we got some new friends, and we've got a story to tell you . . ."

The tune, thick with horns and vocal harmonies, elides into "My City of Ruins," one of the elegiac, gospel-tinged songs on the 9/11 album, *The Rising*. The voices sing "Rise up! Rise up!" and there comes a string of horn solos: trombone, trumpet, sax. Then back to the voices. Springsteen quickly introduces the E Street horns and the singing collective. Then he says, "Roll call!" And, with the music rising bit by churchly bit, he introduces the core of the band: "Professor Roy Bittan is in the house . . . Charlie Giordano is in the house . . ."

When he finishes the roll call, there is a long ellipsis. The band keeps vamping.

"Are we *missing* anybody?"

Two spotlights are now trained on the organ, where Federici once sat, and at the mike where Clemons once stood.

"Are we *missing* anybody?"

Then again: "Are we missing anybody? . . . That's right. That's right. We're missing some. But the only thing I can guarantee tonight is that if you're here and we're here, then they're here!" He repeats this over and over, the volume of the piano and the bass rising, the drums hastening, the voices rising, until finally the song overwhelms him, and, if Springsteen has calculated correctly, there will not be an unmoved soul in the house.

For the next hour and a half, the band plays through a set that alternates tales of economic pain with party time escape. While the band plays the jolly opening riff of "Waiting on a Sunny Day," Springsteen practices striding around the stage, beckoning the imaginary hordes everywhere in the arena to sing along.

A bunch of songs later, after a run-through of the set-ending "Thunder Road," Springsteen hops off the stage, drapes a towel around his neck, and sits down in the folding chair next to me.

"The top of the show, see, is a kind of welcoming, and you are getting everyone comfortable and challenging them at the same time," he says. "You're setting out your themes. You're getting them comfortable, because, remember, people haven't seen this band. There are absences that are hanging there. That's what we're about right now, the communication between the living and the gone. Those currents even run through the dream world of pop music!"

It's a sweet day for Springsteen. *Wrecking Ball* is the No. 1 album in the U.S. and in the United Kingdom, passing Adele's blockbuster *21*. "This is great news, but we'll see where we are in a few weeks," Landau says. Springsteen will never again have huge sellers like *Born in the U.S.A.*, but he will always get an initial burst of sales from his fan base. How sales sustain over time is the question. (The answer is that they don't: after a month, *Wrecking Ball* dropped to No. 19. By summer, it had fallen off the charts.) What makes Springsteen an economic power at this point is mainly his back catalog and his status as a live performer.

Onstage, an impromptu party is forming. The crew passes out flutes of champagne and plates of cake to celebrate the news about *Wrecking Ball*.

"That never gets old," Springsteen says, before heading off to join the party. "I'm still excited hearing the music on the radio! I remember the first time I ever saw someone hearing me on the radio. We were in Connecticut playing at some college. A guy was in his car, a warm summer night, and his window was rolled down, and 'Spirit in the Night' "—a song from Springsteen's debut album—"was coming out of the car. Wow. I remember thinking, *That's it, I've realized at least a part of my rock-and-roll dreams.* It still feels the same to me. To hear it come out of the radio—it's an all-points bulletin. The song's going out . . . *there!*"

———•———

By 1972, Springsteen was fronting a band and writing songs to be performed solo. He wasn't a big reader at the time, but he was so consumed by Bob Dylan's songs that he read Anthony Scaduto's biography. He was impressed by Dylan's coming to New York saga: the snowstorm arrival, in 1961, from the Midwest; the pilgrimages to Woody Guthrie's bedside at Greystone Park Psychiatric Hospital; the first appearances at Café Wha? and Gerde's Folk City; and then the audition for John Hammond, the legendary Columbia Records executive. This was what he wanted, some version of it.

Springsteen's manager at the time was a rambunctious hustler named Mike Appel. Before joining Springsteen, Appel wrote jingles for Kleenex and a song for the Partridge Family. Appel was old school—passionate but exploitative. He signed Springsteen to lopsided contracts. And yet he was so ballsy and unhinged in his devotion to his client that he would do wild things on his behalf, like calling a producer at NBC to suggest that the network have Springsteen perform his antiwar song "Balboa vs. the Earth Slayer" at the Super Bowl. (NBC declined.) Somehow, Appel did manage to get an appointment with John Hammond.

On May 2, 1972, Springsteen traveled to the city by bus, carrying a borrowed acoustic guitar with no case. The meeting didn't begin well. Hammond, a patrician of Vanderbilt stock, made it clear that he was pressed for time, and he was repelled when Appel put on the hard sell about the singer's lyrical gifts. But the vibe changed when Springsteen, sitting on a stool across from the desk, sang a string of songs ending with "If I Was a Priest":

> Well, now, if Jesus was the sheriff
> And I was the priest,
> If my lady was an heiress
> and my mama was a thief . . .

"Bruce, that's the damnedest song I've ever heard," Hammond said, delighted. "Were you brought up by nuns?"

Columbia signed Springsteen to a record contract and tried to promote him as "the new Dylan." He was not the only one. John Prine, Elliot Murphy, Loudon Wainwright III, and other singer-songwriter sensitivos were also getting the "new Dylan" label. ("The *old* Dylan was only thirty, so I don't even know why they needed a fucking *new* Dylan," Springsteen says.) To Hammond's disappointment, Springsteen recorded his first two albums—*Greetings from Asbury Park* and *The Wild, the Innocent, and the E Street Shuffle*—with a band made up of his Jersey Shore mates, including Vini Lopez, on drums, and Clarence Clemons, on tenor sax. Hammond was convinced that the solo demos were better. Despite boosts from a few critics and DJs, the albums hardly sold at all. Springsteen was, at best, a gifted obscurity, a provincial who was running out of chances.

———•———

In June 1973, when I was fourteen, I got on a Red & Tan 11-C bus in north Jersey with a couple of friends and went to the city to see a resolutely unhip and unaccountably popular band called Chicago, at Madison Square Garden. I am not quite sure why I went. We were Dylan fanatics. *Howl*, the Stanley Brothers, Otis Redding, *Naked Lunch*, Hank Williams, Odetta—practically anything I knew or read or heard seemed to come through the auspices of Dylan. Chicago was about as far from the Dylan aesthetic as you could get.

All the same, I'd paid my four dollars, and I was going to see whatever I could glimpse from our seats. Out trundled the opening act: someone named Bruce Springsteen. The conditions were abysmal, as they often are for opening acts: the houselights were up, the crowd was alternately inattentive and hostile. What I remember was a bandleader as frenetic as Mick Jagger or James Brown, a singer bursting with almost self-destructive urgency, trying to bust through the buzzy indifference of the crowd. After that show, Springsteen swore to Appel that he would never open or play big venues again. "I couldn't stand it—everybody was so far away and the band couldn't hear," he told Dave Marsh. It was time to woodshed, time to build an audience through constant, intense performance in clubs, bars, and university gyms.

These were lean times. After Appel had paid expenses and taken his considerable cut, the pay was next to nothing. Sometimes the band slept in the van. Clemons nearly got arrested before a gig for failing to pay child support. Lopez was especially vocal about playing for seeds: "What if I want to take my girlfriend out for a burger?"

In the late afternoon, after lunch, Lopez and I were driving around Asbury Park and he started laughing and pointing. "That's where we went to get food stamps—all of us, Bruce, too," he said.

Lopez was a lot of drummer, too much drummer, perhaps—a chaotic Ginger Baker type. He was also fiery in his style of labor unrest. In early 1974, he roughed up Mike Appel's brother in a dispute over money ("I did *push* him a little"). Soon afterward, Springsteen told Lopez that he was fired.

"I used to keep his guitars at my house, and he had to come get them," Lopez said. "I asked for a second chance, and he said, 'Vini, there are no second chances.' *Christ.* Danny got all kinds of second chances after being a bad boy—for drugs, for not showing up or for being late. But for me no second chances." The argument grew more heated, and Springsteen finally suggested that Lopez was an inadequate drummer.

"I put his guitars down in front of him, and I said, 'There's the door. You know what it's used for.' To this day we haven't talked about it. There's nothing to talk about. I'd have been in the biggest band in the land if that hadn't happened. But, historically, at least, I was in the E Street Band. Bruce knows that, and everyone knows that."

We drove past the low-slung building that used to house the surfboard factory where Lopez lived with Springsteen. The sign on the door now reads, "Immunostics Inc: Quality microbiological, serological and immunological reagents." Around ten times over the years, Springsteen has had Lopez sit in with the band, including at Giants Stadium for a rendition of "Spirit in the Night." When Lopez asked if he could start a band that played all the old Steel Mill songs, Springsteen smiled and said sure, go ahead.

"But it's hard to sell Steel Mill now," Lopez said. "People know that Bruce wrote all the stuff and so they expect Bruce to show up, and that just ain't gonna happen."

———•———

If Vini Lopez is the unluckiest drummer in American history, Jon Landau is surely the most fortunate of rock critics. During a break in the rehearsals for the 2012 tour, I drove up to northern Westchester, where Landau lives with his wife, Barbara. Landau is just three years older than Springsteen, but he is a man of more ordinary physical presence. Landau has been getting a healthy cut of the Springsteen business for more than thirty years. The profits did not go up his nose; they went on the walls. His art collection (mainly Renaissance painting and sculpture, with some nineteenth-century French painting thrown into the mix) is what is called "important." At the risk of alarming his insurance company, I can report the presence of works by, among others, Titian, Tintoretto, Tiepolo, Donatello, Ghiberti, Géricault, Delacroix, Corot, and Courbet.

But Landau has not escaped time unscathed. Last year, he had a growth surgically removed from his brain, and, because the growth was lodged near a tangle of optic nerves, he lost the vision in one eye. The recovery was not easy, and, at times, as we toured the paintings, Landau seemed winded. After the surgery, Springsteen was with Landau nearly every day. "He knew I was going through something, and I thought I was going to die," Landau said. "It wasn't rational, but the fear was there . . . We shared a lot of deep talk." Then he smiled. "The deep thinkers did some deep thinking."

Landau began his life in a profession that didn't really exist. Even by 1966, three years after the rise of the Beatles, there really was no such thing as rock criticism. That year, Landau, a precocious teenager from Lexington, Massachusetts, was working in a Cambridge music store called Briggs & Briggs. His father was a

left-wing history teacher who moved the family from Brooklyn during the blacklists and got a job at Acoustic Research. Landau grew
up on folk music, and in high school he went to every rock concert he could afford. At Briggs & Briggs, he met a Swarthmore student named Paul Williams, who had just started a mimeographed,
three-staple magazine called *Crawdaddy!*, perhaps the first publication devoted to rock criticism. As an undergraduate at Brandeis,
Landau wrote for *Crawdaddy!* When he was a junior, Jann Wenner
invited him to write a column for a biweekly he was starting, to be
called *Rolling Stone*.

As a critic, Landau was nothing if not bold. For the inaugural issue of *Rolling Stone*, in 1967, he panned Jimi Hendrix's classic
Are You Experienced. The next year, he walloped Cream for the loose
bombast of their live shows, adding that Eric Clapton, the band's
lead guitarist, was a "master of the blues clichés of all the post–
World War II blues guitarists . . . a virtuoso at performing other
people's ideas." At the time, Clapton was known as "God." The
review gave God a fit of self-doubt. "The ring of truth just knocked
me backward; I was in a restaurant and I fainted," Clapton said
years later. "And after I woke up, I immediately decided that that
was the end of the band." Cream broke up.

Landau loved the well-wrought single, whether by the Beatles or
Sam and Dave; he was suspicious of arty self-indulgence. "More and
more people expect of rock what they used to expect of philosophy,
literature, films, and visual art," he wrote. "Others expect of rock
what they used to get out of drugs. And in my opinion, rock cannot
withstand that kind of burden because it forces onto rock qualities
which are the negation of what rock was all about in the first place."

In those days, there wasn't much of a line between the rock
industry and rock journalism; in 1969, Jann Wenner produced a
Boz Scaggs record. Landau produced albums with Livingston Taylor and the MC5. Landau admired musically savvy executives, like

Ahmet Ertegun and Jerry Wexler, and he approved of musicians who understood the virtues of popularity. In his senior honors thesis at Brandeis, he wrote admiringly of Otis Redding's willingness to be an entertainer "openly and honestly concerned with pleasing crowds and being successful."

By the end of 1971, Landau was living in Boston and married to the critic Janet Maslin. Although he had Crohn's disease and was ailing, he was the energetic center of a circle of emerging young critics: Dave Marsh, John Rockwell, Robert Christgau, Paul Nelson, Greil Marcus. Landau took notice of Springsteen's first album, *Greetings from Asbury Park*, assigning the review to Lester Bangs, in *Rolling Stone*; he reviewed the second, *The Wild, the Innocent and the E Street Shuffle*, in the alternative weekly *The Real Paper*, calling Springsteen "the most impressive new singer-songwriter since James Taylor," but he added that "the album is not as well-produced as it ought to have been." It was "a mite thin or trebly-sounding, especially when the band moves into the breaks."

Landau, who was twenty-six at the time, accepted an invitation from Dave Marsh to go to Charlie's Place, a club in Cambridge, to check out Springsteen's act. "I went to this club, and it was completely empty," he told me. "He had the smallest of cult followings. Before the show, I asked the guys in the bar where Bruce was, and they pointed outside."

Springsteen was standing in the cold—a skinny bearded guy in jeans and a T-shirt, hopping up and down to keep warm. He was reading Landau's record review, which the management had put in the window.

"I stood next to him and said, 'What do you think?'" Landau recounted. "And he said, 'This guy is usually pretty good, but I've seen better.' I introduced myself, and we had a good laugh."

The next day, he got a call from Springsteen. "We talked for hours," Landau said. "About music, about philosophy. The core of

him then was the same as it is now. And, you know, we've been having that conversation for the rest of our lives: about growth, about
thinking big thoughts, about big things."

A month later, Landau went to see Springsteen at the Harvard
Square Theatre, where he was opening for Bonnie Raitt. It was
the eve of Landau's twenty-seventh birthday, and he was feeling
prematurely worn out. His career was at a standstill. The Crohn's
disease was making it hard to eat or work. His marriage was falling
apart. But that night, May 9, 1974, he felt rejuvenated as Springsteen played everything from the old Fats Domino tune "Let the
Four Winds Blow" to a new song about escape and liberation called
"Born to Run."

The article that Landau wrote for *The Real Paper* is the most
famous review in the history of rock criticism:

> Last Thursday, at the Harvard Square Theatre, I saw my rock
> 'n' roll past flash before my eyes. And I saw something else: I
> saw rock and roll future and its name is Bruce Springsteen. And
> on a night when I needed to feel young, he made me feel like I
> was hearing music for the very first time . . . He is a rock 'n' roll
> punk, a Latin street poet, a ballet dancer, an actor, a joker, bar
> band leader, hot-shit rhythm guitar player, extraordinary singer,
> and a truly great rock 'n' roll composer. He leads a band like
> he has been doing it forever . . . He parades in front of his all-
> star rhythm band like a cross between Chuck Berry, early Bob
> Dylan, and Marlon Brando.

Columbia Records used the line "I saw rock and roll future" as
the centerpiece of an ad campaign. Springsteen befriended Landau, who came to stay with him at his ramshackle house, in Long
Branch. "Modest doesn't even begin to describe the house," Landau
recalled. "There was a couch, his bed, a guitar, and his records. And

we were up till 8 a.m. talking." The two men listened to music and talked about Springsteen's third record. Columbia was not likely to keep investing in Springsteen if the third record failed. Springsteen appreciated Appel's loyalty, but his way of making high-handed judgments grated. Landau was more subtle, asking questions, flattering, suggesting, recommending. Springsteen invited Landau into the studio, where he helped Springsteen cut "Thunder Road" from seven minutes to four and advised him to revise the opening of "Jungleland."

"I had a youthful conviction that I knew what I was doing," Landau said. Springsteen told Appel that he was bringing in Landau as coproducer.

———•———

Born to Run, which was released in August 1975, transformed Springsteen's career, and the ten-show stand at the Bottom Line early in the tour remains a rock date to rival James Brown at the Apollo or Dylan at Newport. At the Bottom Line, Springsteen became himself. By adding Van Zandt as a second guitar player, he was liberated from some of his musical duties, and he became a full-throttle front man, leaping off amps and pianos, frog-hopping from one tabletop to the next.

Landau quit his job as a critic and became, in essence, Springsteen's adjutant: his friend, his adviser in all things, his producer, and, by 1978, his manager. After a prolonged legal battle that kept Springsteen out of the studio for two years, Appel was bought off and cast out.

Landau fed Springsteen's curiosity about the world beyond music. He gave Springsteen books to read—Steinbeck, Flannery O'Connor—and movies to see, particularly John Ford and Howard Hawks Westerns. Springsteen started to think in larger terms than cars and highways; he began to look at his own story, his family's story, in terms of class and American archetypes. The imagery, the storytelling, and the sense of place in those novels and films helped fuel his songs. Landau was also a catalyst in making Springsteen into a big business, pressing him to play bigger halls, overcoming his nightmarish early performances at Madison Square Garden. And he pressed him to think of himself the way Otis Redding did—as both an artist and an entertainer on a large stage.

Some critics have depicted Landau as an avaricious Svengali, a Colonel Parker, or worse. But the people I've talked to in the music business dismiss any idea of malign or overweening influence on Springsteen. "The idea that he'd be manipulated is so preposterous," Danny Goldberg, who has known Springsteen for more than thirty years, says. As Goldberg, who has managed Nirvana and Sonic Youth, puts it, "It's Bruce who uses Jon, to achieve complete artistic control." Landau is sensitive to any claim that he is somehow responsible for his trajectory. "The first principle of being a manager is being a fiduciary for the artist—his interests come first," he says. "So when you are working with him, no matter what the issue is, the first question is, 'What's the best thing for Bruce?'" Springsteen, he went on, "is the smartest person I've ever known—not the most informed or the most educated—but the *smartest*. If you are ever confronted with a situation—a practical matter, an artistic problem—his read of the people involved is exquisite. He is way ahead."

At one point a decade ago, Springsteen rewarded Landau, who had once dreamed of becoming a rock star himself, by calling him onstage. "Bruce told me one night I should strap on a guitar when we got to 'Dancing in the Dark,' and for five or six nights I came out," Landau told me one night backstage. "It's just a tremendous high. But then on the seventh night he said, 'You know, it's great you comin' out onstage. But I was thinking that maybe we should give that a rest tonight.'"

"You mean I'm fired?" Landau said.

Springsteen smiled and said, "Well, yeah. That's about the size of it."

———•———

As Springsteen grew more worldly, he became far more political. He did not start out that way. In 1972, he played a small benefit for George McGovern, at a movie theatre in Red Bank, but, as a young man, his interest in the music was almost completely as a source of personal liberation. He had not made the connection between his father's drift and the politics of unemployment, the depression of Freehold and the wave of deindustrialization.

A political consciousness could be felt on *Darkness on the Edge of Town*, and it grew in the years that followed. He began to find the voice for that by reading—Landau's enthusiasms played a role here—and by traveling, and, crucially, by listening to country and folk music: to Hank Williams and Woody Guthrie. Springsteen knew he had run out of things to say about desperate nights on the Turnpike; he wanted to write songs he could sing as an adult, about marriage, about being a father, and about larger social issues. As he listened again and again to Hank Williams, he said, the songs went from "archival to alive." What had seemed "cranky and old-fashioned" now had depth and darkness; Williams represented "the adult blues," and the music of the working class. "Country by its nature appealed to me, country was provincial, and so was I," Springsteen said in a recent speech, in Austin. "I felt I was an average guy with a slightly above-average gift . . . and country was about the truth emanating out of your sweat, out of your local bar, your corner store." He read Joe Klein's biography of Guthrie. He read memoirs by the civil rights lawyer Morris Dees and the anti-war activist Ron Kovic. All this fed into the working-class anthems of *Darkness on the Edge of Town*, the acoustic howl of *Nebraska*, and even the anthemic pop of *Born in the U.S.A.* He was singing now about Vietnam veterans, migrant workers, class, social divisions, deindustrialized cities, and forgotten American towns, but never in an idiom that threatened "Bruce"—the iconic family-friendly rock star. From the stage, he began to deliver paeans to his causes and ask for donations to local food banks, but the language was never threatening or alienating, and the gate receipts and record sales were beyond fabulous.

Some detected in all this the stink of sanctimony. In 1985, James Wolcott, a punk and New Wave enthusiast, found himself weary of Springsteen's "cornball" sincerity and the level of praise accorded him by the "city-slick Establishment." "Piety has begun to collect around Springsteen's curly head like mist around a mountaintop," Wolcott wrote in *Vanity Fair*. "The mountain can't be blamed for the mist, but still—the reverence is getting awfully thick." For Tom Carson, the problem was insufficient radicalism—the fact that Springsteen remained, at heart, conventionally liberal. Springsteen "thought rock and roll was basically wholesome," Carson wrote in *L.A. Weekly*. "It was an alternative, an escape—but not a rebellion, either as a route to forbidden sexual or social fruit, or, by extension, as a rejection of conventional society. To him, rock *redeemed* conventional society."

In the marketplace of arena rock, that measure of conventionality was a strength, not a limitation. By the mid-eighties, Springsteen was the biggest rock star in the world, capable of selling out Giants Stadium ten shows in a row. He was so unthreatening to American values that, in 1984, George Will went to see him. Wearing a bow tie, a double-breasted blazer, and earplugs, Will watched Springsteen perform in Washington and wrote a column called "A Yankee Doodle Springsteen": "I have not got a clue about Springsteen's politics . . . He is no whiner, and the recitation of closed factories and other problems always seems punctuated by a grand, cheerful affirmation: 'Born in the U.S.A.!'" A week later, Ronald Reagan went to New Jersey to give a campaign speech. Taking his cue from Will, Reagan said, "America's future rests in a thousand dreams inside your hearts; it rests in the message of hope in songs so many young Americans admire: New Jersey's own Bruce Springsteen."

Springsteen was appalled. He later said that "Born in the U.S.A." was "the most misunderstood song since 'Louie, Louie,'" and he began to sing an acoustic version that leached it of its bombast and made its dark shadings plainer. From the stage, he said, "Well, the president was mentioning my name in his speech the other day, and I kind of got to wondering what his favorite album of mine must've been, you know? I don't think it was the *Nebraska* album. I don't think he's been listening to this one." Springsteen played "Johnny 99," the bleak story of a laid-off Jersey autoworker who, in drunken despair, kills a night clerk in a botched robbery.

———•———

Someone once said to Paul McCartney that the Beatles were "anti-materialistic." McCartney had to laugh.

"That's a huge myth," he replied. "John and I literally used to sit down and say, 'Now, let's write a swimming pool.'"

With the *Born in the U.S.A.* album, Springsteen combined political virtue and popular appeal, protest and party time. When he was writing the songs for the album that became *Born in the U.S.A.*, Landau told him that they had a great record, but they still didn't have a swimming pool. They needed a hit.

"Look, I've written seventy songs," Springsteen replied. "You want another one, you write it!" Then he sulkily retreated to his hotel suite and wrote "Dancing in the Dark." The lyrics reflected the played-out frustration of an artist who "ain't got nothing to say," but the music—a pop confection buttressed by a hummable synthesizer line—went down easy. "It went as far in the direction of pop music as I wanted to go—and probably a little farther," Springsteen recalled in a text for his book of lyrics, *Songs*. "My heroes, from Hank Williams to Frank Sinatra to Bob Dylan, were popular musicians. They had hits. There was value in trying to connect with a large audience." *Born in the U.S.A.* went platinum and became the best-selling record of 1985 and of Springsteen's career.

When Springsteen and Van Zandt were young, they had "pink Cadillac" dreams, fantasies of wealth and rock-and-roll glory. "I knew I was never going to be Woody Guthrie," Springsteen recalled, in Austin. "I liked Elvis, I liked the pink Cadillac too much, I like the simplicity and the tossed-off temporary feeling of pop hits, I like a big fuckin' noise, and, in my own way, I like the luxuries, and the comforts, of being a star." He bought a fourteen million dollar estate in Beverly Hills. He remained friends with his old running mates from Jersey, but he also made new friends, rich and famous friends. When he married an actress named Julianne Phillips, in 1985, they honeymooned at Gianni Versace's villa on Lake Como. Later, there were vintage cars and motorcycles, a state-of-the-art home recording studio, horses, and, the ultimate sign of class ascent, organic farming. Tours grew to corporate scale: private jets, five-star hotels, elaborate catering, massage therapists, efficient management.

Springsteen was aware of the comical contradiction: the multi-millionaire who, in his theatrical self-presentation, is the voice of the dispossessed. Very occasionally, twinges of discomfort about this have leaked into his lyrics. In the late eighties, Springsteen played "Ain't Got You," which appeared on his album *Tunnel of Love*, for Van Zandt. The lyrics tell of a fellow who gets "paid a king's ransom for doin' what comes naturally"—who's got "the fortunes of heaven" and a "house full of Rembrandt and priceless art"—but lacks the affections of his beloved. Van Zandt recognized the self-mockery but didn't care. He was aghast.

"We had one of our biggest fights of our lives," Van Zandt

recalled. "I'm, like, 'What the fuck is this?' And he's, like, 'Well, what do you mean, it's the truth. It's just who I am, it's my life.' And I'm, like, 'This is bullshit. People don't need you talking about your life. Nobody gives a *shit* about *your* life. They need you for *their* lives. *That's your thing.* Giving some logic and reason and sympathy and passion to this cold, fragmented, confusing world—that's your gift. Explaining their lives to them. *Their* lives, not yours.' And we fought and fought and fought and fought. He says 'Fuck you,' I say 'Fuck you.' I think something in what I said probably resonated."

Springsteen was also experiencing intervals of depression that were far more serious than the occasional guilt trip about being "a rich man in a poor man's shirt," as he sings in "Better Days." A cloud of crisis hovered as Springsteen was finishing his acoustic masterpiece *Nebraska*, in 1982. He drove from the East Coast to California and then drove straight back. "He was feeling suicidal," Springsteen's friend and biographer Dave Marsh said. "The depression wasn't shocking, per se. He was on a rocket ride, from nothing to something, and now you are getting your ass kissed day and night. You might start to have some inner conflicts about your real self-worth."

Springsteen began questioning why his relationships were a series of drive-bys. And he could not let go of the past, either—a sense that he had inherited his father's depressive self-isolation. For years, he would drive at night past his parents' old house in Freehold, sometimes three or four times a week. In 1982, he started seeing a psychotherapist. At a concert years later, Springsteen introduced his song "My Father's House" by recalling what the therapist had told him about those nighttime trips to Freehold: "He said, 'What you're doing is that something bad happened, and you're going back, thinking that you can make it right again. Something went wrong, and you keep going back to see if you can fix it or somehow make it right.' And I sat there and I said, 'That *is* what I'm doing.' And he said, 'Well, you can't.'"

Extreme wealth may have satisfied every pink Cadillac dream, but it did little to chase off the black dog. Springsteen was playing concerts that went nearly four hours, driven, he has said, by "pure fear and self-loathing and self-hatred." He played that long not just to thrill the audience but also to burn himself out. Onstage, he held real life at bay.

"My issues weren't as obvious as drugs," Springsteen said. "Mine were different, they were quieter—just as problematic, but quieter. With all artists, because of the undertow of history and self-loathing, there is a tremendous push toward self-obliteration that occurs onstage. It's both things: there's a tremendous finding of the self while also an abandonment of the self at the same time. You are free of yourself for those hours; all the voices in your head are *gone*. Just *gone*. There's no room for them. There's one voice, the voice you're speaking in."

————•————

Springsteen's life in the past two decades has been, from all appearances, notably stable. In 1991, he married Patti Scialfa, a denizen of the Asbury Park music scene who had joined the band as a singer. Scialfa's father was a real estate developer, and she had studied music at NYU.

While Springsteen was on the road, I drove to Colts Neck, where he and Patti live on a three-hundred-and-eighty-acre farm. They have three children, two sons and a daughter, and when the kids were small the family lived closer to the shore, in Rumson, New Jersey. Rumson is wealthy in a suburban way. Colts Neck is hardly Freehold; it looks more like Middleburg, Virginia. Horsey people live there. So does Queen Latifah. The Springsteens also own houses in Beverly Hills and in Wellington, Florida.

Springsteen is hardly immune to the charms of his own good fortune ("I live high on the hog"), yet Patti, who grew up near him but with a great deal more money, has a grander eye. When they moved to Colts Neck, she hired Rose Tarlow, an interior designer who had worked for their friend David Geffen, to do the house. When I arrived, a security guard led me to a garage complex that had been remade into a recording studio and a series of sitting rooms. The walls are decorated with photographs of, most conspicuously, Bruce Springsteen; the tables and shelves are heavy on the literature of popular music, with an emphasis on Presley, Dylan, Guthrie, and Springsteen. There's a big TV, an espresso machine, and a framed walking stick that Presley once owned and, in 1973, shattered in a fit of pique.

Patti Scialfa showed up after a while, trailed by two big, shambly German shepherds. A tall, slender woman in her late fifties with a startling shock of red hair, she was warm and smiling, offering water in the modern way; she also seemed a little nervous. Scialfa, like her husband, enjoys a magnificently cosseted life, but hers is a strange position and she doesn't often talk about it publicly. At concerts, she performs two microphones to her husband's left, a perfect vantage point from which to inspect, night after night, the thousands of hungry eyes directed his way. Scialfa has recorded three albums of her own. In the E Street Band, she plays acoustic guitar and sings, but, as she told me, "I have to say that my place in the band is more figurative than it is musical." Onstage, her guitar is barely audible, and she is one of many supporting voices. Yet no one in the crowd is unaware that she is Springsteen's wife—his "Jersey girl," his "red-headed woman," as the songs go—and, at any given theatrical moment onstage, she can flirt, rebuff, swoon, or dance. The E Street Band is an ensemble of characters, as well as musicians, and Scialfa expertly plays her role as Love Interest and Bemused Wife, just as Steve Van Zandt plays his as Best Friend. "Sometimes my frustration comes when I would like to bring something to the table that is more unique," she said, "but the band, in the context of the band, has no room for that."

On the last couple of tours, Scialfa has been an intermittent presence. She sometimes skips concerts to be with the children: the eldest, Evan, just graduated from Boston College; their daughter, Jessica, is at Duke and rides on an international equestrian circuit; and the youngest, Sam, will be a freshman this fall at Bard College. Being around for the kids has been a priority. "When I was young, I felt really, really vulnerable," Scialfa said. "So I wanted things to be relaxed and stable and have somebody in the house and make sure they felt supported when they went off to school." She added, "The hardest part is splitting yourself, the feeling that you're never doing any one job really well."

It took some doing to get Springsteen, an "isolationist" by nature, to settle into a real marriage, and resist the urge to dwell only in his music and onstage. "Now I see that two of the best days of my life," he once told a reporter for *Rolling Stone*, "were the day I picked up the guitar and the day that I learned how to put it down."

Scialfa smiled at that. "When you are that serious and that creative, and non-trusting on an intimate level, and your art has given you so much, your ability to create something becomes your medicine," she said. "It's the only thing that's given you that stability, that joy, that self-esteem. And so you are, like, 'This part of me no one is going to touch.' When you're young, that works, because it gets you from A to B. When you get older, when you are trying to have a family and children, it doesn't work. I think that some artists can be prone to protecting the well that they fetched their inspiration from so well that they are actually protecting malignant parts of themselves, too. You begin to see that something is broken. It's not just a matter of being the mythological lone wolf; something is broken. Bruce is very smart. He wanted a family, he wanted a relationship, and he worked really, really, really hard at it—as hard as he works at his music."

I asked Patti how he finally succeeded. "Obviously, therapy," she said. "He was able to look at himself and battle it out." And yet none of this has allowed Springsteen to pronounce himself free and clear. "That didn't scare me," Scialfa said. "I suffered from depression myself, so I knew what that was about. Clinical depression—I knew what that was about. I felt very akin to him."

In their early days as a couple, Bruce and Patti's idea of a perfect vacation was to get in the car and drive to Death Valley, rent a cheap hotel room with no TV and no phone, and just hang out. Now they are more likely to take a trip with the kids or cruise the Mediterranean on David Geffen's preposterous yacht with the Obamas. On this there is some defensiveness. "I remember when my family became pretty wealthy, and some people tried to make us feel bad about being wealthy," she said. "Here's the bottom line. If your art is intact, your art is intact. Who wrote *Anna Karenina*? Tolstoy? He was an aristocrat! Did that make his work any less true? If you are lucky enough to have a real talent and you've fed it and mined it and protected it and been vigilant about it, can you lose it? Well, you can lose it by sitting outside and drinking Ripple! It doesn't have to be the high life."

As Springsteen sees it, the creative talent has always been nurtured by the darker currents of his psyche, and wealth is no guarantee of bliss. "I'm thirty years in analysis!" he said. "Look, you cannot underestimate the fine power of self-loathing in all of this. You think, I don't like anything I'm seeing, I don't like anything I'm doing, but I need to change myself, I need to transform myself. I do not know a single artist who does not run on that fuel. If you are extremely pleased with yourself, nobody would be fucking doing it! Brando would not have acted. Dylan wouldn't have written 'Like a Rolling Stone.' James Brown wouldn't have gone 'Unh!' He wouldn't have searched that one-beat down that was so hard. That's a motivation, that element of 'I need to remake myself, my town, my audience'—the desire for renewal."

Wrecking Ball is hardly Springsteen's best album, but it's as earnestly as political a record as *What's Going On?*, *Rage Against the Machine*, or *It Takes a Nation of Millions to Hold Us Back*. After Springsteen's political run-ins in the eighties, he grew even more engaged with social issues. He sang of AIDS ("Streets of Philadelphia"), dislocation ("The Ghost of Tom Joad"), abandonment ("Spare Parts"), and Iraq ("Last to Die"). He made speeches from the stage about "rendition, illegal wiretapping, voter suppression, no habeas corpus." For his trouble, he was attacked by Bill O'Reilly, Glenn Beck, and even a *New York Times* columnist, John Tierney, who wrote, "The singer who recorded *Greetings from Asbury Park* seems to have made an ideological crossing of the Hudson: 'Greetings from Central Park West.'" In 2004, Springsteen campaigned for John Kerry, and, in 2008, he was even more enthusiastic about Barack Obama, posting a statement on his website saying that Obama "speaks to the America I've envisioned in my music for the past 35 years, a generous nation with a citizenry willing to tackle nuanced and complex problems, a country that's interested in its collective destiny and in the potential of its gathered spirit." At a concert at the Lincoln Memorial before Obama's inauguration, Springsteen sang "The Rising" with a gospel choir and, with Pete Seeger, Woody Guthrie's "This Land Is Your Land," including, at Seeger's suggestion, the two last, "radical" verses. ("There was a great high wall there / that tried to stop me; / A great big sign there / Said private property; / But on the other side / It didn't say nothing; / That side was made for you and me.")

The songs on *Wrecking Ball* were written before the Occupy Wall Street movement, but they echo its rage against the lack of accountability. "We Are Alive" draws a line between ghosts of oppressed strikers, civil rights marchers, and workers, while the chorus is a kind of communion among the dead and a call to the living: "We are alive / And though our bodies lie alone here in the dark / Our spirits rise / To carry the fire and light the spark." For all that, the political vision—in *Wrecking Ball*, as in its predecessors—isn't really radical. It's shot through with a liberal insistence that American patriotism has less to do with the primacy of markets than with a Rooseveltian sense of fairness and a communal sense of belonging.

One night, I asked Springsteen what he hoped his political songs would do for people who come to concerts for a good time. He shook his head and said, "They function at the very edges of politics at best, though they try to administer to its center. You have to be satisfied with that. You have to understand it's a long road, and there have been people doing some version of what we're doing on this tour going all the way back, and there will be people doing it after us. I think one thing this record tries to do is to remind people that there is a continuity that is passed on from generation to generation, a set of ideas expressed in myriad different ways: books, protests, essays, songs, around the kitchen table. So these ideas are ever-present. And you are a raindrop."

Springsteen admires Obama for the health care bill, for rescuing the automobile industry, for the withdrawal from Iraq, for killing Osama bin Laden; he is disappointed in the failure to close Guantánamo and to appoint more champions of economic fairness, and he sees an unseemly friendliness toward corporations—the usual liberal points of praise and dispraise. He's wary about joining another campaign. "I did it twice because things were so dire," he said. "It seemed like if I was ever going to spend whatever small political capital I had, that was the moment to do so. But that capital diminishes the more often you do it. While I'm not saying never, and I still like to support the president, you know, it's something I didn't do for a long time, and I don't have plans to be out there every time."

Springsteen has been faulted for taking himself too seriously, and the microworld around him takes him so seriously that to an outsider it can seem like a cocoon of piety. But Springsteen can also be funny about himself. On Jimmy Fallon's show, he agreed to dress up as himself circa "Born to Run"—beard, aviator shades, floppy pimp cap, leather jacket—and went on with Fallon, who was dressed as Neil Young, to sing a mock-serious version of the Willow Smith ditty "Whip My Hair." In a more recent show, Fallon, again dressed as Neil Young, again brought out Springsteen, this time dressed in his muscled-up eighties regular-Jersey-guy regalia—complete with sleeveless denim shirt. They sang a duet of the party song pop duo LMFAO's "Sexy and I Know It": "I'm in a Speedo tryin' t' tan my cheeks . . . I'm sexy and I know it!"

As a writer and as a performer, Springsteen is in command of a variety of themes and moods: comic and grandiose, political and mindless. As the tour developed, he altered the set lists so that each show felt specific to the occasion. At the Apollo, he declared that soul music had been the band's education: "We studied all our subjects. Geography? We learned the exact location of 'Funky Broadway.' History? 'A Change Is Gonna Come.' Math? '99 and a Half Won't Fucking Do.'" In Austin, Springsteen celebrated the centenary of Woody Guthrie's birth by opening the show with Woody's itinerant worker's lament "I Ain't Got No Home" and closed it with "This Land Is Your Land."

In Tampa, Springsteen played "American Skin (41 Shots)," which was written in the wake of the police shooting of Amadou Diallo, but was now for Trayvon Martin, the unarmed Black teenager who was killed in Sanford, Florida. On the first of two nights in Philadelphia, Springsteen paid homage to his Shore roots by playing two semi-obscurities from his first years as a recording musician, "Seaside Bar Song" and "Does This Bus Stop at 82nd Street?" On one foray into the audience, he found Max Weinberg's ninety-seven-year-old mother and gave her a kiss. The next night, he pulled his eighty-seven-year-old mother, Adele, onto the stage and danced with her to "Dancing in the Dark." In New Jersey, Springsteen heightened the tribute to Clarence Clemons. During the final song, "Tenth Avenue Freeze Out," he stopped the music after the line

"The Big Man joined the band," and a film of Clemons rolled on the screens above the stage. ("Man, I could barely *stand* that," the percussionist Everett Bradley told me later. "I was crying so bad!")

At each show, the most striking musical difference between the old E Street Band and the new was the increasing prominence given to Jake Clemons. His playing grew stronger, his willingness to take center stage more pronounced. After a few performances, he was moon-walking across the stage. And yet every time Springsteen paid tribute to Clarence Clemons Jake seemed overcome, pounding his chest with a double tap of respect for his uncle and appreciation of the crowd's response. "Everyone wants to be part of something bigger than themselves," Jake said. "A Springsteen show is a lot of things, and it's partly a religious experience. Maybe he comes from the line of David, a shepherd boy who could play beautiful music, so that the crazy become less crazy and Saul the king finally chills out. Religion is a system of rules and order and expectations, and it unites people in a purpose. There really is a component of Bruce that is supernatural. Bruce is Moses! He led the people out of the land of disco!"

———•———

One night, as Springsteen was waiting to perform, I asked how he thought his inner constitution led to his being the artist and performer he is. "I probably worked harder than anybody else I saw," he said. But there was, he thought, a core psychological component as well: "I searched out something that I needed to do. It's a job that's filled with ego and vanity and narcissism, and you need all those things to do it well. But you can't let those things completely swamp you, either. You need all those things but in *relative* check. And in relative check for me, if you ask some of my friends or some members of my family, might not be considered in check to them!

It's in relative check as far as people who do what I do. But you need those things, because you are driven by your needs out there—the raw hunger and the raw need of exciting people and exciting your-self into some higher state. People have pursued that throughout the history of civilization. It's a strange job, and for a lot of people it's a dangerous job. But those things are at the root of it."

In May, the tour set off for a three-month run of stadium perfor-mances in Europe. In Barcelona, Springsteen was staying in a suite, with a private deck and a Jacuzzi, at the Florida, a hillside hotel overlooking the city; the band and the crew stayed at the Hotel Arts, a five-star hotel on the beach. A caravan of black Mercedes vans whisked the musicians (some band members have their own travel-ing assistants) to the Olympic Stadium in the afternoon for sound check. Banish any images of rock legend: forget about dissipated drummers slumped in a junkie haze in some stadium locker room, forget roadies hurling televisions and empty bottles of Jack Daniel's from hotel balconies into the pool. The Springsteen road show is about as decadent as the Ice Capades. Band members talk about missing their kids, jet lag, Wi-Fi reception at the hotel.

"To be a success these days, you are more likely to be an athlete than a drug addict," Van Zandt told me. "You go through the phase of drugs and drinking, and if you get through it you see that all the rewards are in longevity. Longevity is more fun than the drugs. Then, there's the business. For that you need a clean head."

The upper echelon of the pop music touring business is, like Silicon Valley, dominated by a small number of enterprises: Lady Gaga, Madonna, U2, Jon Bon Jovi, Jay-Z, and a very few others. The drop-off in scale from there is precipitous. Springsteen is no longer in the Beatlemania phase of the mid-eighties—a period of mini-riots around his hotels—but he is still able to sell out stadiums on the I-95 corridor and other cities in the United States. He is even more popular in Europe. The rhythmic stomping of his fans at

Ullevi, a football venue in Gothenburg, in 1985, damaged the foundation, an episode known in Springsteen lore as "the time Bruce broke a stadium." In Europe, that spirit persists.

The *Wrecking Ball* tour is likely to go on for a year. James Brown played many more shows a year, but he never played so long or with such absolute exertion. Some nights, Springsteen stays a little longer in his dressing room, ginning himself up for all the running, jumping, and screaming, but there is never the thought of taking a pass.

"Once people have bought those tickets, I don't have that option," he told me. We were alone in a vast, makeshift dressing room in Barcelona. "Remember, we're also running a business here, so there is a commercial exchange, and that ticket is my handshake. That ticket is me promising you that it's gonna be all the way every chance I get. That's my contract. And ever since I was a young guy I took that seriously." Although there are nights when, in the dressing room, he feels tapped out, the stage always works its magic: "Suddenly the fatigue disappears. A transformation takes place. That's what we're selling. We're selling that possibility. It's half a joke: I go out onstage and—*snap*—'Are you ready to be transformed?' What? At a rock show? By a guy with a guitar? Part of it is a goof, and part of it is, 'Let's do it, let's see if we can.'"

One kindness that Springsteen has afforded his body is more days off, leaving time for his family, for exercise, for listening to music, watching movies, reading. Lately, he has been consumed with Russian fiction. "It's compensatory—what you missed the first time around," he said. "I'm sixty-some, and I think, *There are a lot of these Russian guys! What's all the fuss about?* So I was just curious. That was an incredible book: *The Brothers Karamazov.* Then I read *The Gambler.* The social play in the first half was less interesting to me, but the second half, about obsession, was fun. That could speak to me. I was a big John Cheever fan, and so when I got into Chekhov I could see where Cheever was coming from. And I was a big Philip Roth fan, so I got into Saul Bellow, *Augie March.* These are all new connections for me. It'd be like finding out now that the Stones covered Chuck Berry!"

Springsteen was sitting near a low table covered with picks, capos, harmonicas, and sheets of paper with lists of songs written in thick black marker. After sound check, he tries to imagine that night's performance. The rest of the band and the crew are down the hall at "catering"—an improvised commissary. Tonight, the menu is veal shank, grouper, and various vegetarian options, to say nothing of half a dozen kinds of salad and a pâtisserie of desserts. ("Did you try that Spanish banana thingy? Amazing!") The band members wait for Springsteen to distribute the night's set list. The old-timers are calm, but the newer members wait with a measure of anxiety. "I'm always flipping out, having nightmares that he's gonna call something that I never even heard of fifteen minutes before we go onstage," Jake Clemons said.

Thousands of fans, many of whom had been waiting outside since morning, were allowed to enter the stadium grounds at six o'clock for a show that would not begin until ten. I noticed a few young Spaniards carrying a sign, in English, reading, "Bruce, Thanks for Making Our Lives Better." I tried to imagine a sign like that for—Lou Reed? AC/DC? Bon Jovi? ("Richie Sambora, Thanks for making our lives better." Doubtful.) The ultra-sincere interchange between Springsteen and his fans, which looks treacly to the uninitiated and the uninterested, is what distinguishes him and his performances. Forty years on, and an hour before going onstage yet again, he was trying to make sense of that transaction.

"You are isolated, yet you desire to talk to somebody," Springsteen said. "You are very disempowered, so you seek impact, recognition that you are alive and that you exist. We hope to send people out of the building we play in with a slightly more enhanced sense of what their options might be, emotionally, maybe communally. You empower them a little bit, they empower you. It's all a battle against the futility and the existential loneliness! It may be that we are all huddled together around the fire and trying to fight off that sense of the inevitable. That's what we do for one another.

"I try to put on the kind of show that the kid in the front row is going to come to and never forget," he went on. "Our effort is to stay with you, period, to have you join us and to allow us to join you for the ride—the *whole* ride. That's what we've been working on the whole time, and this show is the latest installment, and, in many ways, it's the most complicated installment, because in many ways it has to do with the *end* of that ride. There are kids who are coming to the show who will never have seen the band with Clarence Clemons in it or Danny Federici—people who were in the band for thirty years. So our job is to honor the people who stood on that stage by putting on the best show we've ever put on. To do that, you've got to acknowledge your losses and your defeats as well as your victories. There is a finiteness to it, though the end may be a long time away. We end the night with a party of sorts, but it's not an uncomplicated party. It's a *life* party—that's what we try to deliver up."

A couple of weeks earlier, one of Springsteen's beloved aunts died. And now, the day before the first concert in Barcelona, Mary Van Zandt, Steve's mother, died, in Red Bank. "When I was a child, deaths came regularly," Springsteen said. "Then there's a period, unless accidents happen, death doesn't happen, and then you reach a period where it just happens regularly again. We've entered that part."

A little while later, having changed from his regular jeans to his stage jeans, Springsteen walked with the band through a stadium tunnel and toward the stage. The last thing he saw before heading to the mike and a blast of stage lights was a sign taped to the top step that read "Barcelona." Once, at an arena show in Auburn Hills, he kept greeting the crowd with shouts of "Hello, Ohio!" Finally, Van Zandt pulled him aside and told him they were in Michigan. That could not happen again.

Now Springsteen glanced at the step and stepped into the spotlight.

"Hola, Barcelona!" he cried out to a sea of forty-five thousand people. "Hola, Catalunya!"

July 2012

THE LAST ITALIAN TENOR

The humid January air of Singapore was ideal for the throat of a tenor in late middle age. The arena, a more likely venue for professional basketball than for bel canto, was sold out, with the autocrat and his guests in the front row, diplomats and trade barons just behind. Even Singapore itself, where befouling the street with a dropped Dixie cup brings a stiff fine and a shaming picture in *The Straits Times*, seemed to ensure a soft landing for the Luciano Pavarotti juggernaut. The focus of all this commerce, efficiency, and attention, however, was suffering in his suite at the Regent Hotel. In the days, a quarter century ago, when Pavarotti was establishing himself as the next great Italian tenor in the line from Caruso to Di Stefano, the *New York Times* critic Harold C. Schonberg said of this portly baker's son from Modena that "God had kissed his vocal cords." Now the blessing was, if not gone, then infected.

Luciano Pavarotti had a cold. Somewhere along this tour of sports arenas from Düsseldorf to Honolulu, he had picked up— along with fees of at least a hundred thousand dollars per concert— the sort of affliction that is hardly noticed by most mortals but is a horror for one who depends for his living and his reputation on the clarity of the resonators in his chest and in his head. With a stuffed nose, the King of the High Cs knew only fear at the prospect of the climactic note in "Nessun dorma"—the B-natural. Phlegm in his throat would mock his attempts to control the dark passages of "E lucevan le stelle." The mere threat of a cough hung over "O sole mio" like a machete. One of his concerts in Japan had been especially trying, and the cold still lingered during the flight south to Singapore. Nothing—not the gallons of French springwater, not the inhalers or medicines, not the Ricola drops or slices of apple— would clear the Maestro's throat.

Colds hit the fragile psyche of a tenor with insidious stealth. They play on his vanity, then crush him. Very often, the day before the cold asserts itself the voice can be plush, almost velvet, in tone; the lining of the nose and throat, the resonant tract, is hypertrophic, swollen and damp. For a moment, the voice mysteriously elevates. It soars. But then the rogue secretions increase. Postnasal drip sets in. The lining of the throat reddens and swells. The throat becomes less pliant. Mucus thickens almost to the consistency of rubber cement and rains cruelly down on the vocal cords. Speech, to say nothing of song, requires a Herculean push through the muck. Breathing grows labored. A change in temperature causes changes in the hydration of the throat. The effort to produce a true musical note becomes a painful exercise in anxiety and overcompensation. There is a metamorphosis. The canary becomes a pigeon.

Even without a cold, Pavarotti always dreads the anticipation of singing more than the singing itself. "The ten minutes before the performance you wouldn't wish on your worst enemies," he says. "Then you go out and begin to sing. If the voice is with you, then you are going to share a gift of God, and there is nothing better than that. But if you have a little cough, then you have to try to force a good performance even though you are sick, and that—well . . ."

With one day still left to go before the Singapore concert, Pava- rotti's manager and friend, Herbert Breslin, waited for the singer to descend from his suite to the lobby. Across town, an orchestra and a conductor tuned up and waited.

"This is pretty unusual," Breslin said, glancing at a clock. "Luciano's usually on time for rehearsals."

Breslin is a man of rubbery features and a hard glare. He is sixty-eight and has been Pavarotti's manager for twenty-five years. In that time, he has helped a great, but by no means singular, tenor achieve a visibility previously unknown in the history of classical music. Not since P. T. Barnum promoted Jenny ("the Swedish Nightingale") Lind on her tour of the United States, in the eighteen-fifties, has the world of opera seen such a marriage of talent and hype. Beloved as an image of virtue, Lind mixed standard arias with the treacly pop songs of the day; she sang to adoring crowds, who then rushed off to buy Jenny Lind candies and Jenny Lind dinner services. With Pavarotti, Breslin has been able to outstrip Barnum. Even more than Jascha Heifetz, Arturo Toscanini, Maria Callas, or Leonard Bernstein, Pavarotti has used virtuosity as a stepping stone to mega-celebrity, and in the process he has acquired a fortune. Performing a fairly stock set of arias and popular Italian love songs—all of them packaged and repackaged many times on compact disk, laser disk, and videocassette—he has drawn Woodstockian crowds to the great parks of London, Buenos Aires, San Francisco, and New York. When he sang *La Bohème* in Beijing in 1986, two hundred and fifty million Chinese watched on television. Five hundred million saw the "Three Tenors" concert (Pavarotti costarring with Placido Domingo and José Carreras) at the Baths of Caracalla in Rome in 1990. That same year, the only musicians who sold more recordings than Pavarotti were Elton John and Madonna. Domingo, a tenor of far greater range, cannot, despite his own commercial strivings, match Pavarotti's fame. He does not have the same ineffable warmth in his voice or stage persona, and he does not have Herbert Breslin.

"The thing with Luciano is that he has penetrated the world of classical music like no one else in the history of the art form," Breslin said as he waited in the lobby of the Regent Hotel. "Who would have thought you could sell out arenas for an Italian tenor in all these exotic places? They all know him and they get to see him. The phenomenon is tied to the events in communications: the VCR, the CD, the spread of television. Television has made him known all over the world. He may not be the greatest musician in the world, but his singing speaks to the soul. The Pavarotti sound gets you right in the center of your being. If he's in good form tomorrow, you'll see fifteen thousand Singaporeans going crazy. See, Luciano is really like a rock star for people over thirty. These are the people who have the money. In every city in the world, there is always a substantial number of people who support the arts, and they are the movers and the shakers, the people in the philharmonic societies, the moneyed classes. They love Pavarotti, and that's why he's the greatest fund-raiser in the history of music. He's done more benefits than Carter has liver pills."

Breslin, who began his career as a public relations man for Chrysler in Detroit, was giving the Pavarotti pitch. His patter is extraordinary in its speed and confidence, and he is experienced. His first client in music was, in salesmen's terms, a Pinto: the soprano Elisabeth Schwarzkopf. "A wonderful singer," Breslin says, "but she presented a tough PR problem." (Schwarzkopf had been a member of the Nazi Party.)

As Breslin spoke, he went on watching the hotel elevators open and shut, a loud pinging preceding each arrival. "Placido does arena concerts, too, but not ten or fifteen thousand people all the time," he said. "Only Luciano can do that. He's single-handedly made the opera a world in which the men predominate. Before, it was Callas and Leontyne Price and Joan Sutherland and all the rest. A man couldn't get to first base. Now look! Sure, you've got someone like Kathy Battle now, but she has a very limited repertoire. Luciano and I have been together for twenty-five years, and everything he's done is to make himself an independent spirit. We began twenty years ago, with recitals in Liberty, Missouri, Dallas, and Carnegie Hall, and those concerts gave him independence. If you succeed at that kind of thing, you don't need an opera company. You can just be yourself. We started with concerts with a piano, then moved on to orchestras. I'm telling you he could read the telephone book and people would enjoy it."

Yet another elevator door opened, and this time Pavarotti, trailed by a few unsmiling members of his entourage, stepped out into the marble lobby. Rossini once described the great contralto of his era, Marietta Alboni, as an "elephant that swallowed a nightingale." It does not take a malicious spirit to think the same of Pavarotti. He is huge. And yet he is immediately appealing. He has a great face: squared off, thickly bearded, expressive. You never feel you are looking at a fatty with a comb-over. He is somehow the living embodiment of the romantic Italian tenor. Women, especially, do not mind his bulk. As one member of the retinue was eager to report, Pavarotti receives as many sexual offers "as your average rock star."

But now Pavarotti seemed glum, unhealthy, in pain. As he headed through the lobby for the door, you could hear his chuffing breath from ten feet away. He had not taken many steps. Breslin tenderly put his hand on Pavarotti's elbow, and the two men, speaking Italian, went out to the driveway and eased themselves into a car. The rest of the crew, including a team of German security men with walkie-talkies, followed in a Mercedes caravan.

———•———

The concert in Singapore was to be a kind of farewell. Pavarotti was postponing a series of appearances and would "disappear" for a couple of months. He would go home to his family, in Modena, start a diet ("Maybe I lose eighty pounds"), and endure an operation for an old and nagging knee injury. Breslin knew that the cancellations would be a public relations blow. The past couple of years had punished the legend. Ardis Krainik, the general director of Chicago's Lyric Opera, let loose a skein of bad publicity in 1989 by cutting off all contractual relations with Pavarotti after he canceled a performance of *Tosca*. Krainik says that she "loves" the singer but that, as a business executive, she had no other choice. It had been his twenty-sixth cancellation out of forty-one scheduled appearances at the Lyric.

In 1991, Pavarotti tried to extend his range from the lyric to the dramatic in a concert version of Verdi's *Otello*—an opera that demands of the tenor a richer, darker sound than Pavarotti can carry—and he was rewarded with a string of devastating reviews. Peter G. Davis's piece, in *New York*, was representative, slamming Pavarotti for his "mechanical, score-bound declamation," and going on to say, "Most of the time he simply sounded scared out of his wits. Perhaps he was. When not singing, the tenor sat next to a table with his face buried in a huge white handkerchief, nervously helping himself to an extraordinary variety of potables and refreshments laid out for his convenience." Pavarotti, for his part, said he had a cold.

In another incident, the BBC sued when its executives discovered that a 1992 Pavarotti concert they had bought for broadcast had been lip-synched. Some fans might have wished for more lip-synching: At the opening of La Scala last December, Pavarotti was poorly prepared for his role in *Don Carlo* and sang badly. The expert fans in the balconies, the *loggionisti*, booed.

When the caravan arrived at the rehearsal hall, a member of the advance team said, with a sense of triumph, "We're lucky. The walk isn't too bad. And there's a good elevator." Pavarotti unfolded from his car. As he walked, he rested his right hand on the shoulder of Judy Kovacs, a striking young woman who travels the world with him as his personal assistant and occasional photographer.

He winced a little as he headed slowly toward the elevator. "More slowly, Judy," he said. "More slowly."

Inside the hall, Pavarotti's special stool, which also travels the world with him, and a local orchestra were in place. Pavarotti smiled, nodded at the assembled musicians, sat down, and quickly settled into an easy groove, softly singing his way through his standard arena program of chestnut arias and Italian songs. For Pavarotti, rehearsal is a mix of the casual and the disciplined, an attempt to sharpen the timing without exhausting the body. He worked with his arms folded over his chest; his eyes narrowed and widened with the music, as if he were watching his voice, testing it for signs of strain or illness. There were a few.

Sitting now in the fifth row of the hall, Breslin watched his man noodle through one aria after another: "Una furtiva lagrima," "O paradiso," "Recondita armonia," "E lucevan le stelle," and the signature, the aria used as the theme music for the 1990 World Cup, "Nessun dorma."

No matter what Pavarotti has lost to age, no matter, even, what hellish tricks his cold was playing on him, his sound came shimmering out of him. To sit so close to that voice, even when it was in half-bellow, was thrilling. Breslin alternated between singing along and talking as the spirit moved him. "You know, the idea for a rest is good," he said. "Luciano told me he woke up the other morning, went into the bathroom, looked at himself in the mirror, and said, 'Luciano, you are fat!' The main thing is that he must lose some weight. It's gotten to the point where he is practically immobile." Pavarotti does not reveal his weight, even to his own dietitian, but he was surely well over three hundred pounds in Singapore. In order for him to perform certain operas onstage in recent years, directors have had to eliminate steps, plant cups of water on the set, and otherwise design the production for the health and safety of the tenor. Dorothy Kirsten, a frequent costar with Pavarotti in New York and San Francisco over the years, once told Opera News,

"If he doesn't lose some of that weight, he'll have a heart attack. It's a shame, because now he's more insecure vocally and nervous and not nearly the artist he was when I first sang with him. Let's hope someone can convince him to do something quick before it's too late!" And that was when Pavarotti was forty-one. He is now fifty-eight.

Breslin hummed along with the orchestra as it played the opening bars of "Vesti la giubba," an aria from *Pagliacci* that is all the more familiar for having once been used as the music for a Rice Krispies commercial. I leaned over to Breslin and said that news of Pavarotti's cancellations was likely to be in all the papers at home.

Breslin rolled his eyes and nodded. "Of course, of course," he said. "Luciano complained to me, 'When my colleagues cancel, no one hears about it. When I cancel, the whole world knows about it.' I told him, 'Luciano, you go to the bathroom and the whole world wants to know.'"

The next night, Pavarotti sang to the elite of Singapore. It was, for those who knew him, a middling performance. Singapore hardly knew him. At the end, the crowd was on its collective feet, roaring its collective glee. They were applauding an opera star, the guest on the talk shows who cooks spaghetti, the man in the American Express Card commercial. Even before he sang a single note, Pavarotti extended his arms in embrace, threw his head back, and brought on the applause. "Do you know me?" Pavarotti seemed to ask as the sweat poured down his face, and his chest heaved. "Do you adore me?" And yes—yes, they did.

———•———

The next day, the road show broke up. Pavarotti flew home to lose weight. I flew home to learn more about Pavarotti. I soon came across a line from the late singer Richard Tucker: asked by *Newsweek* about being the world's greatest tenor, Tucker said, "You have no idea what a great responsibility it is." Tucker's remark has about it all the comic self-dramatizing, the narcissism, of the performing arts world. But it is also true. Opera fans are not much different from the most discriminating baseball fans. At once emotional and impossibly knowledgeable, they are the self-appointed guardians of the art, and buy their season tickets at least in part to hold the current practitioners up to constant scrutiny and historical comparison. Just as the memory of Willie Mays lurks behind every exploit and pretension of Barry Bonds, so does Jussi Björling's 1944 "Nessun dorma" haunt the attempts of Pavarotti to match it. "The opera aficionado is a very strange person," Beverly Sills says. "There's this incredible possessiveness in him. Somehow he feels the opera star should be for him alone, and he doesn't want to share, especially with a crossover public."

It sometimes seems as if the composers had written arias with the precise purpose of undermining the ego of that supreme egoist, the tenor. The ghostly composer sometimes wins by a knockout. Once, in Peru, a tenor faced with singing the daunting series of high Cs in "Di quella pira," from Verdi's *Il Trovatore*, stopped the orchestra and suddenly announced that he would now, "by popular request," replace the aria with "Come Back to Sorrento." Pavarotti is braver but no less frightened. He once recalled that, confronted with singing nine high Cs in a single aria in Donizetti's *La Fille du régiment*—a feat that helped make his name—"I was so scared I didn't know which muscle to use most, the throat or the sphincter."

The responsibility of tenors to the aficionados, and to the music itself, is enormous. For Pavarotti, it is unprecedented. Unless some miracle occurs very soon, he is the last in the line of great Italian tenors. The sense of imminent extinction, of lastness, does not allow him to age peacefully. Until recently, competition among tenors was furious. After Caruso, the species only thrived: Beniamino Gigli, Tito Schipa, Ferruccio Tagliavini, Mario Del Monaco, Franco Corelli, Carlo Bergonzi, Giuseppe Di Stefano. "When I was grow-

ing up, there were thirty great tenors, not three," Pavarotti says.
"I don't know why things are now the way they are." Now there
are a few strong tenors—Richard Leech and Jerry Hadley among
them—but, according to most critical reckoning, there are no greats,
and certainly no great young Italians. "Good tenors are so scarce,"
George Bernard Shaw wrote, "that the world has always condoned
any degree of imbecility for the sake of an *ut de poitrine*"—a high C
from the chest. And never more than now. Domingo, Pavarotti's
only real competitor, is a Spaniard, and is himself in his fifties.

When Pavarotti was growing up, there were still teachers and
conductors alive who had worked with Puccini, who had been part
of the Golden Age. Compared with the Metropolitan Opera of the
fifties and early sixties, when Renata Tebaldi would sing one night
and Callas the next, when Rudolf Bing could afford to fire Richard
Tucker if he felt like it, the place is arguably in serious vocal decline,
especially for the nineteenth-century repertoire.

In the criticism leveled against Pavarotti and Breslin, there
is often a grave undertone suggesting that somehow they have
degraded the integrity of opera itself. Few doubt that Pavarotti's
achievements are considerable—especially his recordings with Joan
Sutherland and Richard Bonynge—but there is also a feeling that
he and Breslin have gone a long way toward trashing a cathedral.
Herbert Breslin "has built around the Pavarotti persona a vast pro-
motional apparatus that many in the music world find thoroughly
repulsive," Will Crutchfield wrote in *The New York Times*. "The
publicity shunts even a noble work like the Verdi 'Requiem' off
into small print on posters for what is first and foremost a Pavarotti
Appearance. It makes claims about the tenor's artistic attainments
and status that are frankly preposterous to anyone who knows opera
and vocal history. In exposure and income Mr. Pavarotti surpasses
by light years several tenors whose actual voice and art he may sur-
pass by only a slight margin, or not at all."

The opera critic Peter Conrad told me, "It's neurotic enough when your career depends on two bits of gristle in your throat, but when you are all hyped, and you are a milk cow producing money for everyone, the pressure is just huge. Pavarotti's high notes ran out some time ago. Now it's often a strangled bleat."

William Weaver, a prominent translator and a critic for the *Financial Times*, told me that he has heard Pavarotti sing well in the past—"marvelous clarity of enunciation, the beautiful pure vowels"—but that "all the inartistic things he does have resulted in a loss of sensitivity," and that now he hears a "coarseness" in Pavarotti's tone and delivery. I asked Weaver if he saw the "Three Tenors" concert. "I never heard such ghastly singing in my life, and Pavarotti was the worst," he said. "He added extra vulgarity: I thought he'd drag out 'O sole mio' until the end of time."

Perhaps no remark on the subject has been more devastating than Bing's before the release of Pavarotti's abysmal 1982 movie, *Yes, Giorgio*. "I won't say that I'd fire him on the spot," Bing said in *New York*. "But I must say that seeing that stupid, ugly face everywhere I go is getting on my nerves. It's all so unnecessary, so undignified."

It is hard—at least, historically—to understand what all the fuss is about. Risë Stevens and Geraldine Farrar did cigarette ads. Roberta Peters did a Chock Full o' Nuts spot on television wearing a toga. Rosalind Elias did an advertisement for Playtex in which she announced that her Cross Your Heart brassiere made her high C come out better. Robert Merrill, usually a paragon of career planning, was once fired from the Metropolitan for starring in *Aaron Slick from Punkin Crick* with Dinah Shore. Opera stars have always straddled the shadow line between high art and low camp. "If Elvis or the Beatles can make a grand living, why should an opera singer be prevented from doing it?" says Ardis Krainik, of the Lyric. "Luciano loves it when eighteen thousand people cheer him. I don't begrudge him that. It doesn't cheapen anything." Bruce-Michael Gelbert, a critic for the *New York Native*, told me that, while Pavarotti has lost his high notes and probably should not have taken on heavier roles like *Otello*, "I still think he sounds so much better than almost anyone else," and he added, "When he's at his best, few can touch him. He usually sounds better than I expect, even though the King of the High Cs now can crack on a B-flat."

For singers the process of aging usually makes itself known at, roughly, the age of thirty. The muscle tone of the abdomen begins to decrease. The lungs lose their elasticity. The thorax loses its distensibility. The neck bones become less flexible, and this affects the ability to raise and lower the larynx; the larynx loses bulk and muscle tone; the cartilage in the larynx becomes ossified. Joints on the back of the larynx can stiffen, and the result is increased breathiness. The vocal cords begin to thin out and bow; the surrounding connective tissue grows flaccid. Because the cords do not close as easily as they once did, the singer overcompensates. He pushes. A still-breathier tone results. Also, hearing becomes less acute. The singer's feedback system goes awry. One sign of age is that the pianissimo in the upper-middle range loses its shimmer. And the nature and volume of the secretions in the throat change; hydration is more erratic; high notes become more of an adventure.

"It's a fact of life. Singers are like athletes," says Dr. Scott Kessler, a specialist in maladies of the voice. "Like an athlete, a singer needs constant training and muscle toning. The fine control goes before the stamina."

———•———

When Pavarotti travels, he stays in the same hotels and, if he can, the same rooms. In New York, he has a twenty-third-floor apartment on Central Park South. The fear of a cold keeps him indoors on all but ideal days. When he does go out, it is always with a scarf and a hat. If he forgets, Judy Kovacs will run up from behind and throw the scarf around his neck. "I am a slave to my throat," Pavarotti complains. There is, despite this awful bondage, almost always someone around to do his bidding. Pavarotti is among the more pampered creatures in the world. "Luciano loves to sit on the couch, make phone calls, and order people around—that's what he does," Breslin says. "Mainly, he's a simple country man. His real passion is horses. He's not much of a reader. He always has to have sixteen people around. Luciano is spoiled. He is who he is and he doesn't like change."

For two months after the Singapore concert, Pavarotti stayed home in Modena with his wife, Adua, and near his three grown daughters and his personal dietitian. He made his calls and tried to survive on fifteen hundred calories a day. When the layoff was done, Pavarotti returned to performing looking a little lighter—thirty-two pounds lighter, he informed his dietitian—and more at ease. His knee was still sore from the operation, and no one had made him any younger, but he moved more easily and was eager to sing. In early May, he and the soprano Aprile Millo gave a benefit concert at the Metropolitan Opera of Puccini and Verdi arias and duets. At times, it was hard to imagine him singing better.

The morning after the concert, I went to see Pavarotti at his apartment. He was sitting at his desk, contentedly looking out the window and waiting for the phone to ring. He had the sweet, aimless look of a lion after lunch, though lunch, he assured me, had not been much: "Today, it was a hot dog. Not bad! If you look at the calories of a hot dog—well, it would be, maximum, two, three, four hundred calories. I try to make one meal divide into two. So if I eat pasta in the daytime, one plate, not even big, with some fruit after, then I can have for dinner maybe fish, salad, and a piece of bread. But only a little piece of bread! This means fourteen hundred calories. If I eat normally, I eat three thousand calories. Easy!"

Pavarotti was pleased with his performance the previous night, but he was still smarting from the accumulation of bad publicity over the past couple of years. "I think this is particularly an attitude of today's world," he said. "They are not interested if something is very nice. They want to say something very bad. They want to see a massacre, like in Waco. If people live in a monastery and stay there and just pray to God, nobody cares. People ask what I will do next to extend myself. I have really done everything possible. We have done four performances of *Otello*, four performances of *Pagliacci*, a beautiful recording of *Manon Lescaut*—these three are the most dramatic operas of the entire Italian *repertorio*. 'Extend' is not the word. It is not possible. Last night, it was arias from *Aida*, *Tosca*, *Bohème*—different periods of a life of a singer. When a tenor is a lyric, abundant tenor, he can sing almost anything. He can sing *Elixir of Love*, all the most difficult arias for a light tenor. It all depends on how you treat the voice. If you treat it well, it stays with you a long time. There are tenors singing till the age of seventy, seventy-five. Things are easier for singers than they were," he went on. "You have better food, better medicine, better ways to travel. We did a concert two days ago in Germany. The day after, we woke up at seven, took a private plane from Dortmund to Paris—forty minutes. We took the Concorde here—three and a half hours. I slept one and a half hours. What can be better than that? It cannot be better than that. They talk about stress, but my profession is not work. My profession is pleasant. You suffer the preparation because you are not sure what is going to happen. That is a kind of necessary suffering. But to suffer because you have to sing is slightly ridiculous. When my daughter was seven, she thought I was a thief, because she never saw me work. For her, singing is not work. Probably she is right!"

Pavarotti's talk of pleasure, even ease, was a relief after all my reading about the self-lacerating lives of other singers. But it was still hard to believe. That morning, I had watched, for the twentieth time or so, a tape of Pavarotti singing "Nessun dorma" at the end of the "Three Tenors" concert. The tape provides a close-up that no audience member ever gets, and it reveals a physical exertion and fear of failure known at certain moments to aerialists, matadors, surgeons, soldiers. Just before the climax of the aria—the

B-natural scream—a look of terror sweeps across Pavarotti's huge, sweating face. His eyes bulge, his jaw squares, and then, at the precise moment when he releases the final note—a direct hit—the eyes betray not pleasure but the most exquisite sense of relief. He has done it again. Another trip through the Puccini minefield.

As I recalled the moment, Pavarotti smiled and nodded indulgently. "Look, there are two kinds of singers," he said. "One who is doing everything very easily. The top note for him is like a—peanut! He just picks it off! And then there are the singers who have a little trouble with the top note, but they give you their heart. For me, personally, I like the singer who makes you feel something very important. The first kind comes out of the schools and they have all the pyrotechnics. So? So? I think you need a little effort. A cry. Pain. Something in there to make you think it is true—to the singer and to the audience. As for 'Nessun dorma,' this is an aria I have sung since I had a tiny little voice like that. So 'Nessun dorma' isn't difficult if you approach it with the maximum respect. You cannot be totally wild in this aria. You must think. The most important thing is to make the phrasing true and at the end make the top, because there is the scream, 'Vincerò!'—'I will win!' It's a real scream! The top in an aria is generally a cry or sound of happiness. But in this there is all the hope of a man. So that is why the people, when they hear this aria, they love it. 'I will win!' I will win in life, I will win in love, I will win in work, I will win in every little thing. In the morning, when you hear this aria you are thrilled. It is the hope of man translated into a piece of music. In the opera, it is a man who will die if he does not win."

———•———

Ten days later, after a quick trip home to Modena and a concert in Monte Carlo, Pavarotti returns to New York. On the morning of May 14th, he rides to City Hall to take part in a press conference with Mayor Dinkins announcing that he will give a free concert in Central Park on June 26th. The concert, with a full orchestra and the Harlem Boys Choir, will be broadcast live on PBS; the next day, it will be shown around the world. One may fairly expect the full package: compact disk, laser disk, videocassette, et al.

Pavarotti sits patiently through the speeches at City Hall. He mugs for the cameras once in a while. But he seems down, worse than in Singapore. A cold is plaguing him again. After the press conference, the caravan heads for LaGuardia, where a private plane is waiting on the runway. There will be a concert the next night at Philadelphia's Spectrum arena, the cavernous home of the 76ers and the Flyers. Breslin, as always, is near his man. "I like to be in his eyesight," he says. Once the plane is aloft, a flight attendant comes around with huge plates of sandwiches, fruit, sweets of all kinds. Pavarotti nibbles a little fruit. He is trying to be good. He has to. His dietitian, an elegant Frenchwoman named Marie-Pierre Grenier, is sitting nearby and keeping watch. Breslin pretends not to care less. "Hey, Luciano!" he shouts. "Peanut butter cookies! Mmmm!"

Someone else tucks into the chocolate-dipped strawberries.

Pavarotti winces, operatically.

Grenier's previous employment was the care and feeding of the leading soccer team of Marseilles. "But this is an adventure," she says. "I lose weight, and Luciano, I hope, he loses weight, too. He goes into the bathroom and weighs himself. He won't let me see the scales. He comes out and says, 'Two more kilos!' I hope he is right." Later, she says, "Luciano has the *cafard*, the blues. I ask him in the morning, 'How are you?' He says, 'Fine,' and I say, 'It's not true,' and he smiles. He says, 'How did you know?'"

———— • ————

In Philadelphia, Pavarotti mostly stays in his room, making phone calls and eating the meals dictated by Marie-Pierre Grenier.

Downstairs, just a few hours before the concert, Breslin sits down to a plate of cookies and a pot of coffee at the hotel café and picks up the narrative where he had abandoned it in Singapore. How things really took off when he started working together with Tibor Rudas, formerly of Resorts International in Las Vegas and Atlantic City, putting together concerts in sports arenas and stadiums. "He came to me with the idea of presenting Luciano, and I paid him no attention at first. He says I threw him out of my office. Not true. But close."

Once the coffee is drained, Breslin goes up to Pavarotti's suite, on the ninth floor. Judy Kovacs opens the door. The suite has about it a crepuscular gloom. Scattered all around, like cracked eggs, are open, half-packed bags. Pavarotti sits on the couch, taking calls. His leg is propped on the coffee table, and there is a bag of ice on his knee, a scarf the size of a sheet draped over his belly. He nods solemnly, like a man getting bad news. Finished, he turns to Breslin, and he does not smile. Their brief conversation ends unpleasantly and Breslin knows not to push it. He backs out of the room and closes the door—carefully, the better not to disturb his man.

Pavarotti seems awfully down, not like a man who has to sing "Vesti la giubba" for Philadelphia in two hours, I say after a while.

Breslin smiles darkly. "Look," he says. "There's Luciano Pavarotti the artist and there's Luciano Pavarotti the man. It's two different things, and as a man he is facing the problems of getting older, with all that implies. And there is not a damn thing I, or anyone else, can do for him. Look, I feel it, too. We'll all feel it. I wish I were thirty-five years younger. I hate getting older. They say, 'Oh, it's not how old or young you are, it's how you feel.' Yeah, bullshit. I'm going to be sixty-nine in October, and I hate it. I hate getting older. I'm a basket case."

A little while later, Breslin and I are sitting together in the front row of the Spectrum waiting for the concert to begin. The houselights dim. Pavarotti comes out, he spreads his arms, and, like a child told to smile once for the camera, he smiles. I thought his face would crack in two. The place explodes. He sings. The acoustics are roughly the same as those of the Lincoln Tunnel. Between the sound and the cold, it is not much of a performance. After the encore arias, from *Manon Lescaut*, hundreds of people start calling for "Nessun dorma."

"He won't do it," Breslin says. "He's working too hard."

Pavarotti thanks the crowd and walks off. Behind the stage, a security man in an electric cart meets him and drives him the fifty yards or so to his dressing room. The houselights go up. We are left silent, blinking.

"He's right," Breslin says. "No 'Nessun dorma.' He shouldn't do it."

———•———

After the show, Pavarotti sat in his dressing room signing autographs and icing his knee. Considering his mood and the cold, he might have been better off canceling. "Some people do in these conditions, but I can't," he said later. "To send home ten thousand people is not fair. There are people who fly in, they stay at a hotel. They've seen you on video. They have the records. How do you cancel?"

After signing posters, programs, matchbooks, and casts for an hour and a half, Pavarotti went back to the hotel. Tibor Rudas's people set out steam plates filled with shrimp and lobster and called it a celebration of Rudas's hundredth concert with Pavarotti. It was a clumsy affair—one of those parties where the band's practiced cheer only highlights the gloom of the guest of honor. People were standing around in quiet little clumps. Pavarotti shimmied for a while on the dance floor and waited for the party to get better.

One of the tour workers came over to me and said quietly, "Please don't stand. He wants people sitting around him."

Breslin and I left the party at about midnight and started the drive to New York. "There's just nothing going on in music," he said, turning to a favorite, desperate theme. "No one really commands your attention the way they did. I mean, just try and give me a cast these days for *Macbeth*. You can't! Give me a cast for *La Bohème*. For *Aida*. These are the days of medium. The greatness is just not there. The last time it was there was in the mid-sixties, in the last years when Rudolf Bing was running the Met. Look who could sing, say, *Tosca*. Maria Callas. Renata Tebaldi. Leontyne Price. Birgit Nilsson. Régine Crespin. Leonie Resinek. Or the tenors. Jon Vickers. Franco Corelli. Richard Tucker. You just can't find anyone like that now. The whole opera company system is dead. There aren't even any coaches around. A discerning audience barely exists anymore."

What did Pavarotti have left in him?, I asked.

"I think Luciano might give up opera on the stage in a year or two and just do concerts," Breslin said. "One thing I'm pretty sure of: he doesn't want to learn anything new. He's just gone through learning *Otello* and *Don Carlo*. There's a new production of *I Lombardi* at the Met in the fall, and he's just recorded *Manon Lescaut*. Just concerts: I think that's in the cards. I had hoped he'd do *Otello* on the stage, but now I doubt that will ever happen."

———•———

If and when Pavarotti leaves the opera house for good, the moment of extinction will have come: the last of the Italian tenors. Or, so they say. I went to see Pavarotti one more time a couple of days after the Philadelphia concert, and his mood had been transformed once again. The cold was fading. He would hear nothing of retirement. There was the Central Park concert to think about, *I Lombardi* to study, and, in the fall, the twenty-fifth anniversary of his and Domingo's debuts at the Metropolitan.

"That was probably the program, to stop singing opera in 1995 and just do concerts maybe once a week and enjoy the life, enjoy the weekend," he said. "But this was a man thirty pounds heavier than now and feeling very bad in the knee. Now it is totally different. You are talking to a different person. My project is in a year or two to go back to playing tennis and get back to the stage without having any pain or needing supports here and there. Coming home from Philadelphia, I was thinking to myself that if my body feels good, like now or even better, I think I want to do something new on the stage. I have a couple of operas in mind. I don't have the courage to say which. Basically, you start out an opera singer and you like being one. All the entourage is around. The orchestra, the colleagues, the makeup people, the stage director, the conductor. I like that. So I want to keep making operas. My father is eighty years old, and he called me wishing me the best and told me he had just sung 'Ave Maria' in church. He has a beautiful voice, a fantastic instrument, even now. So why not?"

Pavarotti saw me out. He was leaning heavily on the door and watching the numbers on the elevator rise. He smiled, the better to mask his impatience. When the little bell rang, he said another goodbye and closed the door.

June 1993

Luciano Pavarotti died on September 6, 2007.

RESTLESS FAREWELL

In 1956, rock and roll was busy being born. Ike Turner and the Kings of Rhythm had broken through five years earlier with a jump-blues hit called "Rocket 88"—a credible candidate for the ur rock tune—but crooners and big band acts lingered on the pop charts. Elvis scored a No. 1 *Billboard* hit with "Heartbreak Hotel"; Nelson Riddle and His Orchestra did, too, with "Lisbon Antigua." But kids knew what spoke to them, and it wasn't "Lisbon Antigua." Robert Zimmerman, a pompadoured fifteen-year-old living in the Minnesota Iron Range town of Hibbing, was one of countless kids who went out and put together a rock-and-roll band. He called his the Shadow Blasters.

In his childhood and adolescence, he stayed up through the night, his head by the radio, absorbing everything being broadcast from nearby Duluth and from fifty-thousand-watt stations throughout the Midwest and the Deep South: R&B, gospel, jazz, blues, and rock and roll. He was fascinated, as well, with the storytelling tricks and aural mysteries of radio dramas such as *The Fat Man* and *Inner Sanctum*. "It made me the listener that I am today," he told an interviewer many decades later. "It made me listen for little things: the slamming of the door, the jingling of car keys. The wind blowing through trees, the songs of birds, footsteps, a hammer hitting a nail. Just random sounds. Cows mooing. I could string all that together and make that a song. It made me listen to life in a different way."

As he was rehearsing with the Shadow Blasters, the most thrilling song on the air was "Tutti Frutti," sung by a flamboyant piano player from Macon, Georgia, who had once gone by the name Princess Lavonne and now performed as Little Richard. And what Zimmerman was hearing he wanted to make his own. His father ran an appliance store in town and kept an old piano in the back. When Bobby was supposed to be sweeping the floor or stocking the shelves, he was trying out hand-splaying boogie-woogie chords on the piano instead.

On April 5, 1957, the Shadow Blasters played at a variety show organized by their school's student council—Bobby Zimmerman's debut. "He started singing in his Little Richard style, screaming, pounding the piano," his friend John Bucklen recalled. "My first impression was that of embarrassment, because the little community of Hibbing, Minnesota, way up there, was unaccustomed to such a performance."

The Shadow Blasters soon broke up—high school bands are as ephemeral as mayflies—and Zimmerman formed another group, the Golden Chords. He and his friends had fun playing Van Feldt's snack bar and Collier's barbecue joint, covering songs by Elvis, Jimmy Reed, and, always, Little Richard. But it was soon clear, as he put it later, that he'd been born in the wrong place. He was a middle-class Jewish kid far from everything he was tuned in to. He would need to leave town, change his name, and deepen his musical education to fulfill his outsized sense of destiny.

First in Dinkytown, the collegiate section of Minneapolis, then in Greenwich Village, Zimmerman, adopting the name Bob Dylan, shifted his attention away from rock and roll. He immersed himself in the vast lexicon of folk music and the blues: Woody Guthrie, Robert Johnson, and the Dixie Hummingbirds; Odetta, Blind Lemon Jefferson, and the Staple Singers; the Stanley Brothers, the Delmore Brothers, and the Five Blind Boys of Alabama. Sometimes music further afield, such as "Pirate Jenny," from *The Threepenny Opera*, caught his attention and fed his musical vocabulary. His hunger for the music was boundless, even larcenous. Ask the friends whose records he stole. Playing guitar now more than piano, he memorized the chord progressions, picking patterns, and lyrics for hundreds of songs: hillbilly songs, cowboy songs, traditional English and Scottish ballads, sea chanteys, church hymns, ragtime, barrelhouse, every variation of the blues. He was reading, too—Kerouac's *Mexico City Blues*, Ginsberg's *Howl*, Homer, Keats, Shelley, Blake, Rimbaud. The Hit Parade could wait. "The thing about rock and roll is that for me, anyway, it wasn't enough," he said later. " 'Tutti Frutti' and 'Blue Suede Shoes' were great catchphrases and driving pulse rhythms . . . but they weren't serious or didn't reflect life in a realistic way. I knew that when I got into folk music, it was more of a serious type of thing. The songs are filled with more despair, more sadness, more triumph, more faith in the supernatural, much deeper feelings."

In the Village, Dylan apprenticed himself to older coffeehouse denizens like Dave Van Ronk and Ramblin' Jack Elliott (both born in the Dust Bowl province of Brooklyn). He studied Alan Lomax's field recordings and Harry Smith's *Anthology of American Folk Music*. He played on any stage that would have him and quickly developed a persona that was a melding of Okie troubadour, Beat poet, and Charlie Chaplin. "For three or four years, all I listened to were folk standards," Dylan once said. "I went to sleep singing folk songs. I sang them everywhere: clubs, parties, bars, coffeehouses, fields, festivals. And I met other singers along the way who did the same thing and we just learned songs from each other. I could learn one song and sing it next in an hour if I'd heard it just once."

For all his earnest apprenticeship, not to mention the brazen theft of this one's version of "House of the Rising Sun" or that one's field hand intonation, he was becoming something distinctly original. Like Walt Whitman, Annie Oakley, Gorgeous George, or Little Richard, he was doing that very American thing: inventing a public, performing self. And he was getting noticed. In September 1961, Robert Shelton, of *The New York Times*, wrote a brief review of Dylan's run at Gerde's Folk City: "There is no doubt that he is bursting at the seams with talent."

Dylan was twenty years old. Not long after his nights at Gerde's, he signed a contract with John Hammond, an unerring talent spotter at Columbia Records, and began work on his first album. It came out in March 1962 and consisted mostly of covers. A significant exception was "Song to Woody," which was both an homage to Dylan's dying idol and the announcement of his own intention to carry the music into the future:

> Hey, hey Woody Guthrie I wrote you a song,
> 'Bout a funny ol' world that's a-comin' along,
> Seems sick and it's hungry, it's tired and it's torn,
> It looks like it's a-dyin' and it's hardly been born.

What happened next represents one of the great explosions of creativity in the twentieth century. Dylan wrote song after song in a kind of fever dream that lasted until 1966. "The best songs to me—my best songs—are songs which were written very quickly," he said. "Just about as much time as it takes to write it down is about as long as it takes to write it." He claimed it took him ten minutes to write "Blowin' in the Wind," a political anthem that borrowed from the tune of a spiritual called "No More Auction Block for Me." He merged the form of a seventeenth-century ballad, "Lord Randall," with the ominous weather of cold war confrontation to write "A Hard Rain's A-Gonna Fall."

Sometimes typing furiously, sometimes scrawling lyrics on envelopes and cocktail napkins, he seemed to be an antenna of the zeitgeist. He was capable of writing three songs in one day. There was no accounting for the originality of the songs or the speed with which they kept coming: "Mr. Tambourine Man," "The Times They Are A-Changin'," "The Lonesome Death of Hattie Carroll," "To Ramona," "It's Alright, Ma (I'm Only Bleeding)," "Don't Think Twice, It's All Right," "Highway 61 Revisited," "Subterranean Homesick Blues," "Desolation Row," "Like a Rolling Stone," "Just Like a Woman," "Visions of Johanna." There were narratives, comedies, epics, and romances, some earthbound, some surreal, and they arrived with an expanding sense of ambition. In no time at all, he had progressed from "Talkin' Hava Negeilah Blues" to "Sad Eyed Lady of the Lowlands."

Many fans had a hard time keeping up; some didn't want to. Folk purists, especially, resented his unwillingness to stay within bounds. During a tour of the United Kingdom, in the spring of 1966, he was applauded for his opening acoustic set but then booed—every night!—when he came out with an electric guitar and members of the Hawks (later, the Band).

One night, in Liverpool, a spectator shouted, "Where's the poet in you? Where's the savior?"

Dylan was having none of it. "There's a fellow up there looking for the savior, huh?" he replied. "The savior's backstage, we have a picture of him."

But defiance was not enough. Dylan was struggling. Drugged up, worn down, razor thin, he was on the edge of a breakdown. In London, after the last show on the tour, John, Paul, George, and Ringo dropped by his hotel room. Dylan was too depleted to see them.

He was particularly weary of being a symbol, "the voice of his generation." All his attempts to deflect, to joke his way through press conferences, to mock the requests for sage advice ("Keep a good head and always carry a light bulb"), his determination to lie to journalists and would-be biographers, telling them he'd been a runaway street hustler, not a bar mitzvah boy, only heightened the mystique. And that mystique came to be untenable. Dylan had wanted to succeed Woody. He could accept being Elvis. But he sure as hell knew he couldn't survive being a prophet. "Whatever the counterculture was, I'd seen enough of it," he later wrote. "I was sick of the way my lyrics had been extrapolated, their meanings subverted into polemics and that I had been anointed the Big Bubba of Rebellion, High Priest of Protest, the Czar of Dissent, the Duke of Disobedience, Leader of the Freeloaders, Kaiser of Apostasy, Archbishop of Anarchy, the Big Cheese."

In the summer of 1966, Dylan retreated to a house in Woodstock, New York, with his wife, Sara Lownds, and their children. One afternoon, he went out for a ride on his motorcycle, lost control, fell, and broke several vertebrae. He took the accident as a sign that he should prolong his retreat. "Truth was that I wanted to get out of the rat race," he wrote. "Having children changed my life and segregated me from just about everybody and everything that was going on." The foremost symbol of the sixties, the High Priest of Protest, more or less sat out the rest of the decade, making very few public appearances. He even skipped the biggest hullabaloo of all, the Woodstock festival, which took place just an hour and a half up the road from him. Dylan did not tour again for eight years.

———•———

More than half a century has passed. Dylan is eighty-one, still writing, recording, and performing on what's long been known as the Never-Ending Tour. He is an object of study. A Dylan museum in Tulsa is now open to scholars and visitors. There are countless books about him—books focused on Hibbing or the Village or his influences, on particular albums, phases, and songs. Christopher Ricks, a distinguished scholar of Victorian and modernist poetry, wrote a treatise that takes Dylan's prosody as seriously as that of Tennyson or Eliot. Michael Gray has published three editions of his enormous study *Song & Dance Man*, as well as *The Bob Dylan Encyclopedia*. There's a book called *The Dylanologists*, about the hardy crew of fanatics who make the pilgrimage to the Iron Range, cruise by the singer's Point Dume compound in Malibu, and vacuum up scraps and ephemera in pursuit of . . . clues.

If you've got the bug, you've got it bad. Recently, I've read memoirs by Louie Kemp, Dylan's buddy from summer camp, and Suze Rotolo, an artist from a left-wing family, who was Dylan's girlfriend in his Village days and the inspiration for "Tomorrow Is a Long Time," "Boots of Spanish Leather," and other lasting songs. There are many biographies. Two early ones, by Robert Shelton and Anthony Scaduto, are filled with the juicy fruits of access, and Clinton Heylin's *Behind the Shades* is a work of heavy industry. But none of them are quite worthy of the subject on a musical or historical level—there's nothing comparable to, say, Peter Guralnick's two volumes on Elvis Presley or Maynard Solomon's life of Mozart.

The critical explorations have been ceaseless, from Ellen Willis's 1967 essay in the magazine *Cheetah* on the tension between the public and the private Dylan to Greg Tate's assertion thirty-four years later in *The Village Voice* that Dylan's "impact on a couple generations of visionary black bards has rarely been given its propers." The most interesting writer on Dylan over the years has been the cultural critic Greil Marcus, who has written innumerable essays about the singer and the songs, including a book-length study of "Like a Rolling Stone." No one alive knows the music that fueled Dylan's imagination better. Marcus just published *Folk Music: A Bob Dylan Biography in Seven Songs*. It's another ingenious book of close listening, but, as Marcus would be the first to say, it is not in any standard sense the full life story.

Early on, Dylan seemed to decide that, if he couldn't make sense of his career, he would make sure that no one else could, either. He wasn't about to be both artist and critic. In D. A. Pennebaker's 1967 documentary, *Don't Look Back*, Dylan, in his youthful wise-ass mode, is captured in conversation with an earnest middle-aged writer from *Time*, the dominant midcult magazine of the era. "I got nothing to say about these things I write," he informs the interviewer. "I don't write them for any reason. There's no great message. I mean, if, you know, you wanna tell other people that, go ahead and tell them, but I'm not going to have to answer to it."

One reason that Dylan might be suspicious of biographers at this point is that he is suspicious of his own memory—of any attempt, in fact, to recall the past with accuracy. In Martin Scorsese's recent semi-fictional documentary about the gloriously shambolic Rolling Thunder Revue tour, Dylan starts out gamely answering questions about the events of 1975, until he breaks off and starts laughing at his own "clumsy bullshit": "I'm trying to get to the core of what this Rolling Thunder thing is all about and I don't have a clue! . . . I don't remember a thing about Rolling Thunder! I mean, it happened so long ago, I wasn't even born."

For years, there were rumors that Dylan was planning to tell his story himself. As an editor, I used to check in periodically with David Rosenthal, a former journalist who ran the publishing house Simon & Schuster, and who had a Dylan memoir under contract. In 2004, Rosenthal finally called and said, "I've got a manuscript."

Rosenthal told me I should also connect with Jeff Rosen, a friendly and musically erudite guy who had been running Dylan's publishing, licensing, and other business concerns since the mid-eighties. I asked Rosen if I could read the manuscript. Maybe he could send it along?

Nothing doing. "I can't let the manuscript out of my office," Rosen said. He gave me an address and said I could come by to read it.

The next morning, I arrived at a commercial building near Gramercy Park. The buzzer at the door was not marked "Dylan Office." Instead, in the manner of a CIA front, it was called something like XYZ Carpets. A rickety elevator took me up to a huge newsroom-like space crammed with albums, tapes, disks, posters, T-shirts, jackets, books, endless Dylan stuff. I'd been listening to Dylan since stumbling on a compilation album called *The Best of '66* as a kid. "I Want You," from the *Blonde on Blonde* album, came just after John Davidson's "You Don't Have to Say You Love Me." I didn't understand a word of "I Want You"—not on the level of language or desire—but that voice! I was hooked. For a long time, everything I cared about, every book or song, somehow came out of this obsession. So, if you had told me when I was fifteen that I could take up residence at the Dylan office and never leave, I wouldn't have hesitated.

Rosen, tall and lean, led me to a small room where shelves were lined with Dylan books: biographies, songbooks, criticism, encyclopedias. There was a chair and a table, bare except for a stack of manuscript pages. "Take your time," Rosen said, and left me alone with *Chronicles: Volume One.*

Like all good Dylan fanatics, I'd read his 1971 book, *Tarantula,* a bewildering prose piece influenced by his reading of Rimbaud, Comte de Lautréamont, and the Beats. It had some of the same larkish spirit as John Lennon's *In His Own Write,* but I haven't been tempted to read it again. The anxiety among Dylanologists was that *Chronicles* would be *Tarantula Redux.* It wasn't. As I read the opening chapter, about Dylan's arrival in New York, I saw that this was the real thing—echt Bob, and yet a relatively straightforward narrative, not a musically inflected version of *A Season in Hell* or *Visions of Cody.*

He was writing now in the plainspoken mode of Woody Guthrie's *Bound for Glory*, telling a story of self-creation. Though flecked with debatable details, it was a credible portrayal of his musical and sentimental education, with recollections of his first winter in the city, of the folk scene in the Village, and of listening to and learning from everyone from the Clancy Brothers to Carolyn Hester to the New Lost City Ramblers. His hunger for American music and his urge to master the tradition reminded me of W. H. Auden's habit of sitting on a volume of the *Oxford English Dictionary*, the better to raise his sights and absorb the language whole.

I stayed on my seat, too, reading the manuscript straight through, no breaks. Once I was done, I dropped by Rosen's office and, trying to keep it casual, said that I was eager to publish an excerpt. After a few more conversations, Rosenthal and Rosen said they would let *The New Yorker* run five or six thousand words a few weeks before the book's publication. We all agreed that we'd be in touch sometime before that in order to square things away: fact-checking, copy editing, and so on. I was delighted.

Late that summer, Rosenthal called to say that the book would be published soon. Were we ready? We certainly were.

"One last thing, though," he said.

"What's that?"

"Bob wants the cover."

"What do you mean?"

"Bob wants the cover. Of the magazine."

"David, you told me that Bob *loves* the magazine. We don't have celebrities on the cover. We don't even have *photographs* on the cover!"

Rosenthal paused. Then he said, "Bob wants a cover."

I got the message.

"So, David, what am I supposed to do?"

"If we don't get the cover, I think we're going to take the excerpt to *Newsweek*."

That stung. A music magazine I might have understood. But *Newsweek?*

"Seriously? There's a presidential election going on"—Bush versus Kerry. "They're going to put Bob Dylan on the cover four weeks before the election?"

"That's what they promised."

I'd been careless. We had only a vague agreement. And so that was that. Dylan appeared on the cover of the October 4, 2004, issue of *Newsweek*. By then he was in his mid-sixties and looked like Vincent Price wearing Hank Williams's clothes: pencil mustache, white Stetson, and cowboy suit. I had other unkind thoughts. But what was the point?

More than a year later, I got a call from Jeff Rosen. "Bob's got a new album," he said. "We wondered if you want to hear it."

There was no use in relitigating the past. And, yes, I wanted to hear it.

"Sure," I said. "Can you send over a disk?"

"Can't do that. Come hear it at the studio."

I went over to a recording studio on the West Side. Someone put me in a room with an armchair between two speakers. I sat there alone and waited in silence for a few minutes, and then the album, *Modern Times*, came roaring out. What struck me then, and still does, is that Dylan seemed to realize that he would never again recover what he once called the "thin, wild mercury sound" of the mid-sixties. In his maturity, he continued to write lyrics of great imagination, but the music, the song forms, were no longer breakthroughs. He wasn't inventing contemporary music; he was revisiting the past, making it his own, showing his love. And so, on *Modern Times*, there's "Thunder on the Mountain," which plays with a Memphis Minnie tune called "Ma Rainey"; there's "Rollin' and Tumblin'," which is a Hambone Willie Newbern tune made famous by Muddy Waters; there's "Ain't Talkin'," which takes bits and pieces from an Irish folk song and a Stanley Brothers tune. The

album is filled with tributes, quotations, and inspired reinterpreta-
tions of moments in Jimmy Kennedy, Bing Crosby, June Christy,
and even James Lord Pierpont, who, in 1857, wrote "The One-
Horse Open Sleigh," better known as "Jingle Bells." Dylan detec-
tives soon discovered that he had adapted some lines from Henry
Timrod, a nineteenth-century South Carolinian whom Tennyson
supposedly referred to as "the poet laureate of the South."

That's the way creativity works, Dylan told Robert Hilburn, of
the *Los Angeles Times*. You're always writing into a tradition. "My
songs are either based on old Protestant hymns or Carter Family
songs or variations of the blues form," he said. "What happens is,
I'll take a song I know and simply start playing it in my head. That's
the way I meditate . . . I'll be playing Bob Nolan's 'Tumbling Tum-
bleweeds,' for instance, in my head constantly—while I'm driving a
car or talking to a person or sitting around or whatever. People will
think they are talking to me and I'm talking back, but I'm not. I'm
listening to a song in my head. At a certain point, some of the words
will change and I'll start writing a song."

———•———

The parts that readers enjoy most in *Chronicles*—the bits that I'd
hoped to run in the magazine—are about his becoming Bob Dylan,
the Village years. What's curious is that, in a moment of pure Bob-
ness, he then skips over most of his early fame. In a sixteen-month
period, between March 1965 and June 1966, he put out three of
the greatest albums of the era: *Bringing It All Back Home*, *Highway
61 Revisited*, and *Blonde on Blonde*. We never hear about that period,
much less his reemergence from Woodstock, the collapse of his marriage, and the making of a masterpiece, *Blood on the Tracks*, in 1974.
Instead, *Chronicles* goes deep into precisely that period which most
fans would just as soon forget, the low point of Dylan's creativity—

the mid- and late-nineteen-eighties, when he was ready to give it all up.

"I felt done for, an empty burned-out wreck," Dylan wrote. "Too much static in my head and I couldn't dump the stuff. Wherever I am, I'm a '60s troubadour, a folk-rock relic, a wordsmith from bygone days, a fictitious head of state from a place nobody knows. I'm in the bottomless pit of cultural oblivion. You name it. I can't shake it."

Dylan toured with Tom Petty and the Heartbreakers in 1986 and with the Grateful Dead in 1987, and though the concerts raked in plenty of money and he had a great sense of kinship with both bands, he felt distanced from his own work and struggled to write anything of consequence: "It wasn't my moment of history anymore. There was a hollow singing in my heart and I couldn't wait to retire and fold the tent . . . The glow was gone and the match had burned right to the end. I was going through the motions."

Even in this relatively fallow period, Dylan wrote songs that were among his finest: "I and I," "Dark Eyes," "Ring Them Bells," "Man in the Long Black Coat." A song like "Blind Willie McTell," in particular, hinted at what was to come, with Dylan's gaze peering into the deep musical past. But his most ardent fans would have to admit that the albums of that period were spotty and the concerts, too often, were lackluster. On any given night, his attention might wander; the performances could be rote. Some point to "Wiggle Wiggle," on the 1990 album *Under the Red Sky*, as an artistic nadir, though that wasn't a parlor game Dylan was prepared to tolerate. "You know, no matter what anyone says, I have written my share," he said. "If I never write another song, no one will ever fault me." And, of course, he was right.

In the early fifties, Randall Jarrell published a review of *The Auroras of Autumn*, Wallace Stevens's last collection of poems. Jarrell finds the late work to be inferior to what Stevens had collected in

Harmonium, which had appeared almost three decades earlier. But Jarrell doesn't chastise the poet for the decline; he asks that we see it as natural. "How necessary it is to think of the poet as somebody who has prepared himself to be visited by a dæmon," Jarrell wrote, "as a sort of accident-prone worker to whom poems happen—for otherwise we *expect* him to go on writing good poems, better poems, and this is the one thing you cannot expect even of good poets, much less of anybody else." Stevens followed the familiar pattern of self-imitation, Jarrell wrote in his review, and yet the emphasis fell not on the failures of the late career but on the miracle that a phenomenon like Stevens happened at all: "A good poet is someone who manages, in a lifetime of standing out in thunderstorms, to be struck by lightning five or six times; a dozen or two dozen times and he is great."

The point is that, if Dylan had died of his injuries in Woodstock, he still would have left behind the richest catalog of American songs of his era. At twenty-five, he could have declared himself retired, younger in age than Jimi Hendrix, Janis Joplin, and Otis Redding were when they died. Yet what makes Dylan so extraordinary is that the end of his early incandescence didn't mark a sustained falling off. Since that brush with self-extinction and death-by-motorcycle, he has made more than thirty albums—all of them interesting, and many of them containing songs that rank among his best. It's the pace that's different.

"There was a time when the songs would come three or four at the same time, but those days are long gone," he told Hilburn. "Once in a while, the odd song will come to me like a bulldog at the garden gate and demand to be written. But most of them are rejected out of my mind right away. You get caught up in wondering if anyone really needs to hear it. Maybe a person gets to the point where they have written enough songs. Let someone else write them."

———•———

The first time I saw Dylan was in 1974, when he made his comeback with the Band. They toured behind a good album—*Planet Waves*—and then he went out and recorded one of his greatest, *Blood on the Tracks*. At concerts ever since, the casual fans—the ones who have Dylan pegged as an "icon," a figure of the past—come to the hall hoping that he will sing "Like a Rolling Stone" or "Tangled Up in Blue" just the way they remember it from the records. Precisely because Dylan has continued to develop as an artist, they are invariably disappointed. The tempos have changed. Dylan's voice has changed. Even the lyrics differ from night to night. You never know what you're going to get. (In 1980, during his "born-again" phase, audiences got to hear Dylan, ordinarily as reticent as the Sphinx onstage, deliver apocalyptic sermons between gospel songs about the battle between the Antichrist and the Lord Jesus Christ.) Those casual fans wonder why he can't be more like the Stones, unfailing jukeboxes of their earlier selves. They want to squint and see the young Dylan, with his Pre-Raphaelite hair and his Brando sneer. They want, at least for an hour and a half, a magic act: a man in his eighties who is a man in his youth.

There are some older performers who are able to pull off a worthy form of compromise with their audiences. Bruce Springsteen knows well that, at least on some level, his fans want him circa 1978, a performer determined to drive himself to the point of abandon, a Jersey guy singing about freeing himself from the grip of the nuns and family misery, finding love, and taking it on the road. The bargain, for Springsteen, his magic act, is that he'll stay in shape, he'll move like a younger man, and he will sing you those hits, but he'll also salt the performance with newer songs, about parenthood, aging, mortality—the work that interests him now. Everyone goes home happy.

Dylan is scarcely resistant to his role as an entertainer. When he last performed in the city, a year ago, he played a smattering of old favorites—"Watching the River Flow," "When I Paint My Masterpiece," "I'll Be Your Baby Tonight"—and he occasionally seemed to be having a good time. He'd grab the mike like an old-style crooner, cock a hip like Elvis, and even pause to make a joke worthy of Henny Youngman. But otherwise it was serious business. The concert was called for eight o'clock, and that's when he took the stage. If you were five minutes late, it was like being at the opera; the ushers held you back from your seat until there was a break in the action. And he did what he came to do: he played nearly every song on his most recent album, the distinctly elegiac *Rough and Rowdy Ways*. For a long time now, Dylan has played piano rather than guitar, and, like a lot of performers these days, he doesn't depend on memory for the lyrics. Most have teleprompters. Dylan leans over and sings off lyric sheets. You can hardly blame him. He's older than Joe Biden, and the songs are often long. In the Whitmanesque "I Contain Multitudes," Dylan sings about the multiplicity of selves in him, in anyone, and provides a litany of the voices, from Anne Frank to William Blake, from Poe to the Stones, that have haunted his imagination:

> You greedy old wolf, I'll show you my heart
> But not all of it, only the hateful part,
> I'll sell you down the river, I'll put a price on your head,
> What more can I tell you? I sleep with life and death in the same
> bed.

Dylan is hardly immune to the pink Cadillac. In fact, he's done ads for Cadillac—along with Chrysler, IBM, and Victoria's Secret. He's got a line of bourbon and rye whiskeys on the market called Heaven's Door, which he went on *The Tonight Show* to promote. Not long ago he sold off his catalog for hundreds of millions of dollars, and now he's in the NFT business. But filthy lucre has not slowed him down. He doesn't stand in the same place for very long. Eighty-one and still at it. Why? Or, better, how?

———•———

Which leads us to my unified field theory of Bob Dylan. The theory isn't especially complicated, or even novel. Greil Marcus has been pressing the case for years, and Dylan himself, always typed as "enigmatic" and "elusive," has been trying to make these matters clear to us all along. In order to stave off creative exhaustion and intimations of mortality, Dylan has, over and over again, returned to what fed him in the first place—the vast tradition of American song. Anytime he has been in trouble, he's been able to rely on that bottomless source. When he was in Woodstock, recuperating and hiding from the world, he got together with the Band, in the basement of a house known as Big Pink, and played folk songs: folk songs they remembered, and folk songs they made up. That was *The Basement Tapes*. When he was struggling again, twenty-five years later, he recorded two albums of folk and blues standards—*Good as I Been to You* and *World Gone Wrong*—and four years after that he emerged, reenergized and backed by extraordinary musicians, to issue a string of highly original albums, *Time Out of Mind*, *Love and Theft*, *Modern Times*, and *Together Through Life*. Many of the songs were about mortality, just as they were on the album he recorded when he was twenty and singing "See That My Grave Is Kept Clean." But now they were felt on a deeper level. Shortly before *Time Out of Mind* was released, in 1997, Dylan heard a pounding on Heaven's door—a heart ailment, pericarditis, which forced him to cancel a European tour and consider, once more, the end. "I really thought I'd be seeing Elvis soon," he said.

Dylan kept moving, even having fun. In 2009, he put out *Christmas in the Heart*. If you were stuck thinking of Dylan as a pure ironist, you were wrong; he sang Gene Autry's "Here Comes Santa Claus"—and made it his own—because he loved it. The record was all in the line of tradition: the Christmas albums of Ella Fitzgerald, Nat King Cole, Bing Crosby, and Elvis Presley. The same goes for what are known as his Sinatra albums—*Shadows in the Night*, *Fallen Angels*, and *Triplicate*—which featured Dylan paying tribute to the so-called American songbook. This shouldn't have been a surprise, either. Dylan loves Frank Sinatra, and the feeling was mutual. In 1995, at Sinatra's request, Dylan played his sunless yet defiant song "Restless Farewell" for the old man at a tribute concert. It's not hard to tell why the last verse would appeal to the guy who often closed his concerts with "My Way":

> Oh, a false clock tries to tick out my time,
> To disgrace, distract, and bother me,
> And the dirt of gossip blows into my face,
> And the dust of rumors covers me.
> But if the arrow is straight
> And the point is slick,
> It can pierce through dust no matter how thick.
> So I'll make my stand
> And remain as I am
> And bid farewell and not give a damn.

Those Sinatra standards replenished him and fed his imagination. They helped bring him to the songs on *Rough and Rowdy Ways*. They allowed him to keep forcing himself forward. Long past the pressure to be a voice of anything or anyone, he has released albums that, though deeply self-expressive, speak to and expand what Leonard Cohen called "the Tower of Song."

Dylan has replenished himself in other ways as well. From 2006 to 2009, he hosted *Theme Time Radio Hour*, a weekly program on satellite radio. With the help of a like-minded music nut, Eddie Gorodetsky, Dylan, aping the mannerisms, puns, and bromides of the DJs of his youth, proposed a theme for each program—blood, say, or money or mothers or flowers—and he'd intersperse songs with his Bobbed-out patter. The programs were hilarious, full of campy nostalgia. Most important, you got to hear the often forgotten music that helped form him in some way, like Buck Owens singing "I'll Go to Church Again with Momma," and "Kissing in the Dark," by Memphis Minnie. And, just to let you know the old guy was keeping up and had a broad sense of an expanding tradition, he threw in tracks from Prince and LL Cool J.

And now there's another exercise in engaging the tradition. Rather than follow the first volume of *Chronicles* with, you know, a second volume, Dylan has published a kind of extension of the radio show: a rich, riffy, funny, and completely engaging book of essays, *The Philosophy of Modern Song*. The cover photograph features Little Richard, Alis Lesley, and Eddie Cochran, and it's immediately apparent what you're in for: Dylan wandering through the enormous record bin of his mind. What he tries to get across is the feel of these songs, their atmosphere and internal life, though the general lack of women in the book is, at best, mystifying. It's at the end of his essay on Dion and the Belmonts' version of Rodgers and Hart's "Where or When" that Dylan makes everything clear:

> When Dion's voice bursts through for a solo moment in the bridge, it captures that moment of shimmering persistence of memory in a way the printed word can only hint at.
>
> But so it is with music, it is of a time but also timeless; a thing with which to make memories and the memory itself. Though we seldom consider it, music is built in time as surely as a sculptor or welder works in physical space. Music transcends time by living within it, just as reincarnation allows us to transcend life by living it again and again.

———•———

When Dylan won the Nobel Prize in Literature, in 2016, he got a lot of stick. The man wrote *songs*! But did he deserve the accolade? Leonard Cohen, one of his most literary contemporaries, had it right. Awarding Dylan the Nobel, he said, "is like pinning a medal on Mt. Everest for being the highest mountain."

What makes Dylan's career all the more remarkable is the way it has evolved, with peaks, declivities, crags—all in service to the music he began to revere in Hibbing. In his own way, he is reminiscent of Verdi, Monet, Yeats, O'Keeffe: a freak of creative longevity. Nicholas Delbanco writes about this phenomenon in *Lastingness: The Art of Old Age*; Delbanco's teacher John Updike wrote about it in his essay "Late Works," and exemplified it in the poems he wrote while dying of cancer in hospice care.

"I think that Bob Dylan knows this more than all of us—you don't write the songs anyhow," Cohen said in his last meeting with reporters. "Your own intentions have very little to do with this. You can keep the body as well-oiled and receptive as possible, but whether you're actually going to be able to go for the long haul is really not your own choice."

Genius doesn't owe explanations of itself. But perhaps the nearest Dylan came to explaining both his gift and its durability was in 2015, accepting an award from the charity MusiCares. Reading from a sheaf of papers in his hands, Dylan exploded the myth of sui generis brilliance.

"These songs didn't come out of thin air," he said. "I didn't just make them up out of whole cloth . . . It all came out of traditional music: traditional folk music, traditional rock and roll, and traditional big-band swing orchestra music . . . If you sang 'John Henry' as many times as me—'John Henry was a steel-driving man / Died with a hammer in his hand / John Henry said a man ain't nothin' but a man / Before I let that steam drill drive me down / I'll die with that hammer in my hand.' If you had sung that song as many times as I did, you'd have written 'How many roads must a man walk down?' too.

"All these songs are connected," he went on. "I just opened up a different door in a different kind of way . . . I thought I was just extending the line."

October 2022

VAGABOND

In the days and weeks after Donald Trump was elected president, it seemed hard to imagine that your spirits could go anywhere but down and down some more. And yet one night, cruising along the YouTube highway, I came across footage of the Nobel Prize ceremony that had just taken place in Stockholm. A few months earlier, Patti Smith had agreed to perform one of her own songs, but when it turned out that Bob Dylan had won the prize for literature she decided to sing one of his, "A Hard Rain's A-Gonna Fall." "From that moment, every spare moment was spent practicing it, making certain that I knew and could convey every line," she wrote later. "Having my own blue-eyed son, I sang the words to myself, over and over, in the original key, with pleasure and resolve. I had it in my mind to sing the song exactly as it was written and as well as I was capable of doing. I bought a new suit, I trimmed my hair, and felt that I was ready."

Smith had been a Dylan fan ever since her mother found *Another Side of Bob Dylan* and gave it to her as a gift. And Dylan, in his own way, had been a supporter of hers ever since they met at the Bitter End, in 1975. She was twenty-eight. Dylan was only five years older, though he had been globally famous for more than a decade. In those days, Smith wasn't about to reveal the outsized admiration she harbored for Dylan. He approached her backstage at the Bitter End after she'd performed. She was determined to appear unimpressed. "He came over to me and I kept moving around. We were like two pit bulls circling," she recalled. "I was a snot-nose. I had a very high concentration of adrenaline. He said to me, 'Any poets around here?' And I said, 'I don't like poetry anymore. Poetry sucks!'" Which was a nervous lie; Smith was immersed in the poems and ill-fated life of Arthur Rimbaud. As she grew older and an affecting sincerity replaced reflexive contempt, she was embarrassed about that initial encounter with Dylan: "I really acted like a jerk. I thought: That guy will never talk to me again. And the day after there was this picture on the cover of *The Village Voice*. The photographer had Dylan put his arm around me. It was a really cool picture. It was a dream come true, but it reminded me of how I had acted like a jerk."

In 1995, Smith was depressed, struggling after the deaths of her husband, Fred (Sonic) Smith, and her brother, Todd. Dylan invited her to join him on tour in the U.S., and at every performance they sang a duet on Dylan's song "Dark Eyes." Notoriously, Dylan changes keys and cadences without warning to his fellow musicians. (They are left to watch his hands, listen, and react.) When he is singing a duet, he'll suddenly play around with lyrics and intonations, often leaving his singing partner in a ditch. But when he sang "Dark Eyes" with Smith, he was solicitous, stepping back to let her sing the verses alone.

And so now, in Stockholm, Smith was only too pleased to sing in Dylan's honor. She'd prepared an elaborate version of "Hard Rain," backed by an acoustic guitar, a pedal steel guitar, and a full orchestra. Smith thought the song was right for the moment, displaying all of Dylan's poetic gifts, and a profound understanding of both human suffering and human endurance. Anxiety was predictable. This was hardly CBGBs. As she waited to perform, she looked out over a vast assemblage of grandees, including the king and queen of Sweden and assorted Nobelists—all expectant and hushed. The Royal Stockholm Philharmonic Orchestra played Sibelius's "Serenade" from the *King Christian II* suite. Patti Smith was next on the program.

"The opening chords of the song were introduced, and I heard myself singing," she recalled. "The first verse was passable, a bit shaky, but I was certain I would settle. But instead I was struck with a plethora of emotions, avalanching with such intensity that I was unable to negotiate them. From the corner of my eye, I could see the huge boom stand of the television camera, and all the dignitaries upon the stage and the people beyond. Unaccustomed to such an overwhelming case of nerves, I was unable to continue. I hadn't forgotten the words that were now a part of me. I was simply unable to draw them out."

Starting with just the acoustic guitarist strumming steadily behind her, Smith made her way through the first verse and chorus. She was singing far better than she thought she was, and delivered the lyrics with grace and assurance, but, as the pedal steel kicked in softly for the opening lines of the second verse, something dreadful happened. She botched a line. "I saw a babe . . ." Then another. "I saw ten thou . . ." Then . . . silence. It was if the words on her lyric sheet had been written in disappearing ink. A "whiteout," as she later described it to me.

"I'm sorry," she said. The musicians behind her realized something had gone wrong and stopped playing. "I apologize, I'm so nervous." The grandees were generous. They applauded Smith, and she smiled back in shy gratitude. She gathered herself and went at it again. "Saw a newborn babe with wild wolves all around it, / Saw a highway of diamonds with nobody on it . . ." In the end, it was an astonishing performance, made all the more profound by the initial collapse. But that was not something Smith could easily believe or accept.

"It was not lost on me that the narrative of the song begins with the words 'I stumbled alongside of twelve misty mountains,' and ends with the line 'And I'll know my song well before I start singing.' As I took my seat, I felt the humiliating sting of failure, but also the strange realization that I had somehow entered and truly lived the world of the lyrics."

Not long after, Smith told me that she'd only been flustered onstage twice in her long career—and both times, Dylan was responsible. "It was funny, because they're similar," she said. "Of course, I got very flustered when I sang 'A Hard Rain's A-Gonna Fall' at the Nobel Prize ceremony. The lyrics *disappeared* for me. The ceremony was on global TV, and I imagined Bob Dylan and his family watching this. It was a very difficult moment.

"But then, later, Martin Scorsese was doing this documentary on Rolling Thunder"—Dylan's 1975–76 tour in mainly modest venues that was meant to resemble a traveling carnival, but a carnival featuring Joan Baez, Joni Mitchell, Allen Ginsberg, and more. "He found a clip of me as he was doing his research. What he didn't know was that I was kicked *off* Rolling Thunder. I really blew it. I was the first to be recruited and the first to be kicked off, and it's a mystery to this day why exactly that was. I didn't really fit in. I was probably too arrogant. But that's okay, because then I went and did *Horses*."

———•———

Horses was Patti Smith's first album. The cover photograph by her lover and friend Robert Mapplethorpe showed her as a self-conscious androgynous meld of Baudelaire and Frank Sinatra—short black hair, white shirt, jacket slung over her shoulder. She

sang her plaintive songs—"Redondo Beach," "Land," "Gloria"—
over a raw, minimalist band led by Lenny Kaye. That album
came along forty-seven years ago as part of a punk movement that
included Television, the Ramones, the Sex Pistols, the Damned,
the Buzzcocks, the Clash, Elvis Costello, and Richard Hell and the
Voidoids. When I first saw Smith and her band, in the seventies,
she enacted the temper of the movement with gestures of impudent
contempt, kicking amps and monitors, spitting on the stage between
verses. It was a thrilling stage act, you thought, that would be here
today and gone with the wind.

And yet, Patti Smith is one of the great survivors: She is seventy-
five, a widow, a mother, a grandmother, a holder of honorary
degrees, the singer of choice to honor Dylan in Stockholm or Joan
Didion at her memorial service at the Cathedral of St. John the
Divine. Like Allen Ginsberg, she grew humble and approachable
with age, but without losing herself or crossing over into museum-
piece status. She remains vital, searching, always writing, a road
warrior. As she travels, she posts photos of the wonders she sees
on Instagram: Whitman's grave; the bells of Ghent; high tide near
her house in the Rockaways; Borges's desk; an espresso cup from
the Café Flore; her Abyssinian cat, Cairo. Smith is a vagabond.
Surrounded by musicians who have been in her orbit for decades,
she tours the world, reading her poems, singing her songs, keeping
journals and dream diaries.

In recent years, *The New Yorker* has invited Patti Smith to its
annual festival. I've been lucky enough to interview her there
twice. Both times, she also performed. And, because there were no
band members around, I backed her up on guitar, the first time
on "Because the Night," the second on "Pissing in a River," Neil
Young's "After the Gold Rush," and her political anthem, "People
Have the Power." That she would risk performing with someone
whose experience is limited to Sunday-afternoon lessons was amazing to me. More amazing is that when I asked her if we could

rehearse, she said, "That's all right. We don't have to rehearse. Just play loud. We'll be fine."

The conversation that follows is an edited version of those sessions and has been shuffled and condensed for the sake of coherence.

———•———

A movie theater in Chelsea. Patti Smith, dressed in black jacket, white T-shirt, and blue jeans, enters stage left, to a standing ovation.

It must be nice to get a standing ovation right away. Is that the usual thing every night?

Well, it's like that moment in *Through the Looking Glass* when the White Queen says "ouch" before she pricks her finger. There's something like that about getting an immediate standing ovation. Later, people might be sorry.

One of the memories that's really important to you and important in your books is the memory of reading. Your father was a factory worker, your mother was a waitress, and, at the same time, reading was enormously important in your house.

Neither one of my parents finished high school, but they were both avid readers. They were brought up in New England. Both of them were brought up in a time when books were a true source of entertainment. My mother read romance novels and poetry. My dad read everything: Aristotle, Plato, Jung, Huxley. My poor mother. She would be making meatloaf or something. He'd say, "Beverly, listen to what Aristotle says." And she'd say, "I don't want to hear what Aristotle says." But he was such an interesting man.

It was a religious house, as well.

The Bible and prayer were important in our house. My mother was a Jehovah's Witness, but she couldn't practice, because she couldn't give up smoking. My mother, who was a real Bette Davis, a chain smoker, loved her religion. When she finally gave up smoking at sixty she happily returned to her religion.

What's your relationship to the Bible? The first words I ever heard come out of the mouth of Patti Smith, when I first put Horses *on a turntable, was "Jesus died for somebody's sins, but not mine . . ." And that was your announcement to the world, your self-declaration, as you moved into covering Van Morrison's "Gloria."*

I had a good Biblical education, between my father's constant searching and his playing the devil's advocate about certain passages. I went to Bible school, and the Jehovah's Witness religion is very scripture based. But I had different interpretations of some of the scriptures. I was not the kind of person who could stay in an organized religion. I disagreed with certain things. I recorded that line—"Jesus died for somebody's sins, but not mine"—when I was twenty-seven, but I wrote it in a poem when I was twenty. And it wasn't really opposed to Jesus but to organized religion. I was young, I wanted to take responsibility for my own wrongdoings. I wanted to be free of guilt, free of the idea that Jesus had to die for me every time I did something wrong. I just thought he'd be free of me. I wanted to make my own mistakes. It was really funny: when *Horses* came out people picketed me and sent me death threats, or they prayed for me, saying, "You don't believe in Jesus." And I said, "I believe in him so much that his name is the first word on my record." I didn't say Jesus doesn't exist. But also, as I evolved, I appreciated Jesus more as an individual, as a revolutionary. I have a high regard for him. At the age of twenty, I just wanted to be free.

What flipped the switch for you when you were young? Famously, when you hear about the young artistic Patti Smith, it's often about you reading the poems of Rimbaud. It's kind of amazing to imagine a teenage kid, in south

Jersey, stumbling on Illuminations *and something lights up inside her. Is that really the story?*

Well, one of the first things that really lit up for me was seeing Picassos for the first time. I was like twelve. I had never been to an art museum. My father took us all to an art museum in Philadelphia and I saw Picassos. My father didn't like him. He preferred Salvador Dalí, because he was a better draftsman. That was the first time my father and I locked horns. I started realizing that certain things spoke to me.

As far as Arthur Rimbaud goes, truthfully, I saw a copy of *Illuminations* at a bus station in Philadelphia, in front of one of those dirty bookstores in a bookcase where all the books were ninety-nine cents each. I looked at the cover picture and I just fell in love with him. It was more like a boyfriend. When I opened the book and started reading it, I didn't understand all of it, but the language was so beautiful. It was transporting.

Where did it lead you?

Well, it led me into trouble at the factory where I worked when I was sixteen. That's what the song "Piss Factory" is about. I was an arrogant teenage girl, and I hated the factory. My first job was as a baby buggy bumper beeper inspector in the Dennis Mitchell toy factory, in south Jersey. I just wanted things to move along. And these women there, I mean, God bless them, they worked in this factory all their lives. They knew how to make their quota, and they didn't want to be pushed to work harder. I was sort of screwing up the quota. They didn't like me much—and rightly so. I didn't show them proper respect. Now that I'm older, I understand that. I walked into their world and they had a system, but I was too young to get that. One day I was carrying around my copy of *Illuminations*, and Dotty Hook, who was my supervisor—she had like maybe one tooth—saw the book and said, "What you reading? You're not supposed to be reading." It was a bilingual edition. She said, "What language is this?" And I said, "It's French." They all decided it was a communist book. They told me I wasn't allowed to read the book there. So, of course, I brought the book in again the next day. They took me into the john and gave me a lesson. That's why it's called "Piss Factory," because I got dunked in yellow water!

You paid a high price for Rimbaud.

I paid for my arrogance, really. Back then I thought I paid for Rimbaud.

You regret how you behaved?

Yes. It was only a few years ago that I realized that. I'm not recanting, because it was a terrible place and they treated me terribly, but now I understand that these women were working there since they were fifteen years old, and they were in their forties. Things were never going to get better for them.

And you knew you were leaving.

Yes. I knew I was leaving, and I just came in and disrupted things. I didn't show the proper respect. But I didn't know. I was just a kid, you know?

At the final show at CBGBs, you were singing, "So You Want to Be a Rock 'n' Roll Star." And at a certain point, you tell the audience, "This is the era where everybody creates. It's all open. It's all up to you: What are you fucking going to do about it?" It was a challenge to the younger people in the audience. When you were very young, you came to New York. Did you know that you could get over?

Well, I wasn't pretending to be anything. I came to New York City in 1967, looking for a job. The shipyard had closed in Camden, New Jersey, and thousands of jobs went away. There didn't seem to be a single job in south Jersey or Philadelphia, not even in a factory, for a twenty-year-old girl who had a couple years of college.

So, I came to New York City. There was tons of bookstores and all kinds of places. My first desire was to simply get a job. But my real hope was to evolve as an artist and as a writer, as a painter. I also dreamed of meeting somebody, because I didn't have a boyfriend then. I wanted to meet somebody like me, with a like mind. But my number one issue then was to get a job because I had no money, nowhere to live.

I met Robert Mapplethorpe very quickly. We lived together. I really believed in Robert. At twenty, he was very confident in himself as a fully formed artist. I wasn't in a hurry. I had read biographies of artists, painters, and poets, and they all suffered, they all starved, they were all unappreciated. I was ready for that. In that way, Robert and I were quite different. I was ready to suffer and take awhile. Robert didn't want to suffer. He knew who he was. He knew what he had and that he wanted to be known.

He had an ambition.

I had ambition, too, but my ambition was more conceited than Robert's. I wanted to write great books and win a Nobel Prize or something like that. But I figured Hermann Hesse wrote *The Glass Bead Game* when he was in his mid-fifties, so I wasn't in a hurry. But I also didn't have the confidence. I still had to prove my worth to myself before I could prove it to the world.

And how did you turn so decisively and intensely to music?

Music had nothing to do with it. I feel embarrassed when people call me a musician. I really can't play anything with any skill. My children are accomplished musicians. My husband was a great musician. I can only play a few chords.

You sing. You write music.

I'm a *performer.* I feel proud to say that I'm a performer, and I think of myself as a performer in the best sense. I like being in front of people. I enjoy communicating with people. I was writing poetry and I would read it to Robert, and Robert really wanted me to read it in front of people because he thought I was entertaining. He pushed me. He got me my first poetry reading, but I found myself much too agitated and speedy to just stand up and read poems. I was bored by it.

I'd go to a poetry reading and . . . Snoresville! Ginsberg was a great reader, and I loved seeing William Burroughs and Jim Carroll. There were a few really good poets, but on the whole . . .

I read somewhere that you used to go to poetry readings with Gregory Corso and hate the stuff.

Gregory was the biggest heckler I ever saw. He would yell at the poet, "Get a blood transfusion!" When I was doing my first poetry reading, I didn't want to be boring. I thought if Gregory's going to be in the audience, I better deliver. As I was getting ready I decided to have some sound behind me. I was trying to figure out how to do it and Sam Shepard said, "Why don't you get somebody to play guitar behind you?"

This was 1971. Nobody had brought a guitar into St. Mark's Church yet. I asked Lenny Kaye to play. I'd met him in a record store and he played a little guitar. So, he played guitar behind me on that poem, "Jesus died for somebody's sins / but not mine / melting in a pot of thieves, / wild card up my sleeve, / Thick heart of stone / my sins, my own." People were quite upset that we had an electric guitar in the church. That was encouraging! Things just evolved from there. I didn't have any game plan except to make poetry more visceral.

By the mid-seventies, and peaking maybe at around 1978, you were a rock-and-roll star.

I'll tell you how I knew I was a rock-and-roll star. We had a job in Italy, and it was actually right before I quit. We arrived at the airport in Florence or somewhere. There were all these paparazzi around and I said to my pianist, "I bet you Sophia Loren or somebody's here." We were whisked out of there in an Alfa Romeo. Later that day, I was just walking down the streets of Florence. There were thousands of kids everywhere, camped out, sleeping on the streets. I went into a record store, and I said, "What's going on here?" The guy said, "Patti, it is you!"

You hadn't noticed until then?

I didn't. I knew we had a job, but I didn't know it was in a stadium for like eighty thousand people.

But you had album after album, you were on the cover of Rolling Stone.

Yeah. But I mean, we weren't rich or anything. We were still building.

Did you enjoy what was happening?

I loved working with my band. I loved the camaraderie. I liked connecting with the people. But there was so much stress, too much pressure to do peripheral things: going to radio stations, doing interviews, getting your picture took. At first it was sort of fun. But then I realized I wasn't growing as an artist. I wasn't evolving. I wasn't doing any work. I was also starting to act out.

How?

Like, if there wasn't a car for me, I'd get pissed off. Or if some amplifier didn't work, I'd put my foot through it.

Did you throw TV sets into swimming pools?

Oh, no, I don't mean that kind of thing. It was just mean agitation. I didn't do anything I was ashamed of. There's nothing wrong with being arrogant and having a certain amount of hubris. I wasn't used to being pampered. I wasn't used to having cars. At first it was kind of cool because I had dark glasses on and I could pretend I was in *Don't Look Back*. I enjoyed it for a while. I had my fun. But then it just seemed like, I'm not interested in the trappings.

You spend a lot of time on the road now. Do you enjoy it more than you did when you were thirty?

Well, I'm a lot healthier than I was then. All the halls back then were filled with thick smoke, cigarette smoke, pot smoke, and I was always getting bronchitis. I was unhealthy. But as soon as I went off the road, I got healthier. I did almost fifty concerts this summer.

Some in front of a few thousand and some in front of a hundred thousand, like in Glastonbury.

Our band is lucky because we attract young people. I think it's because of *Just Kids*. It's funny: in the old days, there would be people who'd come in with your record and then it was the CD, and now I look in the front row and everybody's got a copy of *Just Kids*. In concert, I can talk directly to them. We're an old-fashioned band. We don't have any cues. We don't have a lighting guy. We don't have tape loops. We're just a rock-and-roll band. We're pretty raw. If we mess up, we just laugh. And the kids in the audience, sometimes they'll yell out stuff that they're concerned about or that they feel frightened about.

What do they say?

It might be that nobody cares about them or what should they do if they don't have any money or whatever.

They feel they know you somehow?

They know I'm going to talk directly to them, and they know that I don't pamper them.

Meaning what?

Well, one might say, "I don't have any money to put out my CD." And I'll say, "Well, get a job."

Tough love.

Well, that's what we did. When we did *Horses*, I was working at the Strand bookstore and Lenny Kaye was still working in a record store. We all had jobs. And I thought, well, when we finish *Horses* we'll go back to our jobs. I took a little hiatus and they said, "No, you go on tour." And it was like, "Tour where?" And they said, "Finland." And I was ready.

At this stage of your life, you have family. You have duties as a bandleader, as an activist. How do you carve out the time to write?

When I was younger, I just wrote whenever. I'd sit up all night. Or I'd write when I felt like it. But after I got married, in 1980, and had children, that wasn't possible. I had to carve out time. I'd been very undisciplined. I started waking up early and using the time from five in the morning till eight, when the children got up, as my own time. At first it was difficult. But I came to cherish that period because it was mine. Now, even though my children are grown and my life is quite different, I've maintained that discipline. I get up at maybe six or seven and I'll write maybe till ten or eleven, or at least attempt to write.

For Just Kids, *you worked with letters or diaries, talking to old friends and acquaintances to remember things.*

Unfortunately, almost everyone in *Just Kids* had passed away. The only person I talked to was David Croland, who was one of Robert's first boyfriends. He was knowledgeable and understood Robert's work. I talked to him mostly because I wanted to get him right. Luckily, I have a very good memory. I took minimal drugs in the seventies.

What do you consider minimal?

Well, in the sixties, I took none. And in the seventies, I smoked a little pot. Robert and I took acid twice.

With what result?

I just complained all night. I felt like John Brown, angry at the world, and Robert kept saying, "Patti, you're supposed to feel universal love." I was like on a soapbox about the world and about pollution and about Jesus.

Anyway, my primary resource for *Just Kids* was the fact that I kept diaries. My mother, every Christmas, would send me one of these little diaries and I wrote these things in them that were seemingly meaningless. It would be like "cut Robert's hair like a rockabilly star," or "chopped my hair like Keith Richards," or "met Janis Joplin." All these day by day by day.

They jogged your memory.

Yeah. Where the moon was. When Robert and I had an argument. Or when something sad happened, like when Jimi Hendrix died. Daily notations.

In Just Kids, *there's an act of memorialization about a particular period and a friend and a lover. In* M Street, *you're going back to something extremely painful and joyful, your marriage to Fred (Sonic) Smith, your retreat to Detroit away from public life to private life. Fred was still in his forties when he died of heart failure, in 1994. The love described in the book is beyond intense.*

Fred passed away on Robert Mapplethorpe's birthday. November 4th. It's a doubly difficult date for me. My daughter, Jesse, reminds me so much of him in certain ways. She'll have a gesture that's like his and she has the same touch on the piano as he did. Or my son, Jackson, will call me up, and when he's a little sleepy, his voice sounds so much like Fred's. I think my children sometimes magnify memories of him.

———•———

What was the first rock and roll you listened to with excitement, listening on the radio in New Jersey growing up?

I've seen pretty much the whole evolution of rock and roll. I can remember, when I was a little girl, my mother taking me to Bible school, and she was holding my hand. The boys in town had a club-house with a record player. I was just walking with my mother and "Tutti Frutti" came on. I didn't know what it was at the time, but it filled me with such energy. I let go of my mother's hand and just ran right for the clubhouse. It was like the call of the wild. Little Richard was, I would say, my real introduction to rock and roll. And I think that's probably true for a lot of people.

And did you start singing, or fooling around on the piano or guitar? Did you have any thought whatsoever of getting into music?

Not at all. I mean, growing up in rural south Jersey, there weren't any instruments around. I hardly ever saw a musical instrument. And I didn't really have any aptitude. When I was growing up, everybody sang. They sang on the street corners, they sang a capella. I loved opera. So, I used to daydream about singing opera, but, of course, being a sickly, skinny little kid in south Jersey, my mother told me to pick a different vocation. But from the time I was like eight or nine years old, I wanted to be a writer.

What were you reading that gave you the idea: I could possibly do this?

Well, I love books and I learned to read very early, like three and a half, four. Jo March in *Little Women* gave me the idea that a spindly tomboy bookworm could also be a writer. Truthfully, that's the one gender illumination that I can remember having, that a girl was writing books. I was very much like her in a certain way, sort of a tomboy, always with my nose in a book and with a big imagination. I thought, *I could do that.*

And what about poetry? Was poetry something that you started reading young, or did that came later?

I did win a poetry contest when I was in the tenth grade—an elegy to Charlie Parker called "Bird Is Free." It's sort of a corny poem.

Do you still have it?

Well, I forgot about it. But when my father died, he had a cigar box in his desk, and I wanted to see what was in it. The poem had been published in the local newspaper, and he had cut it out and saved it.

What was it like to read a poem by somebody that was you, but somebody so far in the past?

Truthfully, the fact that my father, who never showed real interest in what I was doing, had secretly saved the poem was what meant the most to me.

I love poetry. I really built everything on poetry, improvisation. I liked R&B music. I like to sing a little. And I like performing. Socially, I'm deadly at a dinner party. But I like to perform. It was always like that in school. I loved to talk in front of the class. Nothing that I like better than to get up and talk about *Moby-Dick*, you know. It is just a natural feeling. I thought I'd be a schoolteacher, because I figured, Oh, you can be in front of people talking all the time.

Did you find it easier to talk to a crowd than two or three people?

I'm much happier in front of seventy thousand people than in the middle of two strangers at a dinner party. I don't know what happens to me, but I spend the whole time trying to think of something to say.

One of your recent books, The Year of the Monkey, *is about many things, but primarily it's about loss.*

The year I wrote it started out with one of my closest friends in the ICU, in a coma. Then my beloved friend Sam Shepard was diagnosed with ALS and it progressed through that year. And I was about to turn seventy. I've been like a Peter Pan person my whole life, so, all of a sudden, seventy seemed like a number to reckon with.

Tell me, if you would, about your relationship with Sam Shepard and your last meeting with him.

Sam was still living when I was writing the book, and then I wrote the epilogue. The last time I visited him was in Kentucky. We were just us. He was really laboring and racing to finish his last book. We spent the lion's share of our time together going over his manuscript. And that was not without humor. I mean, there's a part in it where we're sitting there at the kitchen table in the morning, we'd have peanut butter, bread, and coffee. And we're trying to work. We happened to look at each other and it was like we had the same thought. He said, "Patti Lee, we've become a Beckett play." We were these two characters who could almost never leave the table because of circumstances, and we just read the same absurd paragraphs over and over again. But Sam loved Samuel Beckett, so I figured that's a good thing.

I was very struck by a passage in which you're reading Marcus Aurelius's Meditations *and you come across this line: "Do not act as if you had ten thousand years to live." And you say, "This made terrible sense to me, climbing the chronological ladder, approaching my seventieth year, get a grip. I told myself, revel in the last seasons of being sixty-nine . . ." Haven't you been living the way you have wanted to for a very long time? Not that your life hasn't been without responsibility and tragedy and difficulty.*

All the major choices I've made, like leaving public life in 1979, and having my children, I've done with my eyes open. I made my own decisions, and I have pretty much lived the way I want to. And I still do. But I try to balance that with taking care of myself and, also, being responsible to my family and loved ones and friends. I mean, freedom without the balancing aspect of responsibility can get pretty boring.

I don't know if you ever go on YouTube or anything like that, but I just spent the last week doing so and watching you perform in your earlier days. I just wonder what the experience must be like for you to watch the Patti Smith of that period.

I don't like seeing myself or hearing myself. When I go to You-Tube, it's usually like to watch Glenn Gould playing piano, or Pavarotti doing a master class. But, it's really hard for me to watch myself. I'm just so *frenetic*!

And that's hard for you to watch?

There's a part of me that imagined I would be like Ava Gardner or Jeanne Moreau. And I'm sort of a wild thing.

And yet, I'll bet Ava Gardner might have wished she'd been Patti Smith.

If there were two black dresses and we both had to put one on, she'd win.

———•———

As an artist, do you uncover secrets or revelations about your earlier life?

When I look back at myself, I see that we're all blessed and flawed. I can tell you that the thing I've learned as I get older and look back at what kind of child I was, I wish I would've been more appreciative of my mother. I admired my father. He was more the intellectual. I loved the image of him and the way he was. I tried to model myself after him. But in truth, it was my mother who was an amazing survivor, who got us through the hardest of times, when we didn't have enough food to eat. I didn't realize that until I got older. I didn't realize how much she sacrificed and how hard she worked till I had kids of my own.

What's the experience of the road like for you now?

I'm not lonely on the road. I'll miss my kids. I might miss my cat, or my books, my own books, but I'm sort of a vagabond. You just get on a bus, you have your bunk and a book, and you crawl out of the bunk when you get to the next town. Road life isn't bad for me because it appeals to my inner vagabond.

Take the money out of it. Would you do it anyway?

It's a good living. I don't tour quite as much as I used to because as I get older—that was like the illumination I had writing my most recent book: that I really want to write like ten more books. I have many books in my head, many half-finished books, and it's very hard to write with any concentration on the road. So you just got to make a choice: How do you want to spend your next thirty years? I don't know how long I'm going to have, but I'm hoping like one hundred and four or something like that. And I want to spend more time writing.

Is it just as thrilling as it was when you were much younger to be on a stage in front of five thousand, ten thousand people, and roar through this set that takes an hour and a half, or whatever it is, and people are going batshit? And then it's quiet and you go back to your hotel room. That's an experience that very few people have. Could you give it up?

I'm like Jack Nicklaus. He always says he leaves his game on the golf course and goes home and he just lives his life. When I go onstage, whether it's seven hundred people or seventy thousand people, it's for them. You do your work, and you're building a night together. And what you're hoping is that they have some kind of transformative experience, and that they go home and do their thing with more confidence, or more hope, or some kind of joy. And then I go back to my room and watch detective shows on TV.

———•———

Throughout your career, you've been engaged in the political sense. What can an artist accomplish politically?

Sometimes an artist can create one song, like when Neil Young put out "Ohio" after the Kent State killings, and it's capable of rallying people, igniting people. But, in the end, it's the people, in their numbers, who make change. I don't think that an artist has any more responsibility than every single other human being. We all have to vote. And it's every human being's responsibility to do her part, whether it's helping your fellow man, or using less fossil fuel, or whatever one does. So, artists can inspire people. They can rally people with a song. But when people say to me, "Oh, artists have to get up and do this and do that," I say, "Well, so do you. Fucking you get up, too!"

Your most famous song in a political vein is "People Have the Power." Tell me a little bit about the origins of that.

I was pregnant with my daughter, Jesse, and I was in the kitchen peeling potatoes. my husband came in and he said, "Trisha, people have the power, write it." I was like, I'm going to kill you, but, of course, I did end up writing it! After dinner, Fred and I sat for hours and hours talking about what we wanted this song to contain. His great hope was to do something anthemic that would inspire and rally people all over the world. Fred has studied "Because the Night," which used to be my most popular song. He really respected that song and he wanted to give me something as anthemic as that, but also something that saluted the individual and the power of the collective, the people. Fred's dream was for a song that would move people to action. And now it's my most important song. Fred died young, so he never saw that happen. But I've been able to see and hear people sing this song in Greece, in Spain, at marches in France, Palestine—all over. I know Fred would have liked that. It's my most important song now. It had a goal and it's been embraced.

All right, then. I think that's our cue.
Okay!

(Patti Smith takes the microphone in hand and sings "People Have the Power." Her guitar player tries his best to keep up and play as loudly as instructed.)

Acknowledgments

I wrote my first piece for *The New Yorker* in 1992 and I've counted myself beyond fortunate ever since. My deepest thanks to my colleagues, past and present. My love and thanks, always, to Esther Fein; Alex, Noah, and Natasha Remnick; and Caila Litman. My gratitude to everyone at Knopf, particularly Deborah Garrison, Chip Kidd, and Zuleima Ugalde; to keen listeners, draft-readers, and musical kibbitzers Hilton Als, Robert Ankner, Richard Brody, Vinson Cunningham, Amanda Petrusich, Alex Ross, Kelefa Sanneh, and Nick Trautwein. And abiding thanks to Henry Finder, my editor and friend, who has made things better, time and again.

A Note About the Author

David Remnick has been the editor of *The New Yorker* since 1998 and before that was a staff writer for the magazine for six years. He was previously *The Washington Post*'s correspondent in the Soviet Union. He is the author of seven books, including *King of the World*, a biography of Muhammad Ali, named the top nonfiction book of the year by *Time* magazine in 1998, and *Lenin's Tomb*, winner of the Pulitzer Prize.

A Note on the Type

This book was set in a version of Monotype Baskerville, the antecedent of which was a typeface designed by John Baskerville (1706–1775). Baskerville, a writing master in Birmingham, England, began experimenting around 1750 with type design and punch cutting. His first book, published in 1757 and set throughout in his new types, was a Virgil in royal quarto. It was followed by other famous editions from his press. Baskerville's types, which are distinctive and elegant in design, were a forerunner of what we know today as the "modern" group of typefaces.

Typeset by Scribe, Philadelphia, Pennsylvania
Printed and bound by Berryville Graphics, Berryville, Virginia
Designed by Maria Carella